Basic Skills
Project Book

ALISON BAYLISS

LONGMAN

To Bruce and Matthew,
with thanks for your help and support.

Addison Wesley Longman Limited
Edinburgh Gate, Harlow
Essex CM20 2JE, England
and Associated Companies throughout the world

© Addison Wesley Longman Limited 1997

First published 1997

British Library Cataloguing in Publication Data
A catalogue entry for this title is available from the British Library.

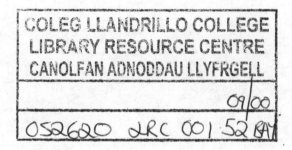
ISBN 0–582–30265–X

Set by 35 in 11.75/14.5pt Sabon

Produced by Longman Singapore Publishers (Pte) Ltd.
Printed in Singapore

Contents

How to use this book

The Basic Skills Project Book offers you an opportunity to practise a variety of Communication and Personal and Social skills. The book is divided into six main topic areas. These are Safety, Recreation, Personal Care, Colour, Pollution and Living with Animals. Within each main topic there is a project for a group of people to work on together and a project for people who are working individually.

Projects

Each project starts with a list of tasks you will be able to carry out. The introduction reminds you to choose activities from the project which best suit your needs and interests. Choose activities which appeal to you and which give you a chance to practise the skills you need.

Activities

Read through each activity before you start work on it. Check it covers the skills you would like to practise and for which you would like to produce evidence. Each activity gives you a chance to practise a range of skills in different ways. By carrying out the work on several activities you can gather evidence of competence in the skills you need for an accreditation or for your own personal goals. Activities often begin with useful background information. You will be able to use this information to start a discussion or research for example.

 Use this icon to find out what action you have to take in the activity. For example, you may take part in a discussion, interview a friend or an unfamiliar person, write a letter, carry out a survey or design a questionnaire.

 Look for this icon for suggestions on how to carry out research tasks. You may be offered an address to write to or ideas about who to talk to. You will be given ideas about where to go to find the information you need to complete the activity.

 When you see this icon you will find some ideas on how to present the work you have done on the activity. You will be offered ideas for presenting posters, mini-guides, fact files or a spoken presentation for example.

 This icon usually appears towards the end of each activity. It marks where you are reminded to check your work. This will mean reading over your work carefully or asking other people for their comments.

1

Optional tasks

Optional Tasks have been added to some of the activities in both the group and individual projects. The tasks offer you the chance to continue the work of the main activity a little further or find out a little more. You can gain more practice in a variety of skills and add to your progress and achievements. If you are working in a group the Optional Tasks may be useful for some of the group to work on while the rest complete work from the main activity.

Worksheets

Many activities have a useful worksheet linked to them. The worksheets are grouped together at the end of each project. A grey band makes them easy to find even when the pages of the book are closed. Some worksheets are multi-use. This means the worksheet is useful both for the activity you are working on and for other activities throughout the projects. They may give tips on writing a questionnaire or a letter or using the telephone for example.

Each worksheet linked to an activity will either give you extra background information, or help with research or with presenting your work, for example, as a survey or report.

Skills

At the end of each activity there is a list of linked skills. When you have completed your work on an activity check the skills you have demonstrated and collected evidence for. You may use the Skills List provided with this book, which links well to many Basic Skills Awards which you may be studying for. You may also use the Core Skills which refer to GNVQ Communication levels One and Two.

The level you have worked at will depend on how much information you have found out for yourself, how you have presented your work and whether you have spoken to people who you don't know as well as familiar people. The project activities give you a chance to practise the same skills many times and in many different ways. You can progress from one level to another as your confidence and ability develop.

Tracking sheets

The tracking sheets at the end of the book give you a complete picture of the skills covered by the activities in each group and individual project. Use the tracking sheet for your chosen project to identify which activities provide you with a chance to practise the skills you need.

Record sheets

It is very important to record your achievements as you work through your chosen activities on a group or individual project. Use the Skills Record Sheet on p. 7 to regularly record details of work you have done and the skills you have covered. It is often difficult to remember exactly when you worked on a topic, so note down dates as you go along. It may be important to remember later the date you carried out an activity. You may wish to compare pieces of work to see how you have progressed. Write down information about resources you use on the Skills Record Sheet. This can be a useful reminder to you if you are later looking for sources of information. It can also be used to offer proof of your ability to use a variety of resources or ask a range of people for information.

When you have finished your work on a project complete the Skills Summary Record on p. 8. This gives you the opportunity to review and record your progress and achievement. Write down information about the evidence you are putting forward for assessment or accreditation or filing for future use. Detail for yourself any skills which need more practice and a date to work towards. Use this record sheet to write down the evidence you have for an award you may be studying for. Write down a personal evaluation of your achievements. Make this a chance to think about and reflect on your progress so far.

Evaluation exercise

At the end of each group and individual project there is an Evaluation Exercise. This simply reminds you to think about the work you have done on a project. You are encouraged to check your Skills Record Sheet is up to date with details of the work you have done. You are reminded to complete your Skills Summary Record.

Back to basics

Back to Basics are some simple literacy tasks. You can practise and improve a variety of reading skills such as fast reading and careful reading. You can practise and improve your proof reading, spelling and punctuation skills. The content of the tasks is linked with the project topic and will either offer extra information or give you the chance to revise information you have already used.

Answers to the Back to Basics tasks are at the back of the book. You can work at your own pace and check your answers when you are ready.

Alternative ideas

Towards the end of each main topic area, some alternative ideas are outlined briefly. They are included to help you find enough activities in each project to enjoy and which suit your individual interests or the interests of a group.

Skills list

Demonstrate the ability to:

1. Manage your own time to achieve an objective.

2. Listen and respond to others appropriately in a group discussion.

3. Respect other people's point of view.

4. Listen to, question and respond appropriately to unfamiliar people.

5. Offer and accept help and support within a group.

6. Understand the nature of the research required.

7. Seek and use advice from an appropriate person.

8. Use appropriate reading skills to locate and select information from written material.

9. Use appropriate reading skills to locate and select information from visual/graphical material.

10. Use questioning, listening or observing to obtain information.

11. Record information in an accessible format for later use.

12. Interpret and evaluate collected information accurately.

13. Communicate information clearly in an appropriate written format.

14. Communicate information clearly in an appropriate visual/graphical format.

15. Respond to written or verbal instructions by completing the task.

16. Use information to make reasoned judgements.

Skills list – student copy

Demonstrate the ability to:

1. Work out how long a task will take and plan your time so you can finish the task in the time allowed.

2. Listen to others carefully during a group discussion and offer your own opinion when it's your turn.

3. Respect the fact that other people think differently to yourself.

4. Listen carefully to, ask questions of, and reply to unfamiliar people.

5. Offer help and accept help from other people, so you give support to each other in the group.

6. Ask questions to check you understand what information you need to find out.

7. Ask for and use advice from people who can help you with your work.

8. Use a variety of reading skills to find and choose useful information from written material, such as books, magazines, or leaflets.

9. Use a variety of reading skills to find and choose useful information from visual material, such as pictures, photographs, diagrams or charts.

10. Use questioning, listening or watching carefully to get the information you need.

11. Write down or tape information you have found out and need to use later.

12. Work out the meaning of and judge the use of information you have collected.

13. Pass on information clearly in a written form such as a letter or report, so it can be easily understood by other people.

14. Pass on information clearly in a visual form such as a picture or chart for example, so it can be easily understood by other people.

15. Follow written or spoken instructions to complete a task successfully.

16. Use information you have collected to make a sensible guess, estimate or conclusion.

Skills record sheet

Record a brief description of the work you have done and the skills you have practised for each activity. Describe the resources you used such as books, writing for information, working with other people or asking unfamiliar people for information.

Name   **Project**

Date	Description of work done	Resources	Skills

Skills summary record

Name   **Start date**

Project   **Group/individual**

Evaluation: What progress have you made? What personal goals have you achieved? What skills do you need to practise next?

Skills (number)	Evidence of competence	Details of work planned	Goal date

Assessed evidence to be put forward for accreditation:

Safety at work

INTRODUCTION

In this group project on *safety at work* you will be able to:

- Find out how to use a computer or word processor safely.

- Write a safety checklist for using a computer or word processor.

- Consider a case study and write a summary of action to be taken.

- Discuss advice on manual handling and try out safe methods.

- Design a poster to show good manual handling methods.

- Discuss the importance of a fire drill and write a checklist on fire prevention at work.

- Compile a guide showing the uses of different types of fire extinguishers.

- Find out about using dangerous substances at work.

- Design a chart showing First Aid for dangerous substances.

- Discuss how to move around the workplace safely.

- Write a handout about moving around the workplace.

- Evaluate your work on the project.

Choose activities which interest you from the wide range of suggestions provided in the project. You can choose to do just part of an activity if you wish. The choice is yours. There are more suggestions in the Alternative Ideas section (p. 52), so you should find enough activities to suit your interests and needs. Finish with the Evaluation Exercise as this will help you think about your work on the project and remind you to record the skills you have covered.

For each activity you choose to do, use the information provided for you in the activity text and worksheets, as well as your own experiences and knowledge. If you need to look for more information consider resources such as books, newspapers and magazines as well as television, radio, video and CD-ROM. You can also use resources such as writing to an organisation or telephoning for information, and talking to people you know as well as other people who may be able to give you the information you need.

Optional task If you have more time available and would like to try another task to develop the skills you have already used in an activity, you can look for the Optional Tasks which are linked to many of the project activities.

You will find the following worksheets useful:

Safety at work

Activity 1 **Write a safety checklist for using a computer or word processor**

If you spend some of your day working on a computer or word processor, typing in information and looking closely at your screen, you should follow a few basic safety routines. If you take care you won't have any problems. People can suffer from Upper Limb Disorders (ULD), which are problems with the hand, wrist, elbow, shoulder and neck, if they spend a large part of their working day using a keyboard. You are more likely to have problems if you have a badly designed work area and too few changes in your working routine.

If using a keyboard is part of your job you should receive training from an employer for your work. Your training should include safe routines for using your keyboard and screen and a safe place to use it.

Discuss the short list below which describes some concerns. Add more information or ideas you have from your own experiences.

■ **Eyes** If you are working for a long time at your computer you may find your eyes get tired. They may feel dry, swollen or look red and you may even get headaches. You can help the situation by
  ■ remembering to blink (lack of blinking can cause dry eyes)
  ■ taking regular, good quality rests away from the screen
  ■ changing your position to help your blood circulate and reduce feelings of tiredness
  ■ sitting in good light and making sure there are no reflections on your screen
  ■ checking the contrast of your screen shows a good difference between light and dark

■ **Comfort** It's important that you sit properly
  ■ check your back is supported by a good sitting position
  ■ check your shoulders, neck and head are at a comfortable angle

- check you are not having to turn your head awkwardly to look at your notes
- check your feet are firmly on the floor in front of you
- check there is plenty of space for you to turn away from your computer or work area.

■ **Hands, wrists, arms** Strain to the hands, wrists and arms can be a problem when you are spending a long time at your computer or word processor. The small movements you make over and over again are the cause. If you don't follow safe routines, such work may lead to the protective layer around the tendons becoming inflamed. Your hands and wrists in particular may suffer. It can be very painful and treatment may mean taking a complete rest from your work.

 Write a safety checklist about safe methods of work for anyone using a computer or word processor during their working day. Choose which safety concerns you would like to find out more about. Work in pairs or small groups, each looking at different safety areas.

 Look in the library for books or magazines on safety in the workplace. Write to your nearest Health and Safety Executive (the address should be in the telephone book) and find out about the Health and Safety (Display Screen Equipment) Regulations. Ask other people whose work involves using a computer or word processor for their comments and ideas.

 Meet up and put your ideas and information together. Use your own situation for your safety checklist, or make it more general for anyone to use. Illustrate your checklist with cartoons, line drawings or diagrams. Use the worksheet provided for ideas on how to set out your checklist.

 Look at your checklist together carefully. Have you missed out any important information? Give a copy of your checklist to friends or people you work with who use a computer or keyboard. Ask them to comment on how useful your checklist is. Does it help them remember to work safely? Amend your checklist if you receive any helpful ideas.

(*See also* Worksheets: computer/keyboard checklist)

	From this activity you may have evidence for:
Skills list	1, 2, 3, 4, 5, 6, 7, 8, 10, 13/14, 15, 16.
Core skills	Communication level 1 and 2.
Element	1.1/2.1 Take part in discussions.
Opportunities	Discuss the problems involved in using computers and word processors.
	Ask people who use computers in their work for information about safe methods of work.
	Ask friends and other people to comment on the safety checklist.
Element	1.2/2.2 Produce written material.
Opportunities	Add to list of safety concerns using own experiences.
	Write a safety checklist.
	Write to the Health and Safety Executive asking for information.
Element	1.3/2.3 Use images.
Opportunities	Use cartoons or diagrams in the safety checklist.
Element	1.4/2.4 Read and respond to written materials.
Opportunities	Read books, magazines or leaflets for information to use in the safety checklist.
	Read information received from the Health and Safety Executive to use in the safety checklist.

Activity 2   Write a summary of action for a case study

Read through the following case study together.

Jim works in a warehouse, loading and unloading vans. It is his company's policy that employees wear toe-protected safety shoes. Jim has just been issued with a new pair of safety shoes which look like trainers, but which have steel toe caps. He needs to protect his feet from heavy boxes, cartons or sacks which could slip and bruise or crush his foot. The safety shoes also have a non-slip sole as the loading bay can get wet and slippery in bad weather.

Unfortunately Jim finds his new shoes uncomfortable. He started wearing ordinary trainers to work but his supervisor spotted this and spoke to Jim about it. He warned Jim to follow the safety regulations and wear his safety shoes. Jim didn't say anything about the new shoes being uncomfortable. The next day Jim started off wearing his safety trainers, but part way through his shift he swapped over to his own comfortable shoes. Just before the shift ended Jim's supervisor noticed that Jim was not wearing his toe-protected trainers.

Discuss what you think happened next. What would Jim's supervisor have said to him? Would it help Jim if he explained the trainers are uncomfortable? Do you think Jim should receive a verbal warning for not following the safety rules, which are there to protect him? Such a warning would be recorded on Jim's work record. Discuss the reasons for your opinions and write a short summary of what you have decided will happen to Jim.

If you are not sure about any of your decisions speak to your own Health and Safety Officer if you have one. Write to your nearest Health and Safety Executive for advice. Telephone an organisation like the Citizens' Advice Bureau which may be able to offer advice.

When you have finished, check your summary is accurate and covers all the main points you want to make.

Optional task

Choose two items from the following list of protective clothing and equipment. Choose from

safety goggles	gloves
helmet	disposable mask
hairnet	boiler suit
ear plugs	

Write down a description of a work situation for each of your two safety items. Talk about and decide how the item protects the person using it from having a nasty accident and add this to your written description. For example, protective gloves must be worn when using chemical solutions in a hair salon. Gloves protect the hairdresser from absorbing poisonous chemicals through the skin.

Use your own experiences of work for ideas. Arrange to speak to your Safety Officer if you have one. Write to or telephone your local Health and Safety Executive area office (the address should be in the telephone book) and ask for information.

From this activity you may have evidence for:

Skills list	1, 2, 3, 4, 6, 7, 8, 13, 15, 16.
Core skills	Communication level 1 and 2.
Element	1.1/2.1 Take part in discussions.
Opportunities	Discuss the case study.
	Ask a Safety Officer or Citizens' Advice Bureau for advice.
	Discuss the use of protective equipment at work (optional).
Element	1.2/2.2 Produce written material.
Opportunities	Write a summary of action on the case study.
	Describe the uses of two pieces of protective equipment (optional).
	Write a letter to the Health and Safety Executive.

Element   1.4/2.4 Read and respond to written materials.

Opportunities   Read the information provided in the case study and use for discussion.

Read information received from the Health and Safety Executive to use in your summary.

Activity 3   Find out about safe manual handling methods

Consider the following advice on manual handling

- lift your load in easy stages (from floor level to your knee, from your knee to the carrying position)

- use the strength of your legs to help you lift and keep your back straight

- reverse the lift stages when you are putting your load down

- hold heavy loads close to your body

- grip the load with your whole hand not just your finger tips

- don't jerk or shove heavy loads to move them

- don't carry such a large load that you can't see where you are going

- check your route is clear before you start lifting and moving a heavy or awkward load

- use lifting equipment whenever possible

- ask for training from your employer

Talk about the advice on manual handling and discuss each point carefully. Use your own work experiences to decide why advice on manual handling is useful for people at work. Add more helpful advice to the list.

Decide on some work situations you are familiar with where safe manual handling methods are needed. Try out some role plays to demonstrate to each other the right and wrong way to lift and carry loads. Decide which parts of the body are most at risk when you lift heavy loads badly and show this in your demonstrations. What kind of injuries can people suffer because they lift and carry poorly at work?

Find some large but lightweight boxes. Imagine they are heavy for the purpose of your role play. Volunteers can lift, carry and put down these 'heavy' loads. Show both the correct method and how dangerous it can be for your back and neck if you lift heavy loads badly (but take care). All have a go, or let some of the group provide a commentary on the action. Look for more ideas about safe handling to add to your list by discussing the action in the role plays.

If you have the equipment, make a video of your demonstration and show it to other interested people. If you prefer, design a poster showing the right and wrong way to go about manual handling. Display these in your building so that others can follow your advice. Use the worksheet provided for ideas on how to design your poster.

Discuss the effect of your poster or video. Have you shown safe methods of handling clearly and accurately so other people could follow your advice? Ask people you work with who do some manual handling if they think your advice could prevent people from being injured at work.

(*See also* Worksheets: ideas on poster design)

	From this activity you may have evidence for:
Skills list	1, 2, 3, 5, 7, 8, 10, 13, 14, 15, 16.
Core skills	Communication level 1 and 2.
Element	1.1/2.1 Take part in discussions.
Opportunities	Discuss advice on manual handling and own experiences.
	Take part in role play and comment on the action.
	Discuss and evaluate your poster design or video.
	Ask other people to comment on your posters or video.
Element	1.2/2.2 Produce written material.
Opportunities	Add ideas to a written advice list on manual handling.
Element	1.3/2.3 Use images.
Opportunities	Design a poster or make a video on safe manual handling.
Element	1.4/2.4 Read and respond to written materials.
Opportunities	Read manual handling advice for use in discussion.

Activity 4 Write a checklist on fire prevention at work

What would you do if there was a fire where you work? Have you practised the fire drill for the building you are in now? People tend to find fire drills a nuisance or rather funny, and even go as far as ignoring them and carrying on with their work. Discuss why fire drills are important. What should you do if there is a fire in your building or workplace? Look around you for a Fire Action notice on a nearby wall or door, which will give you some extra information. Use the ideas below to start your discussion: some are actions you *should* take, some are actions you *shouldn't* take. Discuss which are which.

ADDRESS . . . . ROOM . . . .
FIRE PRECAUTIONS OFFICER

FIRE ACTION
RAISE THE ALARM

CALL THE FIRE BRIGADE

ON HEARING THE ALARM

DO NOT STOP TO COLLECT
PERSONAL BELONGINGS

In the event of a fire

■ try to put the fire out yourself

■ close doors and windows if you have time on your way out

■ collect all your belongings and take them with you

■ ignore the fire alarm, it's probably only a fire drill

■ wait for friends and leave together

■ try and find out where the fire is

■ leave by the nearest exit

■ don't go back into the building unless you are told to by an authorised person

 Find out how to prevent a fire in the workplace by collecting information. Use your own knowledge and experience. Contact your Health and Safety officer if you have one, and ask for information. Write to your Area Fire Authority and ask for information on fire safety and prevention. Look for books, videos or leaflets in your local library about fire prevention. Allocate research tasks to each other to get the work done.

 When you have collected some information, present it in the form of a written checklist with tick boxes. Design your checklist so it can be used as a training paper for a supervisor to use with a new employee. The checklist will help the employee learn about fire prevention at work. Use the worksheet provided to help with the design of your training paper.

 Discuss your checklist and decide if you have included all the important points you want to make. Imagine you are new employees and your supervisor is going over each point with you. Is it clear and easy to understand? Ask friends or people you work

with for comments. If they were starting a new job would they find the advice helpful and easy to understand? Amend your checklist if you receive any useful ideas.

Optional task There are several different types of fire extinguisher. For example there are extinguishers filled with water, foam, carbon dioxide or dry powder. The right one must be used properly to deal with a fire at work. Find out which fire extinguishers can be used for:

fires which involve wood and paper

fires which involve flammable liquids

fires which involve electrical equipment

Explain the colour coding and use for each type of fire extinguisher you find out about. Present this information as a mini-guide, so you can see at a glance which type of extinguisher to use for any fire. Find out what you need to know from your Safety Officer or local Fire Brigade or Fire Authority. Look for a Guide to Fire Precautions in your local library. Find information in a DIY store which sells safety equipment. Allocate the research tasks between you.

(*See also* Worksheets: fire prevention)

From this activity you may have evidence for:

Skills list	1, 2, 3, 4, 6, 7, 8/9, 10, 13/14, 15.
Core Skills	Communication level 1 and 2.
Element	1.1/2.1 Take part in discussions.
Opportunities	Discuss the do's and don'ts for a safe fire drill.
	Ask a Safety Officer for ideas on fire prevention.
	Ask a range of people for information on fire extinguishers (optional).
Element	1.2/2.2 Produce written material.
Opportunities	Write a letter to the Fire Authority for information on fire prevention.
	Write a checklist for fire prevention at work.
	Write a mini-guide on fire extinguishers (optional).
Element	1.4/2.4 Read and respond to written materials.
Opportunities	Read notices for information about the fire drill.
	Read books and leaflets for information about fire prevention.
	Read books, leaflets or labels for information about fire extinguishers (optional).

Activity 5 Design a chart to warn about dangerous substances

When you use dangerous substances at work, for example chemicals, you should follow safety regulations carefully. When an employer buys dangerous substances they also receive a supplier's hazard data sheet, which gives information about each substance. For example it will say how the substance can be stored and used safely. It will give advice on what protective clothing should be worn when using the substance. It will give information on what first aid is needed if the substance is spilled or inhaled.

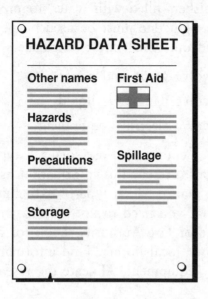

Always follow instructions carefully when using any dangerous substance. This means reading the labels as well as following an employer's instructions. It's easy to become careless with chemicals which you often use. However, spilling industrial strength bleach on your skin for example, can cause a chemical burn which must be treated properly. Some chemicals may irritate or damage your skin and in some cases, if enough is absorbed, can cause death.

Before you start using dangerous substances at work always find out what to do if you spill any on your clothes or skin. This means you will be prepared for any emergency. Make sure you find out who your nearest First Aider or Appointed Person is. A First Aider will have had full training. An Appointed Person will have had some basic training in emergency aid in the workplace. Both should be able to help until further help arrives.

You can recognise many dangerous substances by their warning labels.

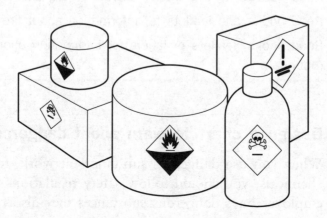

Make a list of dangerous substances which you commonly find in the workplace and which you might use. Find out what First Aid would be needed if you spilled these substances on your skin or breathed them in.

Write out the information as a chart. Share out the work within the group so you each find out about one substance. Use the knowledge and experience you already have in the group. Find more information by using a First Aid manual. You should find one in your local library. Contact your nearest St. John Ambulance headquarters for information or leaflets. The address should be in the telephone book. Use the worksheet provided for ideas on the layout and on what to include in your chart.

Discuss how helpful your finished chart would be for someone who wants to find out how to deal with a dangerous substance. Check your information and advice is clear. Is your chart easy to use? Enlarge your chart by photocopying it and displaying it in a place where others can read it. Reduce it in size and each have a pocket size copy to carry around with you.

(*See also* Worksheets: dangerous substances)

From this activity you may have evidence for:

Skills list	1, 4, 5, 6, 7, 8/9, 13/14, 15, 16.
Core skills	Communication level 1 and 2.
Element	1.1/2.1 Take part in discussions.
Opportunities	Discuss your own knowledge of dangerous substances.
	Discuss and evaluate your finished chart.
Element	1.2/2.2 Produce written material.
Opportunities	Write out a chart of First Aid needs for dangerous substances.
	Write a letter to St. John Ambulance asking for information.
Element	1.4/2.4 Read and respond to written materials.
Opportunities	Read manuals and leaflets for information about First Aid treatment for dangerous substances.

Activity 6   Find out how to move about the workplace safely

You should always be able to move around a work area safely. For example

- there should be enough space to move around any fixed machinery or equipment

- there shouldn't be any hazards such as trailing cables, wires or rubbish left lying about which you might trip over

- the routes or gangways around a work area should be free of obstacles

■ walkways should be clean and dry so that you can't trip or slip

■ steps, sharp corners and the edges of racks should be marked with black and yellow stripes to warn people to take care

■ if you are moving about a work area don't be tempted to take short cuts

■ don't hitch rides on the back of vehicles such as a fork lift truck which is not meant for passengers

 Discuss these suggestions on how to move around the workplace safely. Add more ideas from your own experiences.

Choose four different work situations which you feel you are fairly familiar with. These could be situations from your own experiences of work. You may have experience of working in a busy café, reception or shop. You may have worked in a warehouse or garage or looked after young children in a playgroup. Take each work situation and discuss in detail what should be done by the employer and employee to make sure everyone moves around the workplace safely. Talk about the most common accidents in each situation which have been caused by the way people move around the workplace. Make notes about what is discussed or write up the main points on a board or large sheet of paper.

 Write a detailed summary for one of the work situations in which you are most interested. Work in pairs, each taking a different work situation. Explain the main points you have made in your discussion on how to move around the workplace safely.

 Check through your summaries and make sure you have covered all the important points you want to make.

Optional task Imagine you are an employer who needs to tell a new employee about your company's policy on moving around the workplace safely. Take one of your work situations and design a short handout which you could use to explain the safety routines. Use

drawings or cartoons to illustrate the points you want to make on your handout. The handout will be used for discussion with your employee and may be given to them to keep. Make it attractive to look at and easy to understand. Use the worksheet provided for help to design and write the handout. Test how effective your handout is in a role play. Let someone take the part of the employee and someone the employer. Watch each other and improve any parts of the handout which you see are unclear.

(*See also* Worksheets: moving about the workplace)

From this activity you may have evidence for:

Skills list	1, 2, 3, 5, 10, 11, 13/14, 15, 16.
Core Skills	Communication level 1 and level 2.
Element	1.1/2.1 Take part in discussions.
Opportunities	Discuss suggestions on how to move around the workplace.
	Discuss moving about safely in different work situations.
	Take part in a role play on moving about safely in the workplace (optional).
Element	1.2/2.2 Produce written material.
Opportunities	Write a summary for one work situation.
	Design a handout on moving about the workplace (optional).
Element	1.3/2.3 Use images.
Opportunities	Use pictures or cartoons to highlight points made in handout (optional).

 ## Evaluation exercise

Discuss all you have learned while doing this project on safety at work. What do you know now that you didn't know before? Do you think you will feel safer in a work situation from now on? Have you learned any First Aid skills? Can you respond to a fire drill quickly and safely?

Have your presentation skills improved? Do you feel you are better at putting across your point of view in a discussion? Do you feel more confident about collecting information, using a variety of resources?

Check your Skills Record Sheet is up to date. Have you recorded all the skills you have practised and the resources you have used? Have you completed the Skills Summary Record? Record details of your progress and achievement. Write down details of skills you would like to practise again. Set yourself a goal date for the work. Write down the evidence of competence you have collected during the project. Write down any links to an accreditation you may be working towards.

Computer/keyboard checklist

Choose one of the following presentation ideas for your safety checklist.

■ **Present a list of do's and don'ts** such as do take regular rests, don't work in bad light, etc.

■ **Give a list of safe routines**. Divide your list into different problem areas such as eyes, posture, furniture, space, etc. Draw boxes around each part or use different colours. Add a cartoon or diagram.

■ **Show a diagram of a work station**. Label each part to show safe procedures such as how to sit. Show the position of the keyboard to allow for arm and wrist support. Show where the light source should be, where to place paper work you are reading or copying from, etc.

■ **Design a flow chart** going from one problem area to another. Give each box in the flow chart a title or heading, e.g. Eyes. Use arrows to point to one route which gives information about dangers, e.g. eye strain. Show a second route which offers advice about safe routines, e.g. blinking and rest periods.

■ **Write a start-up checklist** for anyone using a computer or word processor. Detail the actions to take before starting work. For example, checking posture, checking the light source, checking the contrast of the screen, checking the position of hands and wrists.

■ **Present a simple set of suggestions** on safe methods of work. Divide your ideas into sections such as furniture, light source, posture, etc. Write out each set of suggestions on small cards (e.g. credit card size). These could be kept in someone's pocket, wallet or purse to be looked at whenever needed. Use different coloured card to make the different safety areas even clearer.

■ **Draw a cartoon or picture** of a computer work station where everything is hopelessly wrong! Number the points you want to make. List what needs to be put right in a box underneath your drawing.

Multi-use ■ Use this worksheet for ideas about poster design.

Ideas on poster design

Design a poster showing how to lift and carry objects around the workplace safely.

Your **aims** should be one or more of the following:

■ to get someone to notice your poster as they walk by it

■ to get someone to stop and look at your poster

■ to get someone to stop and read your poster carefully

You have got different **pieces of information** to get over in your poster. For example:

■ the stages of lifting or putting down heavy or awkward shapes

■ protecting the spine by keeping it straight

■ keeping movements smooth rather than jerky

■ using the big muscles in the legs to do all of the work

Decide what you want to say.

How can you give this information to someone who looks at your poster? They may only glance at it for a moment. Even if your poster is **attractive** and people **stop to read it** they may not have much time to read a lot of information.

Don't use too many words – most people won't bother to read a lot of words. Keep to simple facts.

Select what is really important and check that your information is **accurate.**

Make the poster relevant to the type of manual handling people who see it are likely to do themselves. Don't show someone carrying drums of chemicals, if the people who look at your poster work in offices.

Make the **message** on the poster **clear**, by using pictures, cartoons, diagrams. This means **use visual images.**

Make your poster **easily visible** from a distance.

Make everything about your poster **bold, colourful** and **large.**

Fire prevention

Use these suggestions on fire prevention at work for your checklist. Add to or replace suggestions with ideas of your own. Keep your checklist general or design it around one area of work you are interested in.

Fire prevention: company policy checklist for new employees

Do you know how to help prevent a fire?

Do you know:

- don't wedge fire doors open in hot weather
- keep your own work area tidy and free of litter
- clear up any spillage of flammable liquids quickly and safely
- do not smoke in a no-smoking area
- throw away cigarette ends safely
- always check your work area is safe before leaving it at the end of your shift

Do you know what to do in the event of a fire?

Do you know:

- where the fire exits are
- which route you should take to leave the building safely
- how to raise the alarm should you find a fire
- how to use a fire extinguisher properly if it is part of your job to do so

---

Change the order of the suggestions so that each one follows on from the one before in a sensible way. This will help a new employee understand why each item is being checked.

Set out your checklist as this example, but with tick boxes. Each item would be ticked as it was explained to the new employee.

Leave a space after each item on your checklist for any notes or follow-up action which is needed. For example a new employee may need fire extinguisher training.

Dangerous substances

At work you may use chemicals and other dangerous substances which could cause serious injury if spilled on your skin or inhaled. It is useful to know what First Aid to give for a chemical burn for example. Use the suggested layout for your First Aid chart. Add more ideas of your own. Some information about one substance, bleach, has already been provided for you to begin your chart.

Substance	First Aid treatment: contact on skin	First Aid treatment: inhaled fumes
Industrial bleach	*Priority* Check own safety (protective gloves?) Identify substance. Flood with water (up to 20 mins).	*Priority* Check own safety (protective mask?) Remove from source of fumes into fresh air. Check breathing. Identify substance.
	Further treatment Remove chemical stained clothing while flooding with water. Take to hospital.	*Further treatment* Take to hospital. Keep check on airway and breathing.

Notes: Make sure used water is thrown away safely. Throw away chemical stained clothing safely.

Use this layout for your chart or something similar:

Substance	First Aid treatment: contact on skin	First Aid treatment: inhaled fumes
	Priority	*Priority*
	Further treatment	*Further treatment*
Notes:		

Consider these substances for your chart:
    Disinfectant
    Caustic soda
    White spirit
    Turpentine

Moving about the workplace

Design a handout to be used by a new employee to remind them how to move around the workplace safely. They may work in an area where there is dangerous machinery, fork-lift trucks being operated, trays of food being carried around or where people are using chemicals.

Keep your handout simple and attractive to look at. Remember a new employee will have a lot of information to think about in the first couple of weeks in a new job.

- use cartoons, diagrams or pictures
- use colour
- use big, bold text
- use language which is clear and accurate

Choose a particular workplace of which you have some experience, or keep your handout more general. You decide.

Include some of the following ideas

- don't hitch lifts on vehicles not meant for passengers
- walk, don't run
- don't take short cuts (which may be quicker but are not safe)
- don't go into any forbidden areas
- keep gangways and routes clear
- clear up any spills quickly
- report any obstacles or hazards you see to your supervisor if you can't do anything about them yourself
- look out for hazards which may be colour marked as you move about, such as shelving or inspection pits
- make sure you have got space to move around people or machinery, etc. If you haven't, talk to your supervisor or Health and Safety Officer about it

Back to basics

Answers on pp. 306–7.

Missing Words

Replace the missing words in these statements about safety at work. The words are provided for you in the box below. If you want to make the task a little harder, cover up the words in the box.

lifting	store	prosecute	First Aider
protective	work	Safety	labelled
dangerous	Appointed	space	clear
Health	tidy	move	correct

a) Inspectors have powers to _____ a firm for breaking the _____ and _____ Regulations.

b) Leave your _____ area _____ and _____ ready for the next shift or person.

c) Make sure you know how to use and _____ your _____ clothing properly.

d) Make sure you know who is your _____ _____ or _____ Person in case of an accident.

e) Your work area should have enough _____ for you to _____ about safely.

f) Do not store _____ substances in spare bottles which are not properly _____.

g) Make sure you know the _____ _____ procedures if you are going to move loads about the workplace.

Muddled Words

Sort out the muddled up words at the top of page 28 which are all types of protective clothing or equipment. Fill in which part of the body is protected by each piece of equipment.

Muddled word	Correct word	Body part	Why protect?
sloggge			From dust or chemical splashes
feasty toobs			From chemicals and falling objects
tenraih			Prevents hair from tangling in machinery
reaglups			Prevent hearing damage and loss

Careful reading

Read the short text below and answer the questions which follow. Try to write your answers in complete sentences.

Each year around 50 people are killed at work from electric shocks. Simple safety rules can reduce the risks for everyone. Here are a few ideas.

■ If you work with electrical equipment make sure you know how to help someone who has received an electric shock. Ask your employer for training or go on a short course with the St. John Ambulance.

■ There should be enough socket outlets provided in your work area so there is no temptation to overload one.

■ There should be a switch or isolator near each fixed machine so the power can be cut off in an emergency.

■ Plugs should be properly fitted, with the flex firmly clamped to stop wires from being pulled from the terminals.

■ Equipment should always be unplugged before you carry out any cleaning or repair work.

■ Make sure any repairs are carried out by a properly trained electrician.

1. How many people are killed at work each year from an electric shock?

2. What should you know how to do if someone you work with receives an electric shock?

3. Why is it important to provide enough socket outlets for electrical equipment in the workplace?

4. Why should you check plugs are fitted properly?

5. Who should carry out electrical repairs in the workplace and why?

Safety in and around the home

INTRODUCTION

In this individual project on *safety in and around the home* you will be able to:

- Carry out a survey on safety in a children's play area.

- Write a short report about safety in a local play area.

- Investigate the safety of children's toys.

- Find out about the work of a Trading Standards Officer.

- Carry out a safety review of your home.

- Find out about common accidents in the home.

- Write a safety checklist.

- Write a short guide to First Aid for DIY accidents.

- Design a handbook for baby-sitting.

- Design a mini-guide on home security.

- Evaluate your work on the project.

Choose activities which interest you from the wide range of suggestions provided in the project. You can choose to do just part of an activity if you wish. The choice is yours. There are more suggestions in the Alternative Ideas section (p. 52), so you should find enough activities to suit your interests and needs. Finish with the Evaluation Exercise as this will help you think about your work on the project and remind you to record the skills you have covered.

For each activity you choose to do, use the information provided for you in the text and worksheets, as well as your own experiences and knowledge. If you need to look for more information consider resources such as books, newspapers and magazines as well as television, radio, video and CD-ROM. You can also use resources such as writing to an organisation or telephoning for information, talking to people you know or talking to other people who may be able to give you the information you need.

Optional task   If you have more time available and would like to try another task to develop the skills you have already used in the project, you can look for the optional tasks which are linked to many of the project activities.

You will find the following worksheets useful:

Safety in and around the home

Activity 1   Carry out a survey on safety in a children's play area

Most young children enjoy playing outdoors on large play equipment. They enjoy swinging, climbing the steps of a slide and going around on a roundabout with other children. These activities can help a child learn new physical and social skills. Many families don't have the space or money to have large play equipment at home. If they use a public play area can they be sure their local play area is safe?

It is estimated that there are around 40,000 injuries to children every year which need a visit to hospital. Children playing on large equipment will get grazes or bruises from time to time, but they will quickly recover. However, they can also injure themselves much more seriously. Falling from a high climbing frame or from the top of a slide onto a hard surface can cause a serious injury. Getting hit by a swing as they walk by can also leave a child seriously injured.

Carry out a survey on a playground near to your home to find out how safe it really is. Think of a list of safety features you would like to find out about. Look for the following safety features in your survey and add more ideas of your own:

■ is there a soft surface underneath equipment for a child to land safely?

■ does the playground have a barrier around it so a child cannot run off, perhaps straight across a road?

■ is there plenty of space between pieces of play equipment so a child can avoid being hit by a swing for example?

■ does the equipment look well maintained or is it rusting and worn?

 Find more ideas for your survey list by contacting an organisation such as the Royal Society for the Prevention of Accidents (RoSPA). Write to their Playground Safety Advisor at Cannon House, The Priory Queensway, Birmingham. Telephone your local council's Leisure and Recreation Department and ask how they make sure playgrounds are safe in your area. Ask for the opinion of friends or family who take children to local play areas. Think about what you would need to do to check large play equipment was safe if you were using it in your own back garden. Use the safety checks you think of in your survey list.

 Write down a good range of safety features to look for in the playground you have chosen to survey. Make sure your survey sheet is clear and easy to fill in while you are standing in the middle of a playground! (If you can't visit a playground, use a detailed photograph to look for a range of safety features.) Decide how you are going to record what you see. Have a rating for each feature such as

   1 = poor
   2 = reasonable
   3 = fairly good
   4 = good
   5 = very good

Use part one of the worksheet provided to help you write out your survey sheet. Take photographs while you are carrying out your survey. Photograph evidence of good, safe equipment and poor, unsafe parts of the play area.

 When you have completed your survey, write a short report on how safe your local play area is for the children using it.

 Use the photographs you took of your chosen playground to remind you about what you saw and to illustrate your report. Use part two of the worksheet provided for help with planning and presenting your report.

Share the results of your survey with friends or other people who use the playground with their children. Did you find a good play area or did you find a lot of dangers?

(*See also* Worksheets: playground safety)

From this activity you may have evidence for:

Skills list	1, 3, 4, 6, 7, 8, 10, 11, 12, 13, 15, 16.
Core skills	Communication level 1 and 2.
Element	1.1/2.1 Take part in discussions.
Opportunities	Ask friends for information about playground safety.
	Ask an organisation for information about playground safety.
	Tell people about the survey results.
Element	1.2/2.2 Produce written material.
Opportunities	Design and complete a playground survey.
	Write a short report on the survey results.
Element	1.3/2.3 Use images.
Opportunities	Use photographs to illustrate your report.
Element	1.4/2.4 Read and respond to written materials.
Opportunities	Read information received to find ideas on playground safety.

Activity 2   Investigate toy safety

When you buy a toy as a gift for a child or a baby, can you be sure you are buying a toy which is safe to play with at home? Unsafe toys which may catch fire easily or have small parts which can be swallowed or choked on are dangerous to young children. Toys which come apart leaving sharp points which can cut or stab can all cause very nasty accidents when played with by a young child at home. Children are also at risk from toxic paint or varnish containing poisonous metals, which they may lick and swallow.

One way you can be sure to find a safe toy is by going to a shop which is a member of the British Association of Toy Retailers. They will be able to give you sensible advice about what to buy. Read the labels on packaging carefully and check the toy has been made to a British Standard. These standards have been written by technical experts for toy makers to follow. Products made to a British Standard are of good quality and safe to use.

One standard on toy safety which is used in Britain at present is BS5665/EN71. If a toy has been made to a British Standard it shows the BS number on its label. You may find the Lion Mark on a toy as well. This is a mark showing a lion's head inside a triangle and was developed by the British Toy and Hobby Association. Toys carrying this mark have been made to the highest standards.

Carry out a short investigation in your local shops to find out how safe toys are. Choose the age range you are most interested in and look for suitable toys. Visit a local supermarket which sells toys, or a toy shop. If you cannot visit a shop use a catalogue instead. Choose a few toys and look closely at the labelling. What information are you given about each toy? Are you told:

- which age group the toy is for
- what uses the toy has
- what materials it is made from
- whether it is flammable or not
- whether it is washable or not
- where the toy was made
- about a British Standard
- is the Lion Mark on the toy or box?

Use the worksheet provided to help you with ideas for your investigation and to record your results.

Look at the results of your investigation. What kind of information do you think is the most helpful for people trying to choose a safe toy? Do you think enough information is given on toy labels? What information do you think should be provided to help people make sensible choices? What guidelines could you provide for someone who is buying a toy for a child? Use the worksheet to note down your ideas.

Write out your guidelines for buying a safe toy for a young child. Show your ideas as a numbered list or as a mini-guide.

Give a copy of your guidelines to someone you know who has young children. Ask them if they would find your guidelines practical and helpful. Amend or add to your guidelines if you receive any useful feedback. Keep your guidelines handy and use them yourself whenever you are buying a toy for a child.

Optional task   Find out about the work of a Trading Standards Officer. What can they do to make sure only safe toys are for sale in your local area? Write a short description of the work they do and how they can help you buy safe items for your home. Find the information you need by getting in touch with your local Trading Standards Office. Look in the telephone book for their number. Ask prepared questions or for a leaflet which explains their work.

(*See also* Worksheets: toy information)

From this activity you may have evidence for:

Skills list   1, 3, 4, 6, 7, 8/9, 10, 11, 12, 13, 15, 16.

Core skills   Communication level 1 and 2.

Element   1.1/2.1 Take part in discussions.

Opportunities   Ask people for comments about your toy safety guidelines.

Telephone for information about the work of a Trading Standards Officer (optional).

Element   1.2/2.2 Produce written material.

Opportunities   Record details of toy safety in an investigation.

Write a set of guidelines for buying safe toys.

Write a description of the work of a Trading Standards Officer (optional).

Element   1.4/2.4 Read and respond to written materials.

Opportunities   Read to find ideas on toy safety.

Read toy labels to find out what information is offered.

Read information about Trading Standards (optional).

Activity 3   Carry out a safety review of your home

Carry out a safety review of your home or your room to see how safe it really is. Keep your review fairly general or consider child safety or the safety of elderly people for example.

Consider in your review the safety concerns which are detailed below. Add more safety concerns of your own.

Poisons

Where are you likely to find poisons in your home and what can you do to make sure they can't hurt anyone?

■ **Medicines**   These should be kept in a cupboard which can be locked or in a bottle with a child-proof top. An overdose of paracetamol or even vitamin tablets can kill a child, who can easily mistake pills for sweets.

■ **Chemicals**   Spilling certain chemicals on your skin or breathing them in can be very dangerous. A child swallowing a chemical, mistaking it for an ordinary drink, can be seriously harmed. Store household chemicals such as bleach, disinfectant and toilet cleaner safely. Don't store the last little bit of paint thinner in an old lemonade bottle: a child may think it is a drink. Don't store chemicals under the sink where they are easily found, put them in a cupboard where you can lock them up.

Think of other chemicals you may have in your home. You will be surprised at just how many there are! Have you got any of the following: caustic soda, silver polish, floor cleaner, lighter fuel, wood polish, methylated spirit, weed killer, paraffin, fly killer, plant food or even nail polish remover? The list is endless!

Burns and scalds

It is not just a fire in the home which can cause danger, equipment in everyday use may cause burns and scalds. In your review check how safely you use some common equipment.

■ **Irons**   Do you switch off your iron and store it in a safe place to cool down or do you leave it on the ironing board where it may get knocked over?

■ **Electric/gas/open fires**   It's easy to fall against or drop something on to a fire which isn't guarded. A young child may be attracted to the red glow and try to touch a fire. An older child may stand too close and their clothes catch on fire. An older person may be a little unsteady and fall against an electric element. Consider who lives in your home and think about the need for a fire guard.

■ **Matches/lighters**   Children can be fascinated by matches. Matches can cause clothing and furniture to burn and a fire in your home can be out of control in minutes.

■ **Water**   The flex of your kettle hanging down over the work surface can be caught or pulled and boiling water splash over your skin causing a painful scald. Keep the kettle well back on the work top and use a safety flex. A hot drink spilt on a child's thin skin is enough to burn it. Don't hold or pass hot drinks above the heads of young children playing around you. A bath run with hot water first is enough to scald a child or elderly person very badly. Always run the cold water first and then add the hot water.

■ **Cooking**   The kitchen is a dangerous place, with sharp objects and electrical equipment. An electric shock can cause serious injury and even death. Don't overload sockets with too many plugs. Turn saucepan handles away from the front of the cooker so they can't be knocked over. Take special care if you are heating oil to cook food quickly. If you go away and forget about it, it may overheat and burst into flames.

Carry out your review by looking at each safety feature throughout your whole home or room. Ask friends and family about their safety concerns in the home and use these ideas in your review. Use the worksheet provided to help you plan and present your review.

When your safety review is finished look carefully at the results. Decide for yourself how safe your home or room seems to be. Are there any safety improvements you think you could make? Do you think carrying out the safety review will mean you have fewer accidents in your home from now on?

Optional task   Write a letter to the Department of Trade and Industry's Consumer Safety Unit, 10–18 Victoria Street, London. Ask for information about the number and type of accidents people have in their own homes. Use the ideas and information you receive to improve your own safety review. Compare the most common accidents reported with the kind of accident you have had in your home before carrying out your safety review. Have you suffered any typical accidents in your home?

(*See also* Worksheets: safety review)

From this activity you may have evidence for:

Skills list	1, 3, 6, 7, 8, 10, 11, 12, 13/14, 15, 16.
Core skills	Communication level 1 and 2.
Element	1.1/2.1 Take part in discussions.
Opportunities	Ask friends for ideas on home safety concerns.
Element	1.2/2.2 Produce written material.
Opportunities	Design and record safety details in a home safety review.
	Write a letter to the Department of Trade and Industry (optional).
Element	1.4/2.4 Read and respond to written material.
Opportunities	Read and evaluate the results of a home safety review.
	Read information received from the DTI (optional).

Activity 4 Write a top ten for DIY safety tips

Enjoying a little DIY or gardening sounds fairly harmless doesn't it? However, standing on your stepladders to hang a picture, using a power drill or knocking down a wall can result in a nasty accident if you don't take care.

DIY and gardening can be dangerous and some sensible methods of work should always be followed. Every year around 350,000 accidents happen to people in and around the garden. There are around 4000 injuries every week caused by people doing a little DIY! Some of these accidents may be small ones but many are serious. A fall from a ladder for example can kill you. Even a simple accident such as hitting your thumb with a hammer can be very painful!

Read the following list of safety tips:

- wear suitable clothing which can't be caught in equipment or trip you over
- wear safety equipment as necessary, such as a dust mask
- make sure the cable of any electrical equipment is safely stretched out behind you
- switch off at the mains before working on any wiring
- don't use electrical equipment outside in wet weather
- don't leave tools lying around, you may trip over them or stab yourself with them

■ keep tools well maintained and stored safely

■ dangerous substances such as weed killer should be safely locked away

■ make sure ladders are at a safe angle, one metre away from the wall for every four metres up

■ use stepladders for small jobs, don't try balancing on chairs or stools to put up pictures or paint the ceiling

■ learn some basic First Aid so that you can cope with an accident, such as how to deal with bleeding or fractures, and keep First Aid equipment handy

■ avoid heat exhaustion or sunburn when working outside on a hot day

■ take care when lifting heavy tools or equipment, remember to protect your back

Think about what you do around the house and garden and add more ideas of your own to the safety tips list. Collect more ideas for your list by asking friends or people you work with for safety tips. They may be able to tell you about an accident they had and how they could have avoided it by taking more care. Find ideas for your list by looking in DIY or gardening magazines. Visit a DIY store or garden centre. Ask for information and collect leaflets. Watch DIY programmes on television for more safety tips. Write to RoSPA at Cannon House, The Priory Queensway, Birmingham, and ask for their leaflets on DIY and garden safety. You should find these very helpful.

Write the whole safety tips list out in order of importance to you. Aim to have a top ten list of safety checks. Your number one DIY safety check will be the most important safety tip in your opinion. Take out any tips which don't apply to you. For example you may not use electrical equipment or you may not have a garden.

Design a logo for each of the safety tips in your top ten. The logo (which is a simple, bold symbol) should give a basic idea about each safety tip at a glance. Use cartoons, find pictures in old magazines or photocopy pictures to illustrate each safety tip on your list.

When your DIY safety tips list is finished, put it in a place where you can see it, to remind yourself to take care! Give copies to friends or people you know who enjoy DIY. Ask them to use your safety tips list next time they decide to do some DIY in their house or garden.

Optional task Choose three examples of DIY or gardening accidents which involve different parts of the body and would need treatment for bleeding. Select both serious accidents and minor ones. For example you may cut your hand on some broken glass while fitting a new pane, or cut your leg because the saw slipped when sawing some wood, or trip over a trailing cable and graze your knee. What First Aid would be needed?

For minor cuts and grazes rinse the wound under clean, running water. Pat it dry and put on a sterile pad and bandage or a plaster. What would you do for a serious wound which is bleeding badly?

Find out what First Aid is needed for each of your chosen examples of DIY accidents which cause bleeding. Write instructions for treatment so someone reading your guidelines could easily follow your advice. Find the information you need in a First Aid manual either by St. John Ambulance or the British Red Cross in your local library.

Illustrate your instructions with simple diagrams or pictures. Write up the instructions as a short leaflet on coping with bleeding, or as a poster which could be put in a shed, garage or kitchen. Use the worksheet provided to help you.

(*See also* Worksheets: DIY safety)

From this activity you may have evidence for:

Skills list	1, 3, 4, 6, 7, 8/9, 10, 11, 12, 13/14, 15, 16.
Core skills	Communication level 1 and 2.
Element	1.1/2.2 Take part in discussions.
Opportunities	Ask friends for their DIY safety tips.
	Ask for safety tips at a DIY or garden centre.
	Watch television for safety information.
Element	1.2/2.2 Produce written material.
Opportunities	Write a DIY safety tips list in order of importance.
	Write to RoSPA asking for information on DIY and garden safety.
	Write a First Aid guide (optional).
Element	1.3/2.3 Use images.
Opportunities	Use logos or pictures to illustrate your DIY safety list.
	Use diagrams or pictures to illustrate the First Aid guide (optional).
Element	1.4/2.4 Read and respond to written material.
Opportunities	Read magazines, leaflets or books for information on DIY and gardening safety.
	Read information received from RoSPA about safety.
	Read a First Aid manual for treating bleeding (optional).

Activity 5   Design a handbook for baby-sitters and parents

If you are a baby-sitter you need to feel confident and safe when you are looking after someone else's child in the home. If you are a parent, you need to feel your child will be happy and safe in your baby-sitter's care.

A baby-sitter should check:

■ how long the parents are going to be out for

■ how they can be contacted in an emergency

■ what jobs they are expected to do, such as bath the children, play games, help with homework, make a meal

■ how many children they will be asked to look after

■ if there are any pets to be looked after

■ if they feel safe and happy in the child's home

A parent should check:

■ what experience the baby-sitter has had

■ if the baby-sitter is punctual and reliable

■ what arrangements need to be made to make sure the baby-sitter gets home safely

■ what jobs the baby-sitter is happy to do, such as preparing food, helping with baths or homework, looking after a sick child

■ if their child feels safe and happy with the baby-sitter

 Find out what baby-sitters and parents would most like to know about how to keep a child safe and happy. Interview a group of friends, or people you work with who have done some baby-sitting or employed a baby-sitter. Prepare some questions which will give you the information you need. Record the answers you get by making notes or taping the conversations. Add more of your own ideas to the following questions.

Ask a baby-sitter:

■ what kind of information can parents give you about their child to make your job easier?

■ what kind of difficulties do you sometimes have?

■ what tasks are you expected to carry out for the child?

■ do you usually get to know the child a little before baby-sitting?

■ are you usually allowed to have a friend to baby-sit with you?

Ask a parent:

■ what kind of information can a baby-sitter give you about themselves to help you decide if they will get on with your child?

■ what kind of difficulties do you sometimes have?

■ what tasks do you expect them to carry out for your child?

■ do you usually like your child to get to know the baby-sitter a little before leaving them alone together?

■ do you usually allow a baby-sitter to have a friend for company?

Design a handbook for baby-sitters and for parents employing a baby-sitter. Include advice from your interviews suggesting checks which should be made. Give advice and information about home security while baby-sitting, such as being careful when going to the door to an unknown caller. Include information about the going rate for baby-sitting in your local area.

Contact your local Citizens' Advice Bureau, Police or Social Services. Find out at what age someone can be paid to look after young children in the home. Include the information in your handbook. Use the worksheet provided to help you with ideas on what to include in your handbook.

Make your handbook attractive to look at and easy to read. Use pictures or cartoons to illustrate the important points.

When your handbook on baby-sitting is complete give copies to friends who hope to do some baby-sitting. Give copies to people you know with young children who need a baby-sitter. Ask them to comment on your handbook. How useful do they find the advice and information? Amend and improve your handbook if you receive any helpful ideas.

Optional task Interview someone about their work as a baby-sitter. Write down a description of the worst situation they have ever experienced. Write the account as if it is for the letters page of a weekly magazine. Look at a few letters pages in magazines to get an idea of how the letters are written and how long they usually are. Write your account in a similar style.

(*See also* Worksheets: handbook on baby-sitting)

From this activity you may have evidence for:

Skills list	1, 3, 4, 6, 7, 13/14, 15, 16.
Core skills	Communication level 1 and 2.
Element	1.1/2.1 Take part in discussions.
Opportunities	Interview friends about baby-sitting experiences.
	Telephone for advice on minimum age for a baby-sitter.
	Ask people for comments about the handbook.
Element	1.2/2.2 Produce written material.
Opportunities	Write a baby-sitting handbook.
	Write a magazine-style letter (optional).
Element	1.3/2.3 Use images.
Opportunities	Use pictures to illustrate the handbook.
Element	1.4/2.4 Read and respond to written materials.
Opportunities	Read letters pages of magazines to check the style and length of letters (optional).

Activity 6 Design a mini-guide to home security

Have you ever had your home broken into and your possessions stolen? It is of course a very upsetting and stressful experience. A burglar can enter your home and steal small electrical items such as a TV, video, computer or CD player in a few minutes. The chances are the thief may give you a few weeks to replace the items you have lost and then return to your home and steal them again! You are left feeling angry and helpless. However, you can do a lot to protect your home and your possessions from theft. You can do a lot to put off a burglar who is just walking along a street looking for a likely house. If your home looks secure and occupied, with no valuables on show, the burglar will go somewhere else!

Design a mini-guide on home security, describing how to keep your home as safe as possible from theft.

Read through local newspapers. Look for any stories about theft or break-ins and note down ideas you get about how to keep your home safe. For example, a newspaper article may describe how a householder left a door unlocked while they popped round to the local shops. On returning home they found they had been burgled. An article may say a ladder left in the garden helped a burglar get into a house. Use these ideas in your mini-guide to suggest what not to do!

Collect more ideas for your mini-guide from friends, family and the people you work with. Ask them if they've ever had a burglary at home, and if so what changes did they make to keep their home safe. Contact your local Crime Prevention Officer by visiting the local Police station and asking some questions. Your local library may have some leaflets on the subject or a video you could borrow. Visit a DIY store and read the information on door locks and home alarms. Ask store assistants for help in finding products.

Add these ideas to your own for use in your guide:

■ leave lights on when you go out so it looks as if someone is at home

■ leave a radio playing when you go out so it sounds as if someone is at home

■ fit good quality locks on all of your outside doors

■ lock doors whenever you go out. Your house can be burgled in just a few minutes

■ don't hide spare keys in obvious places

■ fit window locks

■ if you can't afford an alarm fit a fake burglar alarm, available from DIY stores

■ fit outside security lights

■ don't leave equipment lying about which would help a burglar enter your home, e.g. ladders

■ don't leave valuable possessions where they can easily be seen through a window to tempt a thief

■ if you are going away, arrange for a neighbour to keep an eye on your home for you

■ don't chat about going away in your local shops for example, you never know who may be listening

 Design your mini-guide on home security either as a simple checklist with photographs and diagrams, or as a poster or as a short report with several sections explaining different ways to keep your home safe and secure. Choose the method of presentation which appeals to you most. Use the worksheet provided to help you plan and write your mini-guide.

 When your guide is finished, check you have covered all the important points about home security you planned to include. Photocopy your mini-guide and give a copy to friends, neighbours or people you work with. Ask them for their comments. Does your guide help them to review their own home security arrangements and make any useful changes?

(*See also* Worksheets: home security mini-guide)

From this activity you may have evidence for:

Skills list	1, 3, 4, 6, 7, 8, 10, 13/14, 15, 16.
Core skills	Communication level 1 and 2.
Element	1.1/2.1 Take part in discussions.
Opportunities	Talk about home security ideas with friends.
	Ask the Crime Prevention Officer for information.
	Ask an assistant for help at a DIY store.
	Ask a variety of people for comments on the guide.

Element	1.2/2.2 Produce written material.
Opportunities	Write a mini-guide on home security.
Element	1.3/2.3 Use images.
Opportunities	Use photographs and diagrams in the mini-guide.
Element	1.4/2.4 Read and respond to written materials.
Opportunities	Read local papers for information on keeping your home safe.
	Read information on security devices in a DIY store.
	Read books or leaflets about home security.

Evaluation exercise

Think about the activities you have worked on for this project. What do you know now that you didn't know before about keeping safe in and around the home? Can you recommend a safe play area to people you know who have young children? Will you check your home is safe and secure? Can you carry out DIY around the home more safely from now on, or help keep friends safe?

What skills do you feel more confident about? Do you feel more confident about asking questions or carrying out a survey? Do you feel your skills have improved in presenting information? Do you feel confident about using illustrations to highlight important points?

Check you have recorded the skills you have covered on your Skills Record Sheet. Have you included the date of work and the resources you have used? Complete your Skills Summary Record showing all you have achieved. Record your progress. Record details of the evidence you have for an accreditation you may be working towards. Write down details of further work you plan to carry out.

Playground safety

Part one: **carrying out a survey**

Use this suggested layout for your survey on safety in a local play area. Decide which safety points you want to look for. Add more ideas of your own to the ones listed.

Decide how you are going to record what you see. Rate each statement or question on your survey or write yes/no answers. Choose a rating system with five points, for example: 1 = poor, 2 = average, 3 = quite good, 4 = good, 5 = very good.

Safety points	Rating
A good surface underneath equipment	
Overall surface is:	
Grass/sand/tarmac/rubber/concrete	
Overall surface well looked after	
A safe barrier around the whole play area	
A safe barrier around dangerous equipment (e.g. swings)	
Plenty of space between equipment	
Equipment is suitable for a wide age range	
Play area is well maintained	
Individual pieces of equipment are maintained	
Do any pieces of equipment look unsafe?	
In what ways: rusting	
unstable	
children's fingers or heads could be trapped	

Add more ideas of your own:

Playground safety

Part two: **writing your report**

Set out your report under the following headings and write about what you have seen in your chosen play area.

- **Introduction**   Write down the name and location of the playground. Give a general idea of what you have seen. For example, was the playground busy? What kind of age groups did you see using it?

- **Surface**   Describe the overall surface of the play area and the condition it was in. Describe any different surfaces you noticed underneath pieces of equipment.

- **Access**   Comment on the barriers the site had. Was there a secure gate or access through the barriers? Describe how much space there was around pieces of equipment. Was the play area roomy or very cramped?

- **Equipment**   Describe the different pieces of equipment you saw and what kind of state they were in. Was there evidence of painting or repairs going on? Was there any new equipment? Was a good age range catered for in the play area?

- **Other factors**   Comment on other safety points you noticed in your survey such as the amount of litter about, bins provided, evidence of dog dirt or evidence of vandalism.

Presentation

Check your report for any spelling or punctuation mistakes. You may think you haven't made any mistakes, but if you proof-read carefully you're sure to find something which needs correcting!

Check your report is easy to understand. Someone else will read your report and they need to understand your ideas about safety.

Check you have included all the important points you want to make.

Check how your report looks on the paper. Underline headings and use different print or colour to highlight them on the page. Leave some white space so it is clear where one section ends and the next begins.

Toy information

Use this worksheet to help you plan and record the results of your investigation on toys. Add ideas of your own to the suggestions below. Look at more than three toys if you wish.

Information given	Toy 1	Toy 2	Toy 3
Is an age range suggested?	Yes/No	Yes/No	Yes/No
Does the toy look suitable for that age range?	Yes/No	Yes/No	Yes/No
Are you told how the toy can be used?	Yes/No	Yes/No	Yes/No
Does it have more than one use?	Yes/No	Yes/No	Yes/No
Is the toy washable?	Yes/No	Yes/No	Yes/No
Is the toy flammable?	Yes/No	Yes/No	Yes/No
Does the toy look well made?	Yes/No	Yes/No	Yes/No
Is a British Standard named?	Yes/No	Yes/No	Yes/No
Does the toy carry the Lion Mark?	Yes/No	Yes/No	Yes/No

Decision on investigation

What kind of labelling information is the most useful?

What else do you think you should be told about?

Guidelines for buying toys

Write down some guidelines to help people choose a safe toy for a child to play with at home. For example:

'look for a British Standard or the Lion Mark'
'look carefully at the toy for dangerous small parts'

1.

2.

3.

4.

Safety review

Choose one of the methods explained below to set out the safety review of your home or room.

A. Set out your safety review as a series of questions for each room. Give Yes or No answers. At the end of the review the more Yes answers you have the safer your home is. For example:

Bathroom

1. Do I put all medicines away in a locked cupboard?   Yes/No

2. Do I store toilet/bath cleaner in a safe place?   Yes/No

3. Do I always turn the cold tap on first when running a bath?   Yes/No

B. Award a number of stars for the safety level of each room in your safety review. The more stars you award the safer your home is. For example:

**** = very safe *** = safe ** = reasonable * = dangerous

Choose categories and fill in the stars against each room. For example:

	Poisons	Obstacles	Fire hazard
Kitchen			
Bathroom			
Living room			
Bedroom			
Garage/garden			

C. Set out your review looking at one safety concern at a time throughout your home, for example, poisons. In the bathroom it may be a medicine, in the garage it may be slug pellets. Copy the layout below, repeating it for each safety concern in your review.

Poisons

Do I have poisons in the *kitchen*?   Yes/No

What are they?

1   2   3   4

Do I store all them safely?   Yes/No

Can I improve how I store them?   Yes/No

DIY safety

Select examples of accidents which you can use in your guide to First Aid for bleeding. Pick at least two serious and two minor accidents. For example:

- slipped on gravel path and grazed knee
- tripped over tool and got deep cut on palm of hand
- fell from ladder and gashed leg
- skinned knuckles moving some rubble

Next, find out about First Aid for bleeding. Try any of these methods:

- look in your local library for a First Aid manual or video
- write to St. John Ambulance or the British Red Cross for information
- ask a First Aider at work for information
- watch a television programme about First Aid

Finally, set out your research:

- as a leaflet
- as a pocket-size guide
- as a poster
- as a credit card-size guide
- as a chart (can be increased or reduced in size on a photocopier)

Any other ideas?

Use this example to help start your guide:

Accident	Diagram	Treatment
The casualty slipped while climbing a pair of metal ladders and gashed the palm of their hand on a sharp metal edge.	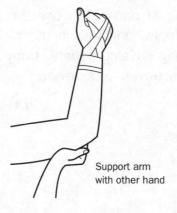 Support arm with other hand	Press sterile pad firmly over cut in palm. Ask person to grip it with fingers. Bandage pad and fingers together so good pressure kept on palm. Support arm in raised position. Take injured person to hospital.

Handbook on baby-sitting

Add more ideas of your own to the suggestions below and put them all into a sensible order. Set out your ideas as a series of questions or headings with the answers provided. Present your handbook as a leaflet or guide book, or on tape as an audio guide.

The baby-sitter

- Find out a little about the child you will be looking after such as their favourite games and activities.
- Ask how the child likes to be soothed if he/she is upset or wakeful.
- Find out what bed time routines the child likes if you are baby-sitting in the evening.
- Check you have been given full details of where the parent is and how to contact them or someone else in an emergency.
- Find out how to lock the house securely. Find out if any callers are expected.
- Find out about any possible problems such as:
  - the child has a cold and is feeling a little unwell
  - the child hasn't been told he/she is going to have a baby-sitter
- Ask a few basic questions about the job such as:
  - how much will you be paid per hour?
  - will you be given a lift home if the parent returns very late at night?
  - are you allowed to invite a friend to sit with you?

Parent/guardian

- Make sure you know what type of person you want to employ. Who would you trust your child with and who would your child feel happy with?
- Ask questions so you find out the information you need about the baby-sitter, e.g. age, experience, etc.
- List what you should tell the baby-sitter about your child, e.g. child has asthma, sometimes wakes and needs a drink of water, likes listening to songs and stories, etc.
- Decide what rules you have and explain them to the baby-sitter carefully, e.g. you may not wish them to smoke.
- Decide how much you can afford to pay. Check the local rate. Can you offer any extras such as a meal, a lift home, more money for a late night for example?

Multi-use ■ *Use this worksheet for ideas on collecting and presenting information.*

Home security mini-guide

Use this worksheet to help you decide where to go to collect information for your mini-guide and how to present the information. Tick the suggestions you will try.

Ask yourself: **Where can I go for information?**

Collect ideas from my own experiences ☐

Ask friends/family for suggestions ☐

Watch useful TV programmes for ideas ☐

Contact useful people or organisations, e.g. my local Crime Prevention Officer: by letter / by telephone / in person ☐

Read local newspapers for helpful articles ☐

Visit the local library for books, videos, magazines, back copies of newspapers ☐

Visit the local Citizens' Advice Bureau ☐

Look through suitable catalogues for ideas ☐

Visit a DIY store to read information on packaging, e.g. locks, alarms ☐

Use Yellow Pages to contact local firms for brochures ☐

Ask yourself: **From all the information I have collected what would I like to include in my guide? What would be a sensible order for the information? How am I going to present the information I have chosen?**

A ten point advice list. ☐

A checklist. Use pictures or cartoons to highlight each point. ☐

A poster. Show a burglary taking place. Use labels to explain how each part of the house could be made more safe against theft. ☐

A leaflet. Give general guidelines with pictures. Use colour to highlight each important point. ☐

An audio tape. Describe your guidelines. ☐

A short report. Each section deals with one point. ☐

Back to basics

Answers on pp. 307–8.

Write a note

You notice the flex on your iron is wearing at the plug and seems to be loose. You haven't got time to check it as you are about to leave for work. You decide to leave a note to warn your partner/friend/daughter/lodger not to use the iron as it could be dangerous.

Write a short, clear note to the person of your choice. Explain why the iron should not be used and say you will check it when you come home from work.

Proof-reading

Rewrite the following information about cold compresses. Put back the missing capitals, commas and full stops.

> cooling an injury such as a nasty bruise or sprain can help reduce swelling place the injured part under cold running water or in a bowl of cold water when injuries need longer cooling use a cold compress if you have no ice cubes handy you can make a cold compress from a bag of frozen peas never put the ice bag directly onto skin always wrap it in a cloth first apply the compress to the injured part and hold it in place for 20 minutes

Advertisement

Imagine you would like to get some paid work, baby-sitting in your local area. Write a card to put in the newsagent's window advertising your baby-sitting services. Include the following information:

> your name and telephone number
> you have your own transport
> you are reliable and experienced in caring for children
> you can provide references

Alternatives Other ideas for activities on safety

Any activity from the suggested group or individual projects can be replaced with an idea from the list below. Use the list to give you more choice of activities to do which suit your needs, interests and the amount of time you have available.

■ Compare different types of job to see which one is the most dangerous or the most likely to cause accidents. Write your opinion of dangerous jobs.

■ Investigate other areas of safety at work such as using electrical equipment or working at heights for example.

■ Arrange a properly supervised visit to a factory or large store or even a building site. Find out about problems with safety and how safety regulations are enforced. Write a report about your visit.

■ Arrange for a speaker to visit, e.g. a Health and Safety Officer. List the questions you would like to ask.

■ Find out about the different safety signs you see around you at work. Write down the meanings of the colour coding and symbols used. Design your own safety sign.

■ Learn some First Aid. Go to a First Aid class, or watch a video on First Aid, or arrange for a demonstration.

■ Write a guide on how elderly people can keep safe in their own homes. Contact a charity such as Age Concern for information.

■ Talk to someone such as a Health Visitor about the safety of children in the home. Write a guide on child safety at home.

■ Learn through role play how to give the Emergency Services all the information they need quickly and efficiently.

■ Investigate the cost of First Aid equipment for the home. Compile a list for the contents of a good basic First Aid box for home use.

■ Make a video showing how to plan and use a sensible escape route from your home in the event of a fire.

■ Survey and work out the cost for installing security equipment in an average home. Cover items such as security lights, alarms and window and door locks.

Time for recreation

INTRODUCTION

In this group project on *time for recreation* you will be able to:

- Discuss the benefits of leisure and recreation.

- Chart the activities people enjoy in their recreation time.

- Design a quiz on leisure activities.

- Discuss the problems people have finding time for recreation.

- Design a guide on how to solve recreation problems.

- Write a resolution to try a new recreation activity.

- Collect information and write a directory listing local recreation opportunities.

- Write your opinion about recreation chances for the whole community.

- Design a schedule for a new Breakfast Show on commercial radio.

- Research and present a written or spoken presentation on a new leisure activity.

- Select and review a television programme about leisure.

- Write a letter to put forward a case for an unusual sport to be shown on television.

- Discuss the enjoyment of eating out.

- Design an ideal menu for a take-away.

- Write a check list for how to complain about a meal.

- Evaluate your work on the project.

Choose activities which interest you from the wide range of suggestions provided in the project. You can choose to do just part of an activity if you wish. The choice is yours. There are more suggestions in the Alternative Ideas section (p. 101), so you should find enough activities to suit your interests and needs. Finish with the Evaluation Exercise as this will help you think about your work on the project and remind you to record the skills you have covered.

For each activity you choose to do use the information provided for you in the activity text and worksheets, as well as your own experiences and knowledge. If you need to look for more information consider resources such as books, newspapers and magazines as well as television, radio, video and CD-ROM. You can also use resources such as writing to an organisation or telephoning for information, talking to people you know and talking to other people who may be able to give you the information you need.

Optional task   If you have more time available and would like to try another task to develop the skills you have already used in an activity, you can look for the Optional Tasks which are linked to many of the project activities.

You will find the following worksheets useful:

Time for recreation

Activity 1   ### Discuss the benefits of recreation and list activities

What is recreation and how does it benefit you? Recreation is something you can do to refresh, entertain and amuse yourself. It is leisure time you can enjoy when you're not working to make money to live on, or studying or looking after your family. Most people have some spare time in their week to relax and enjoy a little recreation. You may do a sport or hobby in your spare time for a variety of reasons. For example, you may enjoy line dancing. You would benefit because:

■ it's a dance done with a group of people

■ you don't need a partner

■ it's quite easy to pick up as there is a caller telling you what to do

■ it's fun and you have a good laugh as people usually make a few mistakes

■ it's good exercise

Discuss the following list of benefits you may enjoy by finding the time for a little leisure and recreation. Add your own ideas to the list. Make your discussion a brainstorming exercise. Everyone can say just what comes into their head about the subject and it can be

written down on a board or large piece of paper. Don't stop to question the ideas at this stage. When all the ideas have been written down look at them and discuss them carefully. For example, someone may suggest taking some time for recreation helps deal with stress. They may be feeling some stress because of problems at work, home or with money troubles. They may be getting headaches or stomach upsets or sleeping badly. Finding time for leisure and relaxation and forgetting about problems for just a short time can really help.

Discuss these benefits. Recreation can:

- help reduce stress
- help you relax
- help you feel less tired and more energetic
- help you meet new people and make new friends
- help you have some fun
- help you sleep better
- help you keep healthy
- help you learn new skills
- involve you in your community, perhaps raising money or organising an event
- get you involved in doing something as a family

Consider carefully all the ideas you have talked about and written down. Did everyone have similar ideas about the benefits of recreation? Did anyone have any very different ideas? Decide which benefits you all feel are the most important.

Think next about how you actually spend your recreation time. Record the hobbies, sports and activities which you all do at the moment. You may find there is quite a variety from computer games, listening to CDs, playing snooker, chatting to friends or going out for a drink, to swimming, Tai Chi and weight-lifting! Record the activities you all enjoy and the benefits you feel you gain from doing them. Write down the problems you have to sort out to be able to do the activities. Include details of the equipment you need and the costs of each activity.

Record the details of your activities either as a chart or as a loose-leaf folder. Use old magazines, catalogues, Sunday supplements and newspapers to find illustrations. Use the worksheet provided to help you with your written record. Allocate tasks to each other. Work in pairs or each write up the information for one activity on the group's list.

Discuss your chart or folder together and decide which recreation activities sound interesting. Is there anything you would each like to try from the ideas you have recorded – perhaps something you have never tried before?

Optional task   Divide into two teams. Write quiz questions for the other team based on the leisure and recreation activities enjoyed by celebrities. Choose people from film, television or sport or pop stars. Use newspapers and magazines to find out how your chosen celebrities spend their leisure time. Work out some rules for your quiz, for example who will ask the questions and how to keep the score.

(*See also* Worksheets: recreation record)

From this activity you may have evidence for:

Skills list	1, 2, 3, 5, 11, 13/14, 15, 16.
Core skills	Communication level 1 and 2.
Element	1.1/2.1 Take part in discussions.
Opportunities	Discuss benefits of recreation.
	Discuss recreation activities enjoyed by group members.
	Take part in a quiz about celebrities' recreation activities (optional).
Element	1.2/2.2 Produce written material.
Opportunities	Write a list of recreation benefits.
	Write a chart or folder of recreation activities.
	Write quiz questions (optional).
Element	1.3/2.3 Use images.
Opportunities	Use pictures or photographs to illustrate the chart or folder on recreation.
Element	1.4/2.4 Read and respond to written materials.
Opportunities	Read newspapers and magazines for information about the leisure activities of celebrities (optional).

Activity 2   Write a guide on how to cope with recreation problems

You may have to solve a variety of problems before you can relax and enjoy your leisure time. For example:

■ **Money**   Some hobbies or sports may be too expensive to try, such as scuba diving. You may be able to hire or buy second hand equipment from a local club. Look for a similar but cheaper sport, such as snorkelling.

■ **Travel**   A leisure activity you enjoy may be held at a club or centre too far from your home. It may be expensive or take too long to travel there. You may not be happy about travelling late in the evening. Go with a friend or arrange for several people to share travel costs.

■ **Equipment**   Equipment may be expensive or difficult to buy or you may not be sure what you are supposed to have. Hire what you need or borrow from a friend or a club. A local club or sports shop should be able to tell you what equipment you need.

■ **Childcare**   If there is no one to help look after your family you may feel you can't enjoy any hobbies or recreation time. Arrange a care swap with a friend, or find a centre which has a crèche. Find a hobby which the whole family can enjoy together.

■ **Shyness**   Sometimes people are too shy to join a new class or club. They decide not to try out a new activity because they think they may not be very good at it. Go along with a friend or try a taster session which has been arranged for beginners.

■ **Pressure**   You may have pressure from family or friends to stop doing an activity. They may think it's a waste of time or money or they disapprove of what you are doing. Explain your reasons calmly to them.

 Discuss the problems which stop people from enjoying recreation time and decide on some solutions which people could try. Discuss your own experiences for ideas. Make sure you all get a chance to speak. Note down your ideas as you go along. Use your ideas to design an attractive guide which describes the problems and offers some solutions for people to try.

 If you need more ideas for problems and solutions for your guide, telephone your local council's Leisure and Recreation Department. Ask for leaflets giving information about how they help people enjoy recreation by providing taster sessions or transport for example. Ask a local charity which helps people with leisure activities for information. Ask friends, relatives and people you work with for ideas. Tape their comments. Listen to the tapes together and note down any ideas you think should be used in your guide.

 Present your guide as a leaflet, poster or an audio tape. Illustrate your guide with photographs, pictures or cartoons. Use music if you are making a tape. Allocate tasks to each other to get the work done. Work in pairs on one part of the guide. Meet as a group again to put the guide together.

 Display your guide for others to read or listen to and arrange for people to borrow it. Ask them to comment on how useful they feel it is. Ask them to comment on how easy your guide is to use. Amend your guide if you receive any helpful suggestions.

Optional task   Each write a resolution to try a new recreation activity for your own benefit. Discuss what resolutions you could all make. Help each other to check you are each being realistic about how much time or money you have to spare. Decide which would be the best day and time to try the new activity and where you can go locally to do it. Discuss what benefits you each hope to gain. What problems will you have to sort out? Record your own decision on the worksheet provided. Agree a reasonable date and time to report back to each other about your progress. At that time, describe your activities to each other and answer questions about your experiences.

(*See also* Worksheets: resolution record)

From this activity you may have evidence for:

Skills list	1, 2, 3, 4, 5, 6, 7, 8, 10, 11, 13/14, 15, 16.
Core skills	Communication level 1 and 2.
Element	1.1/2.1 Take part in discussions.
Opportunities	Discuss the problems which stop people enjoying recreation.
	Ask people for ideas about different problems.
	Make an audio tape on problems and solutions.
	Discuss making resolutions (optional).
	Talk about progress and answer questions about a recreation activity (optional).
Element	1.2/2.2 Produce written material.
Opportunities	Make notes during discussion on recreation problems.
	Write a guide on recreation problems and solutions.
	Record a resolution and update it (optional).
Element	1.3/2.3 Use images.
Opportunities	Use pictures, cartoons or photographs to illustrate the guide.
Element	1.4/2.4 Read and respond to written materials.
Opportunities	Read information about recreation problems.

Activity 3   Write a directory for recreation

Find out how many different recreation activities can be enjoyed in your local area. Collect information and write a directory of recreation for your local area.

Use you own knowledge and experience and add to this by reading local newspapers for more information. Look at adverts and posters in local shops, the library and community centres. Write to local clubs or groups, colleges and sports centres and ask for details of all the recreation activities they offer. Contact the Tourist Information Centre if you have one locally. Allocate the tasks between you to get the research work done. Each research one activity or work in pairs or small groups finding out about one aspect, such as all the travel details for example. Report back to the group to pool information.

Select what information you would like to include in your directory. Decide what details you are going to give about each activity you list. What would people like to know about each activity? For example, if you listed swimming as a local recreation activity, include:

- how to get to the pool (a map, diagram or bus details)
- details of different sessions, times and costs
- special rates for groups
- special classes such as mother and toddler, over 50s, aquafit or fun sessions with a giant inflatable
- any other facilities such as a cafeteria, spectator seating, or hire facilities

Add ideas of your own and use the worksheet to help you set out your directory. Illustrate it with maps, diagrams, pictures or cartoons.

Make copies of your directory to give to friends and people you work with. Put copies in your local library or community centre for people to pick up. Ask people to comment on how useful they find the directory. Amend your directory if you receive any helpful feedback.

Optional task Discuss and then each write your opinion about what is done in your local area to provide chances for recreation for all groups of people. For example, is enough provided for elderly people in your opinion or for people with a disability or for the very young?

(*See also* Worksheets: directory checklist)

	From this activity you may have evidence for:
Skills list	1, 2, 3, 4, 6, 7, 8/9, 10, 11, 12, 13/14, 15, 16.
Core skills	Communication level 1 and 2.
Element	1.1/2.1 Take part in discussions.
Opportunities	Discuss what to include in a directory of local recreation activities.
	Ask people for information on local recreation activities.
	Ask people for their opinion of the directory.
	Discuss whether recreation chances are provided for everyone in your local area (optional).
Element	1.2/2.2 Produce written material.
Opportunities	Write a letter to a local organisation asking for information.
	Write a directory on local recreation activities.
	Write your opinion on recreation chances for everyone (optional).
Element	1.3/2.3 Use images.
Opportunities	Use maps, diagrams and photographs to illustrate the directory.
Element	1.4/2.4 Read and respond to written materials.
Opportunities	Read a variety of information about recreation activities available in your local area.

Activity 4 Write a schedule for a radio Breakfast Show

Listening to the radio can be a relaxing and enjoyable leisure activity. Many people prefer radio to television. They enjoy being able to listen to music, news, information or gossip while doing another task at the same time. They may have particular programmes which they always listen to while carrying out tasks at home and at work. Listening to the radio can be very important for people who live by themselves. The presenters' voices can help people feel as if they have some company and are not alone.

Imagine you are all part of a team starting up a new, small commercial radio station in your area. Discuss and design the format for a Breakfast Show. You have got a young, lively presenter and DJ, and a guest celebrity as it's the first show (you decide who this is). You've got commercial breaks every fifteen minutes, airing four 30-second adverts each time. Write out the schedule for the first day. What features and music would wake people up and put them in a good mood for the rest of the day?

Discuss which radio programmes you listen to while you are waking up, having breakfast and getting yourselves and perhaps other people in your family ready for work. Discuss what you like and dislike about the station you listen to.

Tune in and listen to a variety of breakfast shows on the radio. Make notes about what you hear. Allocate different stations between you and report back to the group with ideas on what was good and what should be avoided! Consider:

- the type of music played

- the relationship the presenter had with the listeners

- the length of the programme

- the news, weather and traffic information

- the length and format of adverts

- was there gossip about celebrities, sports stars, film and music stars?

- was there a phone-in, competition or dedications?

Have a brainstorming session about the schedule for your Breakfast Show. Use the notes and ideas you have gathered by listening to other radio shows. Decide who you think your audience will be. What will they want to hear? Listen to and note down all of your ideas, without commenting much at this stage. Next, look at the ideas you have written down and discuss them in detail. Agree on a planned schedule for the first day of your Breakfast Show. Use the worksheet provided to help you with your written schedule.

Allocate to each other parts of the show to work on, either in pairs or small groups. For example, some people may work on music selections, others on the celebrity guest interview, another on horoscopes, a phone-in or the news and weather information. Meet up often to pool information on your progress and plans. Amend your plans as you work on each part of your Breakfast Show.

Write down details of your final, agreed schedule for the Breakfast Show. Record part of your Breakfast Show if you have access to equipment. Allocate different tasks and roles to each other.

 Play back your show and discuss whether it sounds as you hoped it would. Would it attract the audience you had in mind? Why would listeners tune into your Breakfast Show? Discuss which parts of the show you liked. What would you change or improve if you had the chance?

(*See also* Worksheets: Breakfast Show)

From this activity you may have evidence for:

Skills list	1, 2, 3, 5, 6, 10, 11, 12, 13, 15, 16.
Core skills	Communication level 1 and 2.
Element	1.1/2.1 Take part in discussions.
Opportunities	Listen to radio shows and evaluate them.
	Discuss ideas for a radio Breakfast Show.
	Discuss and assess a recording of the show.
Element	1.2/2.2 Produce written material.
Opportunities	Make notes about radio shows.
	Write a list of ideas to discuss.
	Write a planned schedule for a breakfast radio show.
	Write a finished schedule for a breakfast radio show.

Activity 5   Research and present information about a new leisure activity

Find out about a hobby, sport or leisure activity which you have never tried before. Work in pairs or small groups and help each other to find information about a range of new activities. Research and present a complete picture of your chosen recreation activity, either as a magazine-style written report or as a spoken presentation. Use the worksheet provided to help you plan your presentation.

Read through the list below for some ideas or choose something else you have always wanted to find out about.

slide aerobics	line dancing	Irish dancing
playing the drums	water polo	computer games
arcade games	street hockey	bingo
candle making	karate	Tai Chi
fashion photography	snooker	scuba diving
rowing	kite flying	power walking
meditation	rock climbing	fencing
bowling	travel	cooking
repairing cars	hair and make-up	sugar craft

Help each other by looking out for useful television and radio programmes. Write to clubs or organisations for information. Arrange to visit your local library to do some research there. Look for books, magazines, tapes or videos for information. Use the worksheet provided to help you get the most from your library visit. The children's section can be a useful source for photographs, pictures or diagrams.

Interview an expert in the activity you are finding out about. Record the interview on tape. Use some of the information in your written presentation or play back part of the interview in your spoken presentation.

Present your research about a new leisure activity to the rest of the group. Give a spoken presentation with visual aids or give access to your written magazine-style report.

Give each other feedback about the different written or spoken reports you present to the group. Make sure your remarks are positive and helpful.

(*See also* Worksheets: library research. Presentation checklist)

From this activity you may have evidence for:

Skills list	1, 2, 3, 4, 5, 6, 7, 8/9, 13/14, 15, 16.
Core skills	Communication level 1 and 2.

Element	1.1/2.1 Take part in discussions.
Opportunities	Ask for help with research in the library.
	Ask an expert for information on a recreation activity.
	Give a spoken presentation on a recreation activity.
	Give feedback on each other's presentations.
Element	1.2/2.2 Produce written material.
Opportunities	Write a report on a recreation activity.
Element	1.3/2.3 Use images.
Opportunities	Use photographs, pictures and diagrams in a written or spoken report.
Element	1.4/2.4 Read and respond to written materials.
Opportunities	Read books, magazines and leaflets for information about a new recreation activity.

Activity 6 Watch and review a television programme

A wide range of programmes on television each week give you ideas about how to spend your recreation time. You may watch a holiday programme and decide to visit a place or country because it looked interesting and attractive. You may try out a new recipe or style of cooking because a television chef has demonstrated a delicious meal. You may join a club and go pot-holing, off-road cycling or climbing because you watched a programme which made it look really exciting!

Choose one programme about a recreation activity which would interest you all. Watch it together and review it (or video and view together). Use the worksheet provided to help you with your review. For example, you may decide to watch a programme about the latest film releases because you all enjoy going to the cinema.

Find a programme to discuss and review by studying a weekly television guide or a week's supply of newspapers. Highlight or list the programmes which give ideas about how to spend your recreation time. These could be gardening, cookery, skiing, fashion, exercise, foreign language, motoring or holiday programmes for example. You should find plenty of choice. Use your list to decide which programme you will discuss and review.

Write down the main points as you watch your chosen programme. Discuss the programme and use your notes to refresh your memories about the important points. Ask yourselves:

- did you like the programme?
- was it entertaining and interesting?
- what age group was being targeted?
- was the programme aimed at people who already know a lot about the subject or did it have a wide appeal?

■ did the programme offer useful information?

■ did the programme make you feel enthusiastic about the leisure activity?

Use the ideas from your discussion to each write a short review about the programme. Write your review as if you were a TV critic, writing for a daily newspaper. Collect some newspapers and have a look at the reviews to get an idea of how they are written. There are usually some critic's reviews on the television guide pages. Are they written in a chatty style, do they just give facts or is it a bit of both?

Explain briefly about the contents of the programme. Comment on what you liked about the format of the programme. Do you feel you were given enough information on each item? Comment on any demonstrations of skills, interviews with experts or special offers. Do you feel the programme appealed to a wide enough audience?

Compare your finished reviews. Did you all feel the same about the programme or did people express different opinions in their reviews? Would you recommend the programme to other people? Are you going to try a recreation activity because of information in the programme?

Optional task   Write a letter to a television station of your choice. Put forward an argument for showing a programme about a recreation activity which is not shown at the moment. Write down reasons for why people would enjoy finding out about your suggested recreation activity. Explain how people would benefit from your proposed programme.

Read over all of your suggestions. Take a vote on which ones you would all like to see on television.

If you have access to the equipment you could video your points of view, having one minute each. Explain why your choices should be shown on television. Watch the video entries together and decide which one is the most persuasive and why.

(*See also* Worksheets: programme review)

From this activity you may have evidence for:

Skills list   1, 2, 3, 6, 8, 10, 11, 12, 13, 15, 16.

Core skills   Communication level 1 and 2.

Element   1.1/2.1 Take part in discussions.

Opportunities   Discuss the choice of programme to review.

Watch, discuss and review your chosen programme.

Discuss and vote on programme proposals (optional).

Element	1.2/2.2 Produce written material.
Opportunities	Highlight or list recreation programmes.
	Make notes about a programme.
	Write a review of a television programme.
	Write a letter putting forward an argument for a new programme on television (optional).
Element	1.4/2.4 Read and respond to written materials.
Opportunities	Read a weekly television guide to select a programme to watch. Read a variety of TV critics in newspapers for ideas about writing a review.

Activity 7   Eating out

One leisure activity which many people enjoy is going out for a meal. Eating out can be an enjoyable social event. It is time spent with friends or family members or getting to know new people. Eating out can be relaxing, as you can sit back and let other people do the work. It can be a chance to try out new foods, celebrate a special event or to show other people you care about them.

Discuss what kind of food you all enjoy and where you like to eat out. Do you think it is an expensive recreation activity? Decide if you would rather go out for a meal or have a take-away meal at home. What would be the benefits of both? When you eat out, is it always planned or do you sometimes go on the spur of the moment? Do you enjoy eating in the street or do you prefer to sit down in a café, pub or restaurant?

Have a good discussion about why people enjoy taking the time to eat out. Listen to each other's views and make sure everyone has a chance to speak. Consider:

- what special occasions do you celebrate by eating out?
- what are your favourite kinds of food?
- where do you like to go?
- do you ever eat out alone?
- when do you enjoy fast food?
- when do you enjoy a take-away?
- what kind of food are you happy to eat in the street?

Discuss next what different dietary needs people have in the group, perhaps for a medical condition or for a cultural reason. One person may be allergic to nuts for example, another may be on a low fat diet, a third person may not wish to eat meat. Produce a list of all the special food needs the group has for when they eat out.

Collect some menus from take-away eating places in your local area. Decide where you could find some different types of menus and agree who is going to collect each one. For example, look for Italian, Chinese and Indian take-aways as well as chicken and burger type take-aways and fish and chip shops. Ask for a printed menu or make notes about the meals on offer. Put your collection of menus together and take a good look at the choice on offer.

Choose your favourite meals from the range of menus you have collected. Use your choices to design an ideal take-away menu for yourselves. It must meet all the dietary needs of the group.

 Set your selections out as an actual menu. Organise your meal selections so they are in a sensible order. For example put vegetarian choices together or put a star by meals which meet a special cultural or medical need. If you have the equipment, use a computer and clip art program to get a professional looking finish. Design an attractive border for your menu. Decide on a name. Allocate tasks between you to get the presentation work done.

 Discuss how practical your take-away menu really is. Have you met everyone's special food needs? Do you think you would find an eating place offering a take-away menu with the kind of selections you have put together? Do you think it would be a popular take-away if it did exist? What would attract people to use a take-away with a menu like yours? Ask other people to comment on what would attract them to your take-away menu.

 Next, discuss what would make you complain about a meal you have ordered in a café, pub or restaurant. Are you willing to complain if you think something is not right? Are you most likely to complain about the food, the service or the price? Share experiences you have had of complaining about a meal when eating out. Describe what happened.

Decide together on the best way to make a complaint about a meal when eating out. How can you make sure you get a successful result? Discuss the following ideas:

■ make the complaint promptly – don't sit there feeling cross, do something about it!

■ don't lose your temper, be polite

■ be firm about what you want

■ give them a chance to put things right or offer you an alternative before you storm out!

■ don't be afraid to complain, you have a right to expect value for money

■ don't be put off if other people look at you, they may be admiring your confidence!

Use your own experiences to choose some situations where you need to complain about a meal. Get more ideas on how to complain about poor service from your local Citizens' Advice Bureau or Office of Fair Trading. You should find both of their numbers in your telephone book. Try some role plays of the situations and see what happens. Use your actions in the role play to give you more ideas for how to and how not to complain!

Write out your ideas as a 'how to complain' checklist or make an audio tape guide on how to complain about a meal.

Show your checklist or guide to other people. Ask them if they would find your advice useful in a difficult situation. Make copies for people to pick up and use. Amend your checklist or guide if you receive helpful comments on any parts of it which can be improved.

From this activity you may have evidence for:

Skills list	1, 2, 3, 4, 6, 7, 8, 10, 11, 13/14, 15, 16.
Core skills	Communication level 1 and 2.
Element	1.1/2.1 Take part in discussions.
Opportunities	Discuss ideas on eating out as a leisure activity.
	Discuss different dietary needs.
	Discuss the group's ideal take-away menu.
	Ask other people for their opinion of your menu.
	Ask the CAB or Office of Fair Trading for information on making a complaint.
	Try out role plays to find ways of complaining.
	Ask people for their opinion about your complaint checklist.
Element	1.2/2.2 Produce written material.

Opportunities	List the group's diet needs, likes and dislikes.
	Write an ideal take-away menu.
	Write a checklist for making a complaint about a meal.
Element	1.3/2.3 Use images.
Opportunities	Use clip art to illustrate your menu.
Element:	1.4/2.4 Read and respond to written materials.
Opportunities	Read a selection of menus from local take-aways.
	Read information about making a complaint to use in your checklist or guide.

 ## Evaluation exercise

Discuss the work you have done on this project. Do you feel you now know more about the benefits and problems involved in finding time for recreation? Have you found out more about your local facilities? Are you going to try any new recreation activities?

Do you feel more confident about your research skills? Do you feel more able to present information in a variety of ways? Have you gained competence in asking for information? Do you feel confident about taking part in a group discussion?

Check you have recorded the skills you have practised on your Skills Record Sheet. Write down details of the resources you have used to show the wide variety. Complete your Skills Summary Record. Record your progress and achievements. Write down details of any skills you would like to practise further. Decide on a realistic goal date. Record all evidence of competence you have collected for an accreditation you may be working towards.

Recreation record

Record the recreation activities enjoyed by the group either as a chart or in a folder. Show pictures of each activity or photographs of yourselves enjoying the activities. Include details of the benefits you have noticed such as meeting new people, learning new skills, etc. Comment on possible problems, such as travel, costs and child care difficulties.

Presentation idea: chart

Names of people who do activity	Brief description of the activity	Benefits	Problems and cost
1.			
2.			

Presentation idea: folder

Allow one page for each recreation activity you are going to write about.

Allocate tasks to each other. Work in pairs on one recreation activity.

Give a description of the activity and some facts about it. Include photos of people in the group enjoying the activity.

Give information about costs, equipment, skills you need to start with and what you can learn. Give details on whether the activity can be done alone or in a team or group of people.

List the benefits to be gained from each activity and comment on possible problems.

Make sure your folder is attractive. Use headings, colour, diagrams, pictures and photographs.

Resolution record

Name   Date

I resolve to try   as a recreation

activity on   every week / two weeks / month.

The cost is likely to be   and I will need

the following items of equipment

I can hire

The benefits I hope to gain from doing this activity are

The problems I may have are

I will report back about my progress and experiences on

At that time I will tell the rest of the group whether I kept my resolution.
I will explain what benefits I feel I have gained. I will describe any
problems I have had and how I solved them. I will say if the activity was
worth trying and if I would recommend it to others.

Signed

Directory checklist

Include some or all of these headings in your directory for each recreation activity you describe. Give useful information which helps people decide what recreation activity to try.

- **Description of activity**   Write a brief description of what the activity is like.

- **Location of activity**   Write names of places and how to find them, include diagrams and maps.

- **Transport to reach activity**   Give details of local bus or train services with a telephone number to check times and routes.

- **Costs**   Give an idea of cost and any special rates.

- **Equipment needed**   Give information about what kind of equipment is needed and a suggestion on suitable clothing. Say if equipment can be hired.

- **Skills needed**   Describe any basic skills which are needed to enjoy the activity or say if it can be done by a complete beginner.

- **Fitness rating**   Give an idea of how fit you need to be to enjoy the activity.

- **Social rating**   Give information about whether you can do the activity alone or with a partner or in a team or group.

- **Child care facilities available**   Give details on any crèche facilities and what age the child must be.

- **Benefits the activity may offer**   List what benefits you may gain from the activity such as meeting people, weight loss, relaxation, etc.

- **Possible problems**   Give an idea of any problems involved with doing this activity such as a long waiting list because it's popular, it is easy to get injured, etc.

Breakfast Show

Record your decisions about the Breakfast Show. Write a brief note about each part of the broadcast and who is responsible for it. Write detailed plans for each of the work areas on separate sheets as your ideas develop. Use this worksheet so you all have a copy of the overall plan.

Name chosen for Breakfast Show

Details   **Who is responsible**

DJ: profile of personality and style

Jingles
Introduce the news
The weather
Horoscopes
Guest
Local events

Details of commercials
Slot 1
     2
     3
     4

Music
Details of selections and playing order

Guest celebrity
Time slot for interview
Format for interview
Questions to ask celebrity

Phone-in subject
Time slot for phone-in
Theme for phone-in

Dedications
Time slot for dedications
Theme for dedications

News and weather, national and local
Time slots
Length

Specials
Free adverts for charities
Horoscopes

Multi-use ■ *Use this worksheet to help with library research.*

Library research

Name   **Date**

Details of activity to research

What I need to find out

Who I am going to work with

Library Catalogue reference numbers

Titles of books which may be useful

1.

2.

3.

4.

Details of other resources which may be useful

Specialist magazines

Audio tapes

Video tapes

Newspapers

Reference Library materials

People who can help

Organisations to write to

Multi-use ■ *Use this worksheet for ideas on presentation.*

Presentation checklist

Present your research as a magazine-style written report or a spoken report with visual aids.

Written presentation

■ Collect all the information you can on your chosen subject.

■ Hold a planning meeting – decide what you are going to include in your report and allocate sections and tasks to each other.

■ Decide on a clear structure and style which you all agree to follow. Give each section a heading. Start with an introduction and go on to cover the main points. Sum up at the end of your report. Say why you chose this activity to research and why you found it interesting.

■ Meet again and go over your rough work to check you have included everything you planned.

■ Check all the finished work for spelling or punctuation mistakes. Put the report together.

■ Check you have all included pictures, diagrams and photos in a suitable place in your written work.

Spoken report

■ Collect all the information you can on your chosen activity.

■ Hold a planning meeting and decide what you are going to include in your spoken report. Allocate sections and tasks to each other.

■ Plan your presentation. Have a clear structure and you will each feel more confident about your role.

■ Have a trial run through and check you have included all the information you planned to put in. Make notes about what you each have to say on small pieces of card, for example.

■ Decide how best to use any photos, diagrams, demonstrations of skills or taped interviews with experts.

■ Finally, speak clearly and remember to smile! Sound interested in what you are saying and your audience will be interested. Don't worry if you make a mistake, just pause to calm yourself and start again.

Multi-use ■ *Use this worksheet for programme reviews.*

Programme review

Details of programme

Title of programme

Day   Date

Time: From   To   Channel

Review

Explain briefly the contents of the programme

Do you think the television guide gave you enough information about the
programme?   Yes/No

Did you enjoy the programme?   Yes/No

Explain why

Did the programme give you enough information about each item?   Yes/No

Did you find the programme interesting?   Yes/No

Explain why

What was the format of the programme?

What did you find out which you didn't know before about the recreation
activity?

What didn't you like about the programme?

Would you recommend the programme to others?   Yes/No

Back to basics

Answers on pp. 308–9.

Muddled words

Sort out the muddled up words listed below and write each one out correctly.

creationer	vitaticy	rusilee
tenoymenj	nuf	feebtin
melbrop	lexar	miet

Careful reading

Read the short text below and then answer the questions which follow. Try to write your answers in complete sentences.

Kerry felt nervous. She paused before the closed door. Her heart was pounding and her mouth felt dry. She could see the people in the classroom through a little glass panel in the door. They were all laughing at something the tutor had just said. Kerry turned the handle and opened the door. Several people looked up as she came into the room. The tutor glanced round from the board where he was writing and saw Kerry. He smiled and walked towards her.

'Kerry Baker? I was told to expect you today. Come in and take a seat. My name's Peter. I'm the tutor for this class. Here, why don't you sit next to Chris.'

As Kerry sat down she looked around nervously and several people smiled at her in a friendly way. Peter was talking again.

'Now Kerry, don't worry about joining the class a little late. These people have only been here for a couple of sessions, so you haven't missed much. Chris, next to you, only started herself last week.'

Chris smiled at Kerry. Peter went on to explain that the group were having a discussion about recreation and trying to decide which their favourite activities were and why. Peter introduced Kerry to everyone and they all started talking again.

Kerry felt herself relax a little. Chris leaned forward and whispered.

'I think I know your son Scott. He's at college on the same course as my Clare, doing Catering isn't he?'

1. How was Kerry feeling when she walked into the classroom?

2. What was Peter doing when Kerry walked in?

3. What were the group talking about before Kerry arrived?

4. Who did Kerry sit next to and why?

5. Can you suggest why Kerry was feeling so nervous about joining the class?

Read and order

Read through the following instructions on how to meditate and then rewrite them in the correct order.

- Don't try to change your breathing.
- Set an alarm clock or timer so you don't have to worry about the time.
- Count up to four on each breath as you breathe out.
- If your mind wanders just bring your attention back to your breathing.
- Choose a warm, quiet place.
- Close your eyes and relax.
- Finish your meditation with a stretch.
- Breathe deeply.

Recreation and exercise

INTRODUCTION

In this individual project on *recreation and exercise* you will be able to:

- Carry out a survey of home exercise videos and recommend a best buy.
- Write a personal exercise record.
- Investigate sports energy foods and drinks.
- Write a guide to leisure and exercise in your local area.
- Find out what your local authority are doing to promote healthy exercise.
- Find out about safe footwear for exercise.
- Draw a diagram of footwear for different types of exercise.
- Write a mini-guide about clothing for leisure and exercise.
- Produce a safety checklist for a warm-up and cool-down routine.
- Find out about the problems caused by home exercise equipment.
- Evaluate your work on the project.

Choose activities which interest you from the wide range of suggestions provided in the project. You can choose to do just part of an activity if you wish. The choice is yours. There are more suggestions in the Alternative Ideas section (p. 101), so you should find enough activities to suit your interests and needs. Finish with the Evaluation Exercise as this will help you think about your work on the project and remind you to record the skills you have covered.

For each activity you choose to do use the information provided for you in the activity text and worksheets, as well as your own experiences and knowledge. If you need to look for more information consider resources such as books, newspapers and magazines as well as television, radio, video and CD-ROM. You can also use resources such as writing to an organisation or telephoning for information, talking to people you know and talking to other people who may be able to give you the information you need.

Optional task   If you have more time available and would like to try another task to develop the skills you have already used in an activity, you can look for the Optional Tasks which are linked to many of the project activities.

You will find the following worksheets useful:

Recreation and exercise

Activity 1   Carry out a survey of exercise videos

Many people enjoy taking some exercise in their leisure time but can't go to a class or don't want to join a group. A popular idea is to follow an exercise plan at home using an exercise video for help. How safe are the routines and do the videos offer good value for money? Is exercising at home worthwhile?

Some advantages are:

■ you don't have to travel to a class

■ you don't have to exercise at a set time

■ you don't have to worry about what you look like

■ you don't have to pay for classes

Some of the disadvantages are:

■ you may not have much space at home

■ you don't have anyone to check you are exercising safely

■ you don't have the support of a group

■ you could easily do too much or too little exercise

Carry out a survey of exercise videos which are designed to help you exercise in your own home. Look at videos which offer yoga or dance, weight-training, or step or aerobic type work-outs, for example.

Survey the claims made by each video you look at and decide if you would benefit from the exercises demonstrated. Decide if it would be possible to carry them out safely in your own home. Consider the following points in your survey:

■ are the exercises explained clearly?

■ are you advised to exercise safely and told how to do so?

■ how much space to you need to do the exercises?

■ do you need to buy equipment to be able to follow the video exercises, e.g. a mat, a step, weights?

■ is the music well chosen and easy to follow?

■ are you given a chance to start at a simple level and work up to a better level of fitness?

■ does the video make any special claims – such as helping you to lose weight?

■ is the video presented by a well qualified person or team?

■ how much does the video cost and do you think it is good value?

Visit shops and note down details of the exercises on offer by reading the covers of videos. Ask an assistant for more information. Borrow videos from the library and watch them for yourself. Ask friends or family members who have exercise videos for information and comments. Collect and read reviews of videos shown in magazines or catalogues. Find out about a good range of videos. Use the worksheet provided to help you carry out and record your survey.

Once you have finished your survey write out your results in the form of a simple chart or table. You can compare several videos more easily by this method. Would you recommend any of the videos you looked at? Decide which video seems to have scored well in most of the important areas and record your choice on the worksheet you have used for your survey.

Write a short explanation of why you would recommend this video as the best buy. Show your recommendation to friends or people you work with. Do they are agree with your choice? Do they think your video sounds worth trying?

(*See also* Worksheets: exercise video survey)

From this activity you may have evidence for:

Skills list	1, 4, 6, 7, 8/9, 10, 11, 12, 13, 15, 16.
Core skills	Communication level 1 and 2.
Element	1.1/2.1 Take part in discussions.
Opportunities	Ask for information about videos from friends or from an assistant in a shop or the library.
	Ask people to comment on your recommended video.
Element	1.2/2.2 Produce written material.
Opportunities	Design and complete a survey sheet.
	Record results of your survey on exercise videos as a chart.
	Write your reasons for selecting a video as the best buy.
Element	1.4/2.4 Read and respond to written materials.
Opportunities	Read video covers for information about contents.
	Read magazine reviews or catalogue descriptions about exercise videos.

Activity 2   Compile a personal exercise record

Being fit means having strength, stamina and suppleness. Using your recreation time to exercise can have a lot of benefits for you. Exercise can limit the effects of stress because you can learn how to relax. When you are exercising your mind is kept busy and away from any stressful thoughts. If you are busy cycling, dancing, or playing football or snooker you can't think about worries or problems as well!

Spending your leisure time exercising has good physical effects on your body. Your heart, circulation, muscles and joints will all benefit from your efforts. Your heart will pump more efficiently and your spine will feel more flexible. Your muscles will stretch and feel stronger and will support your bones more easily. If you can exercise three times a week for at least twenty minutes each time, you should begin to feel a little more fit and well.

Write a personal exercise record and use it to plan how to include more exercise in your recreation time. What activities can you do which will help improve your fitness level? Record the leisure activities you do at the moment which involve some exercise. Write down what else you could fit into your routine.

Look at the following list. Decide if you can add any of these simple activities to your usual routine.

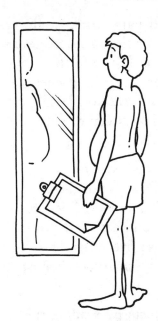

- take the dog for a walk
- go for a longer walk at the weekend
- walk around the shops doing a bit of window shopping
- go for a swim at your local pool
- go dancing with some friends
- walk down to the pub for a drink
- play football
- have a game of street hockey with some friends
- play tennis with a friend
- join an orienteering club
- join a ten pin bowling league
- put a ring in your back garden and play basketball
- go on an easy cycle ride
- take a picnic and walk a little bit further than usual

Include details of how fit you feel now on your exercise record. Use a mirror and take a good look at yourself, or ask a good friend to help. Be honest about how fit, strong and supple you look and feel.

Complete your personal exercise record by writing down how you hope to benefit from your new routine. Comment on physical benefits, such as improving muscle tone. Other benefits you may think of could be weight control, coping with stress, or just having a break from work or study and getting into the fresh air. Use the worksheet provided for the layout and ideas on what to write in your personal exercise record.

Read through your plan carefully and decide if it is realistic. If you plan too much for yourself each week you may get tired and give up. Ask someone who knows you well to look at your personal exercise record and help you decide if it is a practical one for you. Set a date to review your progress and to record all the changes you notice about yourself.

(*See also* Worksheets: personal exercise record)

	From this activity you may have evidence for:
Skills list	1, 3, 7, 8, 11, 12, 13, 15, 16.
Core skills	Communication level 1 and 2.
Element	1.1/2.1 Take part in discussions.
Opportunities	Talk to a friend about your fitness level.
	Ask someone to comment on your exercise record.
Element	1.2/2.2 Produce written material.
Opportunities	Complete and update a personal exercise record.
Element	1.4/2.4 Read and respond to written materials.
Opportunities	Read information and choose new exercise activities.
	Read and complete the exercise record.

Activity 3   Investigate sports energy foods and drinks

The labels and packaging on sports energy food bars, drinks and sweets claim the products can help you enjoy exercise. You are told the sports energy bars or drinks can give you the fast, effective energy needed for leisure and sports. The makers claim that energy foods eaten before, during and after exercise will give you lasting energy. Sports glucose drinks and sweets, the makers claim, will give you the fast energy you need to enjoy sports.

Carry out an investigation into the benefits claimed for sports energy food bars, drinks and sweets. Find out how useful these products really are and if they are good value for money. Look for isotonic drinks, dried drink mixes, sports glucose sweets and drinks and sports energy cereal and chewy bars. Choose five different items which you can find easily in your local supermarket, chemist or High Street chemist or health food store.

Find out more about each of your chosen products by reading the labels carefully. Use a dictionary to check your understanding of any terms you are not sure about. Ask people who have tried sports energy foods questions about the benefits. Find out if people feel they benefit from eating or drinking sports energy foods. Do they feel they perform better in sport or exercise? Make notes on what they tell you or tape their comments. Write to a maker about their product. A famous energy sweet is Kendal Mint Cake. It is popular with walkers and climbers. Read information on the packaging about how the mint cake provides energy. Write to the maker and ask why they think their product is helpful to people taking exercise. Ask for information about products in chemists or large stores. Ask for leaflets about the products. Use the worksheet provided to help record the information about each of your chosen products.

 Set out your investigation results as a chart. Write down the name of each of your chosen products, the size and the cost. List the ingredients clearly and the claims made for the product. List the benefits you have read about or people have told you they have experienced.

 Look at the information you have set out and decide on your replies to the following questions:

■ do you think any of your chosen products help people feel energetic while enjoying exercise?

■ can the products make a difference to the way people enjoy activities?

■ which product seems to offer the most benefits?

■ are the products good value for money?

■ do you think you could get the same benefits by simply eating a good diet?

Write your opinion about one of the products you investigated as if you were writing a news item for a leisure or health magazine. Say if you think the energy bar, drink or sweet is worth trying or is a waste of money.

(*See also* Worksheets: sports energy food/drink investigation)

From this activity you may have evidence for:

Skills list	1, 3, 4, 6, 7, 8, 10, 11, 12, 13, 15, 16.
Core skills	Communication level 1 and 2.
Element	1.1/2.1 Take part in discussions.
Opportunities	Ask a variety of people for information about sports energy foods.
	Ask friends for comments about their experiences of energy foods.
Element	1.2/2.2 Produce written material.
Opportunities	Write to a maker of sports energy foods for product information.
	Make notes during your investigation.
	Write out the results of your investigation as a chart.
	Write your opinion of energy foods as a magazine news item.
Element	1.4/2.4 Read and respond to written materials.
Opportunities	Read labels and packaging for information.
	Read information received from makers of energy foods.

Activity 4   Write a guide to fitness and recreation

Write a guide to the leisure activities in your local area which can help you keep fit and well.

Collect information from sports centres, swimming pools, local community centres and clubs. Ask about sports, dance and keeping fit. Read posters and adverts in newsagents, clinics and local centres for more information. Ask people you work with for information.

Decide how you will set out your Guide and what information you will provide. Give the name of the activity, where it can be done, what day and time, what equipment you need and how it can help you keep fit. Design a star rating where one star means very little benefit up to five stars which means very good benefits. Use maps, diagrams and photographs to illustrate important points in your guide and make it attractive to look at. Put in some personal comments about activities people have tried. Use the worksheet provided to help you plan what to include.

For example, suppose you give information about a local cycling club which anyone can join. List the day, time and place where the group meets and a contact telephone number. List the basic equipment you need. Show pictures of what you need, e.g. a bike, helmet, gloves, water bottle and comfortable, safe clothing (if clothes are too baggy they may get caught in the cycle chain). Give an idea of the size of the group, the age range and whether beginners are welcome. List how the activity can benefit you and in which ways, e.g. very good for stamina. Include some diagrams of cycle routes the club takes. Include information on how to warm up properly. Offer some advice about how to take care of yourself in new situations, such as letting someone you trust know where you are going and how long you expect to be.

Show friends, family and people you work with a draft copy of your guide. Ask them to comment on how useful they think it is and whether they like the kind of details you have included. Improve your guide by using the comments you receive. Give people a finished copy of your guide to keep for their own use.

Optional task Write to your local council's Leisure and Recreation Department. Ask for information about how they promote leisure activities in your area which help people keep fit. Do they lend out equipment for groups to get started with a sport? Do they run special taster days which give people a chance to try a new activity? Do they help young people enjoy different activities? Do they help elderly people keep fit? Do they encourage women to take part in sport? Check your letter is clear, neat and polite. Use their reply to improve your guide if you receive useful information.

(*See also* Worksheets: writing a guide to leisure activities)

From this activity you may have evidence for:

Skills list	1, 3, 4, 6, 7, 8/9, 10, 13/14, 15, 16.
Core skills	Communication level 1 and 2.
Element	1.1/2.1 Take part in discussions.
Opportunities	Ask people for information about local activities.
	Ask people for comments on a draft copy of the guide.
Element	1.2/2.2 Produce written material.
Opportunities	Write a guide to leisure activities in your local area.
	Write a letter to the local council asking questions about exercise facilities (optional).
Element	1.3/2.3 Use images.
Opportunities	Illustrate the guide with pictures, maps or diagrams.
Element	1.4/2.4 Read and respond to written materials.
Opportunities	Read information about local leisure activities from posters, adverts and leaflets for use in your guide.

Activity 5 Find out about safe footwear for exercise

Do you think about the comfort and support you need from a sports trainer when you choose a pair to wear for your leisure exercise? Do you look for any of these design features?

■ **Cushioning** A good pair of trainers for aerobics gives cushioning under the heel and ball of the foot where you will feel the impact on your foot. Less cushioning would be needed for a stretch and tone class.

■ **Stability**   A pair of trainers for an activity which involves changing direction quickly like badminton should be well structured and have secure strapping.

■ **Flexibility**   Look for flex-grooves in the sole and a low-cut heel allowing your foot to move naturally but with support, which you would need in a dance exercise class.

■ **Weight**   You don't want heavy shoes slowing you down if you are running.

■ **Breathing**   Your feet will get hot and sweaty if you are working hard in any activity which you are doing to get fit. You need a shoe which will allow your foot to cool. You may be less concerned with this design feature if you are doing a less energetic activity.

■ **Laces**   The wrong lace pattern can cause blisters or poor circulation in your foot if you are running or doing aerobics and working hard. You need a shoe with a good lace pattern or advice about how to lace up properly.

Choose two popular recreation activities which involve exercise but which need different kinds of support for your feet. For example, aerobics and stretch and tone classes or basketball and walking. Find out which type of sports trainer you should choose for both of your selected activities. Describe the best design features to look for.

Collect information about suitable sports trainers for each of your chosen activities. Use your own experience. Ask people you know who enjoy your chosen activities for ideas. Look in catalogues and sports brochures for information. Ask for information in sports shops. Read information on the box, label or card attached to new trainers for ideas about special features.

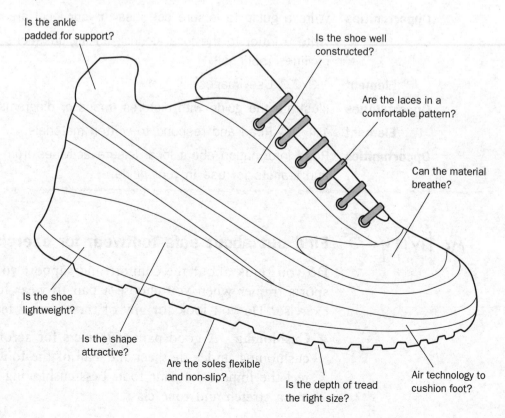

Is the ankle padded for support?

Is the shoe well constructed?

Are the laces in a comfortable pattern?

Can the material breathe?

Is the shoe lightweight?

Is the shape attractive?

Are the soles flexible and non-slip?

Is the depth of tread the right size?

Air technology to cushion foot?

Present your collected information by drawing a diagram of an ideal trainer for each of your chosen activities. Label in detail the design features which show the important points about each type of sports trainer. Show in your labelling the differences between the two trainers and the reasons for the design features.

Include in your diagrams information about:

- the type of material used and why – does it breathe?
- the flexibility of the shoe – does it flex evenly?
- the depth of tread on the sole – does it absorb impact?
- the construction of the shoe – is it well made?
- cushioning – is the ankle cushioned as well as the foot?
- air technology – is there extra cushioning in the sole?
- non-slip soles – is the tread going to stop you slipping?
- the weight – is it a reasonable weight for the sport?
- the shape and colour – are the shoes attractive?

Show your labelled diagrams to friends and other people you know who enjoy your chosen recreation activities. Ask them if they would find advice about selecting the best trainer useful. Are your diagrams easy to follow? Do they think they are wearing the right kind of footwear for their favourite exercise at the moment? Reduce your diagrams in size using a photocopier and give copies to people for them to make use of.

Optional task Whether your favourite recreation activity is rock climbing, cycling or tap dancing, you are likely to enjoy it more if you wear suitable clothing. There may be pressure on you to wear a certain type of clothing or a particular label because of fashion or comments from friends. Most activities however can be enjoyed wearing a simple tee shirt and shorts or loose jogging trousers.

Natural fibres such as cotton are usually cooler to wear and will soak up sweat more easily than man-made fibres. When you are finishing your activity and beginning to cool down, put on a sweat shirt or jumper to stop yourself from getting too cold. Jeans are not good to wear for exercise as they are heavy and can rub your skin. Lycra cycling shorts can be attractive and useful but if you're wearing them for aerobics or dance you can get very hot. Some activities such as canoeing for example do need some special clothing such as water-proof protection.

Choose your four favourite leisure activities. They don't have to be activities you do at the moment, just things you would like to do. Write a mini-guide showing suitable and affordable clothing for your chosen activities.

List the activity and describe the clothing you suggest is best. Describe where it can be bought and what the cost is likely to be.

Have a look in shops or catalogues for ideas. Suggest what clothing you *don't* need, for example leggings, leotards or specialist clothing where you are just paying for the name.

Ask friends to model their favourite, comfortable leisure wear and photograph them. Use the photographs to illustrate your mini-guide.

From this activity you may have evidence for:

Skills list	1, 3, 4, 6, 7, 8/9, 10, 12, 13/14, 15, 16.
Core skills	Communication level 1 and 2.
Element	1.1/2.1 Take part in discussions.
Opportunities	Question friends and others about their choice of sports footwear.
	Ask in sports shops about footwear.
	Ask friends for information about clothing for exercise (optional).
Element	1.2/2.2 Produce written material.
Opportunities	Write a mini-guide for choosing leisure clothing (optional).
Element	1.3/2.3 Use images.
Opportunities	Draw and label diagrams of footwear for two recreation activities.
	Use photographs of leisure wear in a mini-guide (optional).
Element	1.4/2.4 Read and respond to written materials.
Opportunities	Read brochures or catalogues for information on footwear.
	Read labels and packaging for information on footwear.
	Read catalogues and labels for information on clothing (optional).

Activity 6   Write a safety checklist for exercise

It's easy to feel enthusiastic about exercise and throw yourself into it without warming up properly. It's also easy to hurt yourself by doing too much too quickly, or by trying to compete with someone who is more fit than you are. You will be left with sore, aching muscles. Even wearing the wrong shoes can cause problems, leaving you with blisters and bruised feet. Tight clothing can cause rubbed, sore skin. Preparing properly for exercise is very important.

Warming up properly allows you to stretch out muscles you are going to be using in your recreation activity. It can help avoid injuries and prepares your body, leaving you feeling alert. A good warm-up routine also helps to prepare you mentally for the activity you are about to enjoy. Take your time and prepare properly for leisure activities which involve exercise.

Produce a safety checklist for people to use who are exercising in their recreation time. Give advice on a good warm-up routine. Make suggestions about safe clothing and shoes. Give information about how to take care of yourself while you exercise. For example, warn people not to carry on with exercise if they are feeling unwell. Include in your safety checklist some advice on how to cope with minor injuries such as blisters and sprains. Finally, give advice on a good cooling down routine which will help muscles you have been working to stretch and relax.

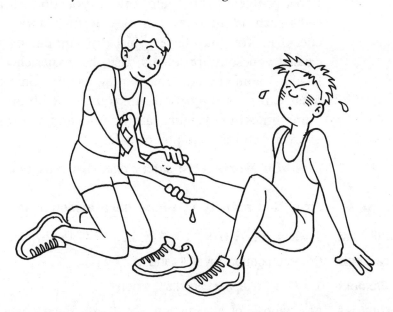

 Collect information about a good warm-up routine from health and fitness guides in your local library. Look through magazines or watch fitness videos. Watch television programmes for information; often a morning programme includes exercise advice. Pick up leaflets from a local fitness centre. A First Aid manual will give you information about how to deal with minor injuries. If you have a local sports injury clinic in your area or a college running a course in sports therapy, ask for information about safe exercise. Ask friends or people you work with who enjoy exercise for ideas about safety checks. Use the worksheet provided to record information from questions you have asked.

 Design your safety checklist either as a mini-guide to fit in a pocket, or as a poster to put on the wall near to training equipment to remind people to take care. Use photographs or diagrams to explain important points. Use the worksheet provided for suggestions on what to include in your safety checklist.

 Show your safety checklist to friends or people you work with who you know do some sport or exercise in their leisure time. Ask them to comment on how useful they think your safety ideas are. Do they think using your safety checklist could prevent people from hurting themselves while exercising? Give copies of your safety checklist to people who are interested.

Optional task Choose one piece of home exercise equipment. For example:

exercise bike	dual action cycle	multi-gym
stepper	rowing machine	cross country walker
treadmill	weights and bench	aerobic rebounder

Draw a diagram of the equipment or cut out a picture from a catalogue or magazine. Label your diagram or picture showing all the problems or injuries you could suffer if the equipment wasn't used properly.

Label problems you could have if you don't follow sensible safety steps such as the ones you have written about in your safety checklist. You may have a piece of equipment at home which has caused you some problems. Use this experience for ideas. Ask friends about the equipment they use at home for more ideas of what can go wrong. Look in your local library for books about home fitness or weight training and find information about how to use your chosen equipment safely.

(*See also* Worksheets: safety checklist part one and part two)

From this activity you may have evidence for:

Skills list	1, 3, 4, 6, 7, 8/9, 10, 11, 12, 13/14, 15, 16.
Core skills	Communication level 1 and 2.
Element	1.1/2.1 Take part in discussions.
Opportunities	Ask people for information about exercising safely.
	Telephone a sports injury clinic or local college for information.
	Ask friends for comments about your safety checklist.
	Ask people for ideas about problems with home exercise equipment (optional).
Element	1.2/2.2 Produce written material.
Opportunities	Design and write a safety checklist.
	Record responses to your questions about safe exercise.
Element	1.3/2.3 Use images.
Opportunities	Use photographs or diagrams in the safety checklist.
	Draw and label a piece of home exercise equipment showing possible problems (optional).
Element	1.4/2.4 Read and respond to written materials.
Opportunities	Read information about exercising safely from books, leaflets, magazines.
	Read a First Aid manual for information on injuries.
	Read books on fitness for information about home equipment (optional).

 ## Evaluation exercise

Think about the work you have done on this project. What do you know now which you didn't know before about fitness and keeping safe during exercise? Can you choose a safe exercise video which is good value for money? Have you found out about any new leisure and fitness classes in your local area? Do you know more about choosing the best sports trainers for your favourite recreation activity?

Do you feel confident about researching for information and about reading and selecting information? Do you think your presentation skills have improved? Do you feel more confident about asking people for information or listening to their opinions?

Make sure all the skills you have practised are written down on the Skills Record Sheet. Check you have recorded details about the variety of resources you have used. Record your progress and achievement on the Skills Summary Record. Write down the details of evidence you have for an accreditation you may be working towards. Write down details of skills you wish to practise further and how you intend to do this. Write down realistic goal dates for the work.

Exercise video survey

Select the videos you are going to include in your survey. Write down as much detail as you can about each video. Use the guidelines below. Add more ideas of your own.

Title of exercise video and cost   **Where available**
                                                        e.g. shop, by post

1.   £

2.   £

3.   £

4.   £

Answer these questions about each video in your survey

Does the video:

Offer a safe warm-up section?   Yes/No

Comments:

Offer a cool-down section?   Yes/No

Comments:

Offer different levels of exercise, e.g. beginner, advanced?   Yes/No

Comments:

Explain the exercises clearly?   Yes/No

Comments:

Does the video use:

An interesting format?   Yes/No

Enjoyable and suitable music?   Yes/No

A celebrity presenter?   Yes/No

Do you feel the presenter knows what they are doing?   Yes/No

Do the exercises need any special equipment?   Yes/No

Does the video make any special claims e.g. weight loss, stress
control, muscle toning?   Yes/No

Do you think the video is good value for money?   Yes/No

Which video do you recommend as a best buy?

Your reasons:

Personal exercise record

Record how fit you feel now, what extra exercise you are going to try and how you are going to review your progress.

What exercise do I do now each week?

How fit do I feel now? (Circle one choice)

Very fit / fit / fairly fit / not very fit / very unfit

What extra exercise am I going to try?

How can I check this is safe for me to do? (e.g. check with GP, check with a club)

When will I start my new activity?

How do I feel it may benefit me, e.g. weight loss, better muscle tone, feel more relaxed?

Which is the most important benefit I hope to gain?

When will I review my progress?   After two weeks
                                         After four weeks

At my first review:

How fit do I feel now? (Circle one choice)

Very fit / fit/ fairly fit /not very fit / very unfit

What differences have I noticed? e.g. feel well, sleeping better, more flexible joints, less breathless

Have I suffered any injuries?   Yes/No

At my second review:

How fit do I feel? (Circle one choice)

Very fit / fit / fairly fit / not very fit / very unfit

What changes or benefits have I noticed?

Do I feel it is worth continuing with the activity?   Yes/No

Why?

Sports energy food/drink investigation

Use this worksheet to help you record the information you find for each of your chosen sports energy drinks, sweets or food bars. Repeat this suggested outline for each item.

Product name

Size   Cost

Main ingredients

Flavour

Maker's name

Maker's claims for the sports food/drink/sweet

Information about the sports food/drink/sweet from another source, e.g. a sports centre, a chemist, a friend

Results of questioning people about the product

Comment on taste

Does the sports food/drink/sweet improve your feeling of energy *before* exercise?	Yes/No
Does the sports food/drink/sweet improve your feeling of energy *after* exercise?	Yes/No
Do you feel the activity is easier because of the sports food/drink/sweet?	Yes/No
Do you feel you recover from exercise more quickly because of the sports food/drink/sweet?	Yes/No

Writing a guide to leisure activities

Use the headings below to help you decide what information to give about each activity you include in your guide. Make your guide clear and attractive. Use different lettering to make headings stand out, colour, diagrams or computer clip art.

Name of activity

Give a brief description of the sport or activity.

Time and place

Give information about where you can go to do the activity. State which days of the week and times it is available. Give a contact name or a telephone number so people can check details for themselves.

Cost

Give examples of cost per person or for a group. Include information about special rates or discounts. Cost could be an important factor for someone using your guide.

Equipment

Provide some information about basic equipment you need and what you can easily hire or borrow until you are sure you like the activity. Suggest what type of clothing it is sensible to wear.

Attitude

Give an idea of how competitive each activity is. Can you just do it on a friendly basis? Do beginners mix with people who are more skilled? Do people take the activity quite seriously because it involves a lot of competitions?

Skills

Explain if you can begin the activity with little or no skill. Give information about any instruction people will get. Are you expected to practise and improve your skills?

Numbers

Give information about whether you can do the activity alone or with a partner. Can you join a group without a partner? Is the activity done in pairs, fours or a larger group? Give information about how popular the activity is in your local area. Is there likely to be a waiting list?

Time

Give an idea of how much leisure time this activity is likely to take up, in a week for example.

Benefits and problems

Explain what the benefits are likely to be from doing this activity, e.g. it may improve your stamina or strengthen your joints or spine. Warn about possible problems such as common injuries.

Safety checklist – part one

Design your safety checklist as a poster to display near to exercise equipment, or as a mini-guide to carry around. Make copies to give to friends.

Explain how to warm up safely

List what to do, such as stretching out the muscles you are going to use. Gradually increase your heart rate ready to try some exercise.

Draw out a flow diagram to describe the routine step by step, or a series of little pictures, line drawings or cartoons.

List safety tips

List tips such as wearing sensible clothing and choosing comfortable shoes, for example. Warn against carrying on exercise if you feel unwell. Advise people to start exercise slowly and build up to being more active.

Describe a cooling down routine

Describe a routine which includes a chance to stretch the muscles you have been using. The routine should bring your heart rate down slowly if you have been working very hard. Put in advice about wearing an extra jumper to keep warm. You don't want to cool down so much you actually become chilled!

Describe some common minor injuries

Suggest what to do about the small injuries you may get while exercising. For example, list problems like blisters or strained muscles. Name some useful products such as blister healing gel, muscle rubs and elastic supports. Give instructions for some simple First Aid.

What not to do

Have a section which lists things you should definitely not do before, during and after exercise. For example:

- don't exercise straight after eating a big meal
- don't smoke or drink alcohol before, during or after exercise (alcohol will affect your concentration, smoking will make you breathless and wheezy)
- don't rush into exercise, take your time and warm up
- don't carry on if you feel sick, dizzy, in pain or you can't get your breath. Get help
- don't do a lot of exercise and then just stop. Cool down properly to prevent sore muscles

Safety checklist – part two

Ask friends, family and people you work with about their safety routines for exercise. Use their ideas and tips to improve your safety checklist.

Ask:

What safeguards do you take when you are exercising in your leisure time? For example

Do you always warm up?   Yes/No

What do you do?

Why do you think it's important to warm up properly?

Do you always cool down?   Yes/No

What do you do?

Why do you think it's important to cool down properly?

How do you keep yourself safe while exercising? Do you:

Wear suitable clothing for the activity?   Yes/No

Wear suitable shoes for the activity?   Yes/No

Exercise at a sensible pace for your level of fitness?   Yes/No

Rest if you feel tired, unwell or get a cramp?   Yes/No

Take care to exercise in a safe place with people you know?   Yes/No

Have you ever suffered from any minor injuries while exercising?   Yes/No

If yes:

Describe the injury

How did you treat it?

What have you done to make sure you are not injured again?

Back to basics

Answers on p. 309.

Careful reading

Read the text below and answer the questions which follow. Try to write your answers using complete sentences.

> Just twenty to thirty minutes of exercise, three times a week, can help you feel active and energetic. As you get better at your chosen activities and a little more fit, you will enjoy each activity more and more. Feeling fit means being supple, strong and having plenty of stamina. Regular exercise can have other benefits as well such as helping to control high blood pressure or helping you to relax for example. It's never too late to start a new activity to improve your fitness level. You can work at your own pace and improve a little each week.

1. How much weekly exercise is suggested to keep you feeling active?

2. What benefits can be gained from exercise as well as getting fit?

3. What does feeling fit mean?

4. Do you have to be under a certain age to begin a new activity?

Missing words

Put back the missing words in these sentences about recreation and exercise. The words are provided for you in the box below. Cover up these words to make the task harder for yourself if you wish.

support	age	activities
instructions	supple	cushioning
refreshing	flexible	injury

a) Choose _____ that you enjoy.

b) Try to follow the _____ carefully in an exercise class to avoid _____.

c) Yoga and gymnastics keep you _____ and _____.

d) Walking is a good all round exercise for all _____ groups.

e) For jogging you need a pair of shoes which give _____ and _____.

f) Swimming is a _____ form of exercise.

Fast reading

Read the advert below which is for a ski course at your local sports centre. Answer the questions by looking for the information in the advert.

SKI SATURDAY

ONE DAY SKI COURSE THIS SATURDAY

10 AM TO 3 PM

SUITABLE FOR BEGINNERS AND IMPROVERS

ALL EQUIPMENT PROVIDED. MUST TAKE AT LEAST SIZE 5 BOOT.

COST £9.50

FOR FURTHER INFORMATION CONTACT 659981

1. What sport can you try for a day?
2. What time does the course begin?
3. How can you find out more about the course?
4. How much does the course cost?
5. Do you need to bring your own equipment?
6. Can you attend the course if you take a size 4 boot?

Alternatives Other ideas for activities on recreation

Any activity from the group or individual projects can be replaced with an idea from the list below. Use the list to give you more choice of activities to do which suit your needs, interests and the amount of time you have available.

■ Visit a local craft fair. Look at the crafts on display and watch any demonstrations of craft work. Discuss the different crafts you have found out about, decide what is interesting about one and whether there are any you would like to try. Write a description of what you have seen and the skills you have found out about.

■ Carry out some research into traditional pastimes. Find out how people used to spend their leisure time. Find out about local festivals which are still being celebrated. Find out what it was like for people to go to the cinema for the first time, travel to the sea-side for the first time, or visit the first public parks. Choose one idea from these which interests you and write an account of your research. Illustrate it with old photographs, maps or drawings.

■ Consider what recreation activities can be enjoyed by the whole family. Ask families what they like to do or find out what is available locally. Design a poster to advertise what families can do together in your area.

■ Find out within your group, or from family and friends, who enjoys watching sport on television. Find out which sports people like to watch. Make up a television schedule for sport lovers. Ask people why they enjoy watching a sport rather than taking part in it.

■ Find out about relaxation. How do leisure activities help people to relax? Ask people for ideas. Write a list of common leisure activities and show how they match up to relaxation benefits. Give each one a relaxation rating.

■ Find out about being a volunteer as a recreation activity. It could be for a local charity shop, for a local historic house or for a countryside organisation which repairs paths and walls and clears ditches! Interview some volunteers about why they enjoy doing the job in their spare time. What benefits do they get from being a volunteer? List some local places or groups which need volunteers.

■ Go to see a film and review it. Discuss whether you think there is too much violence in films today. Decide if you feel people are influenced by violence in films.

Personal care: feet and hair

INTRODUCTION

In this group project on *personal care: feet and hair* you will be able to:

- Research and present information on footwear fashion.

- Draw up a chart of shoe fashions and problems they can cause.

- Design a questionnaire about foot care and evaluate the results.

- Write a mini-guide for caring for your feet.

- Investigate foot problems and treatments and design a chart.

- Discuss targets for a shoe design and design a new shoe.

- Investigate hair style and colour choices.

- Write a checklist for successful hair style changes.

- Design a quiz about famous faces.

- Discuss hair care routines and write a top ten of hair care products.

- Investigate and test hair products.

- Research into common hair problems and produce a chart showing some solutions.

- Design an advert for a new hair care product.

- Evaluate your work on the project.

Choose activities which interest you from the wide range of suggestions provided in the project. You can choose to do just part of an activity if you wish. The choice is yours. There are more suggestions in the Alternative Ideas section (p. 151), so you should find enough activities to suit your interests and needs. Finish with the Evaluation Exercise as this will help you think about your work on the project and remind you to record the skills you have covered.

For each activity you choose to do, use the information provided for you in the activity text and worksheets, as well as your own experiences and knowledge. If you need to look for more information consider resources such as books, newspapers and magazines as well as television, radio, video and CD-ROM. You can also use resources such as writing to an organisation or telephoning for information, talking to people you know and talking to other people who may be able to give you the information you need.

Optional task If you have more time available and would like to try another task to develop the skills you have already used in an activity, you can look for the Optional Tasks which are linked to many of the project activities.

You will find the following worksheets useful:

Personal care: feet and hair

Activity 1 **Research and present information on footwear fashion**

Fashion changes have seen the platform sole and wedge heel go in and out of favour many times. It's a shoe fashion which has proved difficult for some people to wear. It has caused sprained ankles and posture problems for many people. Have you ever worn a really high platform shoe? Stiletto heels remained in fashion for some time, in spite of the damage they did to floor coverings! High heels have been in and out of favour for both men and women. Why do you think people are attracted to high-heeled shoes?

Sports shoe designs have changed due to fashion and the demands of different sports. Sports trainers are now worn as everyday items of footwear and not kept just for the track or gym. Can you remember wearing thin-soled plimsolls at school or doing exercises in bare feet?

Research and collect information about how shoe styles have changed through time and fashion. Choose either a period in history from long ago, or a more recent time such as the styles from the 60s, 70s or 80s, for example. Choose the same period and do the research together, each looking at a different aspect, or pick different times or well-known styles of shoes and share the results of your research.

Help each other by making a list of where to look for ideas and information. Visit your local library and bookshops and look in the history or fashion sections for information on footwear. Ask for old copies of magazines in your local library, or celebration issues showing how fashion in footwear has changed.

Write to a large shoe manufacturer such as Clarks (any good shoe shop should have their address). Ask about changes in shoe fashions and styles over the last few decades in the UK.

Look out for shops in your area which specialise in selling second hand clothes and shoes. They may have some old styles of footwear in stock to look at. Ask an elderly relative or friend who has kept some favourite old shoes which you could photograph.

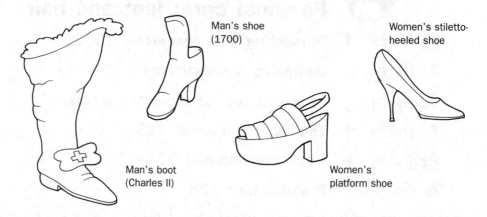

Man's shoe
(1700)

Women's stiletto-
heeled shoe

Man's boot
(Charles II)

Women's
platform shoe

Write to a large museum such as the Victoria and Albert Museum in London. You may be able to buy postcards showing footwear styles from the past. Make notes about your research and collect as many pictures, photographs and diagrams or samples of shoes as you can.

Present your results either by writing about them in a short description, using photographs or sample shoes, or by giving a short spoken presentation. Use the worksheet provided to check your presentation. Share your written presentations or listen to each other's spoken presentations.

Give each other feedback about the presentations. Keep your comments positive and helpful, suggest how to make improvements and praise the parts you all enjoyed.

Optional task   Use the information you have about footwear fashions from the past to design a simple chart showing different styles through the ages. Show how each style you feature may have caused foot problems. For example, narrow, pointed shoes would have caused squashed, overlapping toes, clogs may have caused hard skin and corns, and stiletto heels caused problems because the foot was pushed so far forward. Give each type of shoe a comfort rating.

Allocate a shoe style to each person in the group to find out about. Talk to other people about problems they remember having. Discuss your chart and decide which you all feel was the most dangerous fashion as far as your feet are concerned!

(*See also* Worksheets: presenting your research)

	From this activity you may have evidence for:
Skills list	1, 2, 4, 5, 6, 7, 8/9, 11, 13/14, 15.
Core skills	Communication level 1 and 2.
Element	1.1/2.1 Take part in discussions.
Opportunities	Visit shops and ask questions about footwear fashion.
	Ask friends and family about shoe fashion and problems.
	Present research in a spoken presentation.
	Give feedback on presentations.
	Discuss foot problems caused by shoe fashions (optional).
Element	1.2/2.2 Produce written material.
Opportunities	List areas for research.
	Write a letter to a manufacturer and/or museum for information.
	Make notes about research findings.
	Present your research as a written presentation.
	Present a chart showing problems caused by footwear fashion (optional).
Element	1.3/2.3 Use images.
Opportunities	Use pictures, photographs and samples of shoes to illustrate the presentation.
	Use pictures of shoe fashions in a chart about foot problems (optional).
Element	1.4/2.4 Read and respond to written materials.
Opportunities	Read books, magazines, brochures and replies to letters to use in the presentation.

Activity 2 Design a questionnaire on foot care

Your foot has over a third of your body's movable parts. With every step you take your foot absorbs two and a half times your body weight! Foot problems are often caused by badly fitting shoes. This can mean swollen ankles, cramp in the toes, knee pain, poor posture, backache and headaches! Shoes should fit you well, allowing room for the spread of your toes. As you stand you should have a good, even spread of body weight through your feet. If you put a lot of weight on the ball of your foot you can get corns, for example.

Keep your feet clean by washing and drying well as part of a regular routine. Dry between your toes carefully, as warm, damp skin can encourage fungal infections such as athlete's foot. Cut your nails straight across to prevent ingrowing toenails, which can be a painful problem. It's a good idea to walk about in bare feet sometimes to strengthen your muscles and encourage a good blood supply to your feet.

Design a questionnaire on foot care and use it to find out just how much people know about looking after their feet. What kind of habits do they have?

Discuss the following ideas for your questionnaire and add some more of your own. Find out if:

- people have their feet measured to make sure they are buying shoes which fit correctly
- people think about how comfortable a shoe is: heels not too high, foot supported, room for toes, etc.
- people remember that socks should fit properly as well as shoes
- people can say how they keep their feet clean
- people think about drying their feet properly after a bath, shower or swim
- people know how to cut their toenails correctly
- people exercise their feet

Find more ideas for questions by asking friends about their routines. Look in books and magazines on health care. Look for leaflets at a chemist on foot care products and read labels on product packaging.

Write out your questionnaire. Make sure the questions you ask will give you the information you would like to find out. Check you have provided enough space for people to write their replies. Give your questionnaire to friends, people you work with or family members. Agree on how many people you will each ask. Use the worksheet provided for tips on how to design your questionnaire.

Once you have some completed questionnaires, discuss the results. Are there any surprises? Decide together whether you can draw any general conclusions from the questionnaire. For example, can you say:

- most people look after their feet fairly well?
- most people know how to cut their toenails properly?
- most people don't bother to have their feet measured as they think their foot size never changes?

Write up a short summary or description of how much you think people know about caring for their feet. Write about any good or bad or even odd habits people seem to have.

Optional task Discuss and write a pocket-size mini-guide on how to look after your feet. Give sensible advice for daily care. Explain how to give yourself a pedicure once a week. For example:

- suggest a daily washing routine
- suggest products to keep feet smelling fresh
- draw a diagram on how to cut toenails safely
- suggest moisturisers for feet
- suggest products and routines to get rid of hard skin

Allocate tasks to each other to get the work done, each writing one part of a good care routine.

(*See also* Worksheets: designing a questionnaire)

	From this activity you may have evidence for:
Skills list	1, 2, 4, 6, 7, 8, 10, 11, 12, 13/14, 15, 16.
Core skills	Communication level 1 and 2.
Element	1.1/2.1 Take part in discussions.
Opportunities	Discuss foot care routines.
	Ask friends for foot care ideas.
	Discuss the results of the foot care questionnaire.
Element	1.2/2.2 Produce written material.
Opportunities	Write a questionnaire on foot care.
	Write a summary of questionnaire results.
	Write a mini-guide on foot care (optional).
Element	1.3/2.3 Use images.
Opportunities	Use diagrams to explain foot care in the mini-guide (optional).
Element	1.4/2.4 Read and respond to written materials.
Opportunities	Read magazines, leaflets and product labels for foot care information.
	Read and evaluate questionnaire results.
	Read information about foot care (optional).

Activity 3   Design a chart about common foot problems

Many people suffer from problems with their feet. Athlete's foot is a very common foot problem. It's a fungal infection between the toes and on the foot. It's often picked up at a swimming pool or from being barefoot near an infected person, and is very infectious. The skin can crack between your toes, turn a whitish colour and weep. It then peels, leaving red, raw patches which can be very itchy. Make sure you keep your feet dry and clear up the infection with cream or dusting powder. Don't share a towel with anyone else and wear fresh socks daily.

Corns are another common problem. They are areas of hard, sometimes painful skin often caused by a shoe putting pressure on your foot. Sometimes a pad is required to protect the foot and a visit to the chiropodist may be needed.

Design a chart showing some common foot problems. Include the name of the problem and a brief description of what it is. Say when and how you could treat it for yourself and when you should get treatment from a doctor or chiropodist. Describe the products you can buy from your local chemist to help with each problem.

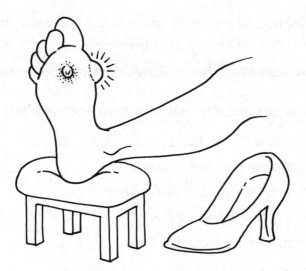

 Decide which common foot problems to put in your chart by discussing how much you already know, using your own experiences.

Discuss these foot problems:

- corns and bunions
- overlapping toes
- blisters
- athlete's foot
- verrucae
- ingrowing toenails

Visit your local chemist and ask for names of creams and for advice about each problem you feature in your chart. Read labels and packaging for information. Look through magazines for ideas. Telephone a local chiropodist for information or call in for a leaflet. Find out about some natural remedies. Allocate the research tasks between you. Make notes about products and treatments you find out about as you go along.

 Design your chart using the worksheet provided to help you. This will give you some ideas of what to include and how to set out your work. Show a photograph or diagram of each problem next to a description of treatment and products. Allocate tasks to each other to get the work done.

 Have a good look at your finished chart and discuss how useful you think it is. Print copies and give them to friends or people you work with, and ask for their comments. Make improvements to the finished chart if you receive any helpful suggestions.

(*See also* Worksheets: checklist for common foot problems)

From this activity you may have evidence for:

Skills list   1, 2, 3, 4, 6, 7, 8, 10, 11, 13/14, 15, 16.

Core skills   Communication level 1 and 2.

Element 1.1/2.1 Take part in discussions.

Opportunities Discuss your own experiences of foot problems.

Ask a chemist or chiropodist for information about foot problems.

Discuss and assess the finished chart on foot problems.

Ask friends for comments on the usefulness of the chart on foot problems.

Element 1.2/2.2 Produce written material.

Opportunities Make notes about research material.

Design and write a chart about common foot problems.

Element 1.3/2.3 Use images.

Opportunities Use photos, diagrams and pictures to illustrate the chart.

Element 1.4/2.4 Read and respond to written materials.

Opportunities Read books, magazines and leaflets for information on foot problems and treatments.

Read labels and packaging information for ideas on treatments.

Activity 4 **Design a shoe**

Design a completely new shoe for a special activity or occasion. For example, design a new type of trainer for tennis, walking, basketball or ten pin bowling. Design a shoe for a wedding, an anniversary, a party or for going clubbing. Design a shoe for someone who has oddly shaped feet and who is always complaining how difficult it is to buy shoes.

Brainstorm for ideas as a group and note down suggestions for shoe designs. List the problems people have with different kinds of shoes for different activities. Discuss how your design could solve these problems. For example if you decide to design a completely new trainer, consider how important such things as flexibility, weight, cushioning and appearance are to someone wearing your new design. Work in pairs or small groups to create your designs for a new piece of footwear.

Before you begin to sketch out your designs, discuss and agree as a group a list of targets. These should be things which you all feel would be part of a good shoe design. Write them out so you all have a copy to refer to. Consider the following targets for your list:

- the importance of colour
- what materials your shoe would be made from
- how important it is that someone's foot balances well in your design (this means the foot should not tipped too far forwards by a high heel, for example)
- the shoe should be attractive and comfortable
- any special features (a non-slip sole, glow-in-the-dark, air pumped in, etc.)

■ the shoe should be strong enough for the activity

■ how flexible the shoe needs to be

 Let your imagination loose now, as you don't actually have to make this shoe, only present a detailed drawing of your design! Use the worksheet provided to help you with your design process step by step.

 When you have finished your designs, check you have met the targets you all agreed on. For example, if you are designing a new shoe to go ten pin bowling, you might have decided that it's important to have a flexible shoe with a non-slip sole and lace-free fastenings. Check your designs to see if you included all the special ideas you had.

Show your finished designs to each other. Take a good look at everyone's ideas and ask each other questions about them. For example:

■ do the designs meet the targets you all agreed on?

■ are there any designs which you feel could actually be made up into a shoe?

■ are there any designs which you would all enjoy wearing?

Discuss how difficult it was to think of new ideas and meet the agreed targets. Listen to each other's comments.

Optional task   Hold a Design Awards Exhibition and display your shoe designs. Give a short presentation about your designs, either to each other or to a small invited audience. Explain how you tried to meet the targets you had decided on and any special features in your designs. Explain just what you had in mind for your designs and answer any questions people may have. Arrange a vote by ballot for the:

■ Design Award for the most original design

■ Design Award for the most practical design

■ Design Award for the most amusing design

■ Design Award for the most 'impossible shoe to wear' design!

(*See also* Worksheets: the design process)

From this activity you may have evidence for:

Skills list	1, 2, 3, 5, 6, 10, 11, 14, 15, 16.
Core skills	Communication level 1 and 2.
Element	1.1/2.1 Take part in discussions.
Opportunities	Discuss design ideas and shoe problems.
	Discuss and evaluate shoe designs.
	Invite people to a Design Award Exhibition (optional).
	Give a spoken presentation on shoe design (optional).
	Vote on Design Awards (optional).

Element	1.2/2.2 Produce written material.
Opportunities	List common shoe design problems.
	Write a list of design targets.
Element	1.3/2.3 Use images.
Opportunities	Design and label a drawing of a completely new shoe.
Element	1.4/2.4 Read and respond to written materials.
Opportunities	Read and follow the suggested design process to produce a shoe design.

Activity 5   Investigate hair style and colour choices

Discuss how different you would all look and feel if you each changed the colour or style of your hair. Has anyone ever fancied a complete change? Has anyone ever looked really different to how they do today because of a hair style or colour, or perhaps they once had more hair?

Collect some photographs of yourselves which show your faces clearly. Next, cut out as many different hairstyles as you can find using old magazines, photos and newspapers. Ask a local hairdresser for unwanted style magazines. Weekly magazines or Sunday supplements should provide plenty of source material. Include punk styles, shaven heads or styles from the 40s, 50s and 60s. Find pictures of hair styles used in Victorian times or Elizabethan times for example, or from other cultures or countries. Make your selection of cut-outs as wide as you can.

Lay out the photographs of yourselves and cover them with a variety of different cut-outs of different hair styles. Experiment and see how different you can make your faces look. Try to find a cut-out which gives each person a really new look. Help each other with choices and listen to each other's opinions.

Talk about how it makes you all feel seeing your faces changed by a new colour, length or shape of hair style. For example, have you found out if long hair suits you? Perhaps you worry about hair loss, and seeing a picture of yourself with less hair is really not so bad! Do you tend to agree with each other about the changes or do some people have very different views to others?

Discuss next any awful hair experiences you have had. Consider these ideas:

■ have you ever experimented on yourself with a colour or perm and it all went wrong?

■ have you ever had a bad experience at a salon, being left with a terrible hair style?

■ have you ever taken in a photo of a style you would like and come out with something completely different?

■ do you think people have an unrealistic idea of what a hairdresser can actually do?

■ do you think it would be a good idea to have a computer terminal in all hair salons so a customer can see exactly what they are going to look like?

■ why does a poor hair style affect people's confidence?

Use your discussion ideas to write a simple checklist. Present helpful tips for people to follow whenever they are thinking about having a completely new hair style, length or colour. For example, suggest they try your cut-out system to see if their face would suit the style they have in mind. Suggest they ask people who know them well for advice. Advise them to check the hairdresser is well recommended by other satisfied customers. Suggest they find a photograph of the style they would like and discuss it fully with their stylist before making a decision.

Read over your checklist and make sure your advice is in a sensible order. Make copies and give them to friends or people you work with and ask for comments. Would they use the checklist and find it helpful? Amend your checklist if you receive any useful ideas. Keep a copy each to use whenever you have any hair changes to make.

Optional task   Design your own 'Rogues Gallery'. Cut out pictures of celebrities from magazines and newspapers. Fit a cut-out of a completely new hair style, length or colour of hair over each face.

Display all the photographs of famous people you have given a new look to in your 'Rogues Gallery'. Ask other people to guess who each celebrity is. They may find it hard! You tend to look at someone's whole face, so if your hair is changed a great deal, people may not recognise you very easily. Have a bit of fun and see how well people get on!

From this activity you may have evidence for:

Skills list   1, 2, 3, 5, 6, 9, 10, 11, 12, 13/14, 15, 16.

Core skills   Communication level 1 and 2.

Element   1.1/2.1 Take part in discussions.

Opportunities   Discuss the results of the cut-out choices.

Discuss unpleasant hair experiences.

Ask people to guess famous faces in a Rogues Gallery (optional).

Element	1.2/2.2 Produce written material.
Opportunities	Write a checklist for making changes to your hair style.
Element	1.3/2.3 Use images.
Opportunities	Collect and use a variety of pictures of hair styles.
	Design and display a Rogues Gallery of famous faces (optional).
Element	1.4/2.4 Read and respond to written materials.
Opportunities	Scan newspapers, magazines and books for pictures of hair styles.

Activity 6 Investigate hair care routines and hair products

Television and magazine adverts for hair care products are common. You are made to feel hair care is important if you want to get on in a job or make a good impression on friends. Adverts encourage you to feel it is important to know what type of hair you have. You are encouraged to buy a large variety of products to care for your hair.

Discuss the different hair care routines you all have. Do you like simple, wash-and-go routines or do you have a more complex one? Do you stick to one product for your hair or do you often try out new ones? Would you use a different hair care routine to normal if you were preparing for a date, a party or a special occasion? Are you sometimes just too busy to wash your hair?

Consider these questions:

- do you use shampoo and water to wash your hair, and how often?
- do you often try out new hair products?
- do you use mousse, spray or conditioner?
- do you like to colour your hair?
- do you oil your hair?
- how often do you have your hair cut?
- has anyone in the group never had their hair cut?
- does anyone have religious or cultural traditions they must follow?

Use the worksheet provided to remind yourselves about personal hair care routines and share your ideas together.

Use the ideas from your discussion on hair care to write down a top ten of the most popular hair care products used by the group. Write them down in order of popularity. Include shampoos, conditioners, gels or mousses, colours and hot oil treatments, for example. Next to each item on your list, write a short explanation of why you selected it. For example, you might all like the smell, the creamy lather it makes or think it's good value for money.

Next, visit a large supermarket and list the top ten best selling hair care products. You may be able to spot this for yourselves by observing what people buy. Ask an assistant for information.

If you are not able to visit a supermarket, collect the information by looking through a range of magazines. Select the top ten most popular products being advertised. Watch TV adverts for ideas of popular products. Agree on and write down a top ten of best selling hair care products.

Compare your two top ten lists. Are there any products which appear on both lists? Have they been given the same placing? Are your Number One slots occupied by different products or the same ones? Overall, has the group chosen a top ten which is very similar to the ten best selling items of hair care products? If your own top ten is very similar, talk about why you think that has happened.

Optional task

Select five different shampoos. Try to choose a good price range, with one of your five an expensive brand and one a cheap supermarket own brand. Investigate and test the claims made by the makers of your chosen products.

Read the labels and packaging carefully for information. Write down the size and cost. Comment on the smell, texture and feel of each shampoo. Do they lather well or too much? Is the smell too strong or too weak?

Allocate tests between you and pool information to write out the results as a table. Include the makers' claims and your investigation results.

Use your results to decide on the following:

◼ is it worth paying more for a shampoo or are the cheaper brands good value?

◼ are the makers' claims for their products accurate?

◼ do the different shampoos have anything in common?

◼ which is the best shampoo in your opinion and why?

(*See also* Worksheets: hair care routines)

From this activity you may have evidence for:

Skills list	1, 2, 3, 4, 6, 7, 8/9, 10, 12, 13, 15, 16.
Core skills	Communication level 1 and 2.
Element	1.1/2.1 Take part in discussions.
Opportunities	Discuss hair care routines.
	Ask questions to find best selling hair products.
	Discuss hair product investigations (optional).
Element	1.2/2.2 Produce written material.

Opportunities	Write a group top ten of popular hair products.
	Write a top ten best selling products list.
	Write out the results of hair product investigations (optional).
Element	1.4/2.4 Read and respond to written materials.
Opportunities	Read magazines, books and adverts for information on best selling hair products.
	Read labels and packaging for information on makers' claims for hair products (optional).

Activity 7 Carry out research into common hair problems

You have an average of 100,000 hairs on your scalp. Each one is a string of cells containing keratin, overlapping to give strength to your hair. The cells divide all the time from the base of each hair, which is called the hair follicle. Each hair has a root under the skin of your scalp with a tiny gland to supply it with oil and keep it smooth and glossy. Each of your hairs will remain in place for about three years unless they are badly treated by heat or chemicals. As each hair becomes oily, dead skin cells and dirt get stuck to it and need to be washed off with mild shampoo.

You may sometimes have problems with your hair, for example, your hair may sometimes look limp. Limp hair can be caused by a build-up of oil on the hair or styling products which weigh the hair down and flatten it against your head. A clarifying shampoo is recommended for limp hair. This has a slightly stronger detergent level which dissolves the leftover styling products, leaving your hair totally clean.

Carry out some research to find out about common hair problems and produce a chart describing the problems and suggesting some solutions.

Choose some of the following common hair problems. Pick ones which you have some experience of already. For example:

dry hair   split ends

greasy hair   dandruff

loss of hair   greying hair

frizzy hair   dull hair

Research one problem each or work in pairs on a problem, making notes about your research as you go along. Get together as a group to compile your whole chart by pooling the information you have found. Allocate tasks to each other to get the work done. Use the worksheet provided to help you with your research.

Find information in books and magazines. Magazines are a good source of general information. Borrow back copies from friends or relatives so you have quite a few to look through. Read the labels of products which are on sale to correct or prevent some of the most common hair problems. Ask friends about their hair problems and favourite remedies. Ask your hairdresser or barber for advice.

Show your information as an attractive chart with diagrams and text. Write a short description about each hair problem you feature or draw a diagram to show the problem. Explain how to treat or improve the problem and give information about useful products to use on hair.

Photocopy your chart and each keep a copy to use whenever you have any hair problems. Laminate your charts so they can be kept in your bathroom and be wiped clean of splashes.

Give copies of your chart to friends and ask them to comment on how useful they think it is. Is it helpful to have the information on one chart rather than having to read product labels for information? Listen to comments you receive and report them back to the group. Discuss any useful ideas and amend your chart if necessary.

(*See also* Worksheets: problem hair)

From this activity you may have evidence for:

Skills list	1, 2, 4, 5, 6, 7, 8/9, 11, 13/14, 15, 16.
Core skills	Communication level 1 and 2.
Element	1.1/2.1 Take part in discussions.
Opportunities	Discuss and allocate tasks for work on the chart.
	Ask for information on hair problems from friends or your hairdresser.
	Ask for and discuss feedback about the chart from friends.
Element	1.2/2.2 Produce written material.
Opportunities	Make notes on research to share with the group.
	Write up a chart on common hair problems.
Element	1.3/2.3 Use images.
Opportunities	Use diagrams to explain hair problems on the chart.

Element   1.4/2.4 Read and respond to written materials.

Opportunities   Read information about hair problems in books, magazines, adverts and product labels to use on the chart.

Activity 8   **Design an advert for a hair care product**

Design an advert for a new hair care product. Discuss what your product will look like and smell like. What shape bottle and labelling will you give it? Brainstorm for ideas on names, claims you will make for your product and packaging. Write down all your ideas as they come to you and then go back and discuss them in detail. Choose the features you all like and agree on your new hair product. Write a description of exactly what you have decided so everyone is clear about the chosen product design.

Design an advert to advertise your product. It could be an advert for a magazine or television, or for commercial radio.

Collect adverts of hair care products from magazines for ideas on how they are set out. Watch television adverts for ideas. Record a selection so you can view them together. Tape some radio commercials and listen to them.

Have another brainstorming session. Ask yourselves what makes people notice an advert and then go out and buy that product. Write everyone's ideas down just as they come. Next, look carefully at your ideas and decide what you need to keep in mind when designing your own advert. For example, consider these suggestions:

- use colour to catch people's attention
- use colours which people associate with cleanliness
- use large print to catch someone's eye
- use a catchy phrase which is easily remembered
- give your hair care product a good name
- use attractive photographs or funny cartoons
- use a picture of a famous person
- use words which make people remember your hair care product
- make claims about the product, e.g. it makes hair glossy and shiny, it clears up dandruff, etc.
- use music if you are making a video or tape

Draw the advert out by hand or use a computer paint program, or tape your advert. If the advert is for a commercial radio station, write a jingle for your product. Make a model of the bottle or package to use in a video, or photograph it for your advert. Allocate tasks to each other so you are each responsible for part of the work. Try different methods and vote on the most successful outcome. Work in pairs or small groups and get together regularly to pool information for your advert.

Look at your finished advert for a new hair care product. Have you made the product sound attractive? Does it sound worth trying? Decide if you would be persuaded to go out and buy it and why. Show your advert to other people you work with. Ask them if they like the sound of your product and if so, why.

From this activity you may have evidence for:

Skills list	1, 2, 3, 4, 5, 6, 9, 10, 12, 13, 14, 15, 16.
Core skills	Communication level 1 and 2.
Element	1.1/2.1 Take part in discussions.
Opportunities	Brainstorm for ideas for a new hair care product.
	Discuss ideas for an advert for a new product.
	Allocate tasks for work to be done on the advert.
	Record an advert for commercial radio.
	Evaluate the effectiveness of your advert design.
Element:	1.2/2.2 Produce written material.
Opportunities	Write a description of a new hair product.
	Write the text for an advert.
Element	1.3/2.3 Use images.
Opportunities	Use images in an advert for television or a magazine.
Element	1.4/2.4 Read and respond to written materials.
Opportunities	Collect a variety of adverts and analyse the content for use in a new advert.

Evaluation exercise

Discuss your experience during this project on the care of feet and hair. What have you found out about which you didn't know before? Will you think differently about shoes from now on, having designed your own piece of footwear? Have you learned any new routines for the care of your feet? Will you be able to select the right product for a hair problem?

Do you feel you are more confident about research activities? Are you more confident about presenting your work in a number of different ways? Do you feel more able to ask questions? Can you take part in a discussion, listen to others and put your own point of view?

Check you have completed your Skills Record Sheet, writing down the important skills you have covered. Record your comments and details of the resources used. Remember to include the dates you practised different skills. Record evidence you have of competence in a range of skills on your Skills Summary Sheet. Write down any links to an accreditation which you may be working towards. Write down details of skills you wish to practise further and give yourself realistic goal dates for completing the work.

Multi-use ■ *Use this worksheet for checking presentations.*

Presenting your research

(Tick each area of work as you complete it)

Collect information

Make notes from books, TV, video, talking to people

Collect photocopies of charts, diagrams or articles

Tape interviews with people

Find useful pictures and photographs

Write to organisations for information   ☐ ☐ ☐ ☐ ☐

Plan work

Use a spider plan

Use a numbered list

Use a storyboard   ☐ ☐ ☐

Select information

Select information from notes

Select information from charts, diagrams or articles

Listen to tapes and select parts to use

Decide how pictures can be used to add information

Select information from replies to letters   ☐ ☐ ☐ ☐ ☐

Present information

As a written report

As a spoken presentation

As a video or audio tape

As a chart or diagram

As a poster   ☐ ☐ ☐ ☐ ☐

Check written presentation

Correct spelling mistakes

Correct punctuation

Make sure sentences make sense

Is all planned information included?

Does work look neat and attractive?   ☐ ☐ ☐ ☐ ☐

Check spoken presentation

Check notes cover all key points

Check preparations are complete, e.g. visual aids ready

Deal with nerves

Speak clearly   ☐ ☐ ☐ ☐

Evaluate presentation

Are you happy with your finished presentation?

What have you learned?

What would you change if you could?

How would you do things differently another time?   ☐ ☐ ☐ ☐

Multi-use ■ *Use this worksheet for planning a questionnaire.*

Designing a questionnaire

Use these tips to help you design a good questionnaire.

■ explain the purpose of the questionnaire to the people completing it for you

■ choose questions which produce useful information

■ keep your questionnaire as short as possible

■ don't ask for personal information which people may be unhappy about giving

■ put your questions in a sensible order

■ check your questions are clear and can't be misunderstood

■ use a mixture of 'open' and 'closed' questions

■ include a 'thank you' at the end of your questionnaire

Open questions can be very helpful.   These are questions which let someone explain how they think or feel. For example:

What kind of shoes do your feel most comfortable in?

Other types of open questions ask people if they strongly agree or disagree with a statement you make. You then provide a scale for the person to tick or circle their choice. For example:

You should have your feet measured every time you buy a pair of shoes.

Closed questions can also be very useful.

It is easier for you to look at the results of these types of questions as you are giving people a limited choice of answers. Questions may need a Yes or No, or you may provide a multi-choice with tick boxes. For example:

Which of the following foot care products have you used in the last three months?

Provide a list of common products with a box next to each one with room for a tick.

Checklist for common foot problems

Use this suggested layout for your chart about foot problems.

Name of foot problem:

Brief description of main symptoms (include diagram or drawing if possible)

Can the problem be treated at home?   Yes/No

Suggested treatment to be carried out at home

Recommended product (with reason for choice)

What results you can expect

How long the treatment will take

When should the problem be treated by your GP?

When should the problem be treated by a chiropodist?

Repeat this layout for each foot problem you find out about and include in your chart.

Show the information as the layout above and draw a box around each separate problem you show.

Use colour to show the different problems or different kinds of treatments or use diagrams of each problem.

List each heading across the top of a large piece of paper and write the facts you find out underneath. Reduce the size of your final chart on a photocopier for individual copies.

The design process

Think carefully about your ideas for a completely new shoe. Look at the list of targets you agreed as a group. Think about the special event or activity you want the shoe to be used for.

Sketch out your first ideas. It doesn't matter if the sketches are very rough at this stage. Write your ideas down in words if you prefer.

Look at shoes which you have at home, or in catalogues or shops. Notice any particular features which seem important. It might be that the colour is good, the material needs to be waterproof, or the sole needs to have a good grip for example.

Add your research to your first ideas and see if you can improve your design. Draw it out again showing your new ideas.

Look carefully at your design and decide if you are happy with it. Have you met your targets? Have you included all the special features you wanted? Make a good drawing of your final design. Label all the parts to explain your design to others. Use graph paper or a grid to help you draw the shape, or find shapes to draw around.

Look at your design, show it to others and discuss what you think about it. Does it meet the targets you listed? Is it attractive? Would you like to wear the shoe if you had the chance?

Write down an evaluation of your design. This could be a mixture of your own opinion and the comments you received from other people. Be positive about your design. There may be parts of the design you are not pleased with, but there will also be parts which work very well!

Hair care routines

Read the list of prompts below and underline or put a circle around the ones which apply to you. Note down which products you use for each part of your hair care routine.

Daily routines

Do you   **Products?**

Brush hair quickly / thoroughly

Comb hair quickly / thoroughly

Oil hair

Polish hair

Use mousse / spray / gel

Use mild shampoo

Use curlers / curling tongs

Use hot comb / brush

Wash hair with any kind of shampoo

Use a special shampoo

Use conditioner or shampoo/conditioner

Dry hair with hair dryer / in the air

Tie hair into fashion style

Tie back hair for work

Plait or bead

Cover hair completely

→

Weekly routines

Do you   **Products?**

Use a special shampoo

Use shampoo for dandruff

Use conditioner or shampoo/conditioner

Use hot oil treatment

Colour hair – a tint

Style with curlers / tongs / brush

Monthly (or less often)

Do you   **Products?**

Have a hair cut / trim / re-style

Have your hair cut at a salon / by a friend

Colour hair: semi-permanent / permanent

Bleach hair

Use hair treatment masks

Problem hair

Use this suggested layout for your chart on hair problems. An example of how to complete it is provided. Enlarge your chart on a photocopier for a wall display, or reduce it for a pocket-size copy.

Hair problem:

Brief description:

Possible causes:

Recommended treatment:

Recommended product or where to find one:

How to carry out treatment:

Possible cost:

Duration of treatment and possible results:

Hair problem: Limp hair

Brief description: Hair has no bounce or volume and hangs flattened to the head.

Possible causes: a build-up of sebum or remains of styling products left on the hair.

Recommended treatment: A shampoo with a stronger detergent action than normal to dissolve the products or sebum which remain on the hair.

Recommended product or where to find one: A clarifying shampoo. Should be widely available in chemists or directly from a hair salon. Ask for help in choosing one or read the label carefully.

How to carry out treatment: Wash hair as with any normal shampoo and rinse really well.

Possible cost: Up to £3

Duration of treatment and possible results: Hair may only require one treatment, can be repeated when needed. Hair should have bounce and shine.

Back to basics

Answers on pp. 310–11.

Careful reading

Read through the following routine for washing hair. Re-write it putting the routine into the correct order.

■ Blot your hair dry gently with a towel. Comb your hair with a wide-toothed comb to get rid of any tangles.

■ Rub shampoo between the palms of your hands then smooth into your hair. Massage gently over your whole scalp.

■ Wet hair with warm water and gently comb fingers through hair to make sure it's completely wet.

■ Comb dry hair with wide-toothed comb to prevent tangling when wet.

■ Smooth conditioner over hair with the palms of your hands, concentrating on the ends of the hair. Rinse well again.

■ Rinse hair well using clear, warm water. A common cause of dull hair is poor rinsing.

Answer these questions about the hair care routine, now you have put it into the correct order.

1. Why should you comb your hair before washing it?

2. How should you apply the shampoo?

3. What is a common cause of dull hair?

4. How should you apply conditioner?

Muddled Words

Sort out these muddled-up words about foot care and write out each one correctly.

slain	theleat's tofo	creavrue
sunobin	tofoware	conott ckoss
reab tofo	blexifle	trislbe

Leaving a note

Jackie and Sandra work in the same hair salon. Jackie took a telephone message from a customer just as she was leaving for home, writing it down in a hurry. When Sandra arrived at work the next day she read the note but found she wasn't certain what the customer wanted. Read the note Jackie left for Sandra. Think about what Sandra needs to know and rewrite the note putting in the extra information.

Tuesday

Sandra

One of your ladies, Mrs Waters, phoned and cancelled her appointment. Some emergency in the family she said. She wants another appointment next Wednesday. Just for the usual. Can you write it in the book?

Jackie.

Personal care: teeth, skin and body

Choose activities which interest you from the wide range of suggestions provided in the project. You can choose to do just part of an activity if you wish. The choice is yours. There are more suggestions in the Alternative Ideas section (p. 151), so you should find enough activities to suit your interests and needs. Finish with the Evaluation Exercise as this will help you think about your work on the project and remind you to record the skills you have covered.

For each activity you choose to do, use the information provided for you in the activity text and worksheets, as well as your own experiences and knowledge. If you need to look for more information consider resources such as books, newspapers and magazines as well as television, radio, video and CD-ROM. You can also use resources such as writing to an organisation or telephoning for information, talking to people you know and talking to other people who may be able to give you the information you need.

Optional task   If you have more time available and would like to try another task to develop the skills you have already used in an activity, you can look for the Optional Tasks which are linked to many of the project activities.

You will find the following worksheets useful:

Personal care: teeth, skin and body

Activity 1   ## Write a checklist for caring for teeth and gums

What's your regular care routine for your teeth and gums? Is it a quick brush before you go to bed, or do you clean your teeth carefully after every meal?

Your teeth are made of a substance called dentine. The dentine is covered with a hard outer layer called enamel, for protection. In the centre of the tooth there is a soft tissue called the pulp which contains blood vessels and nerves.

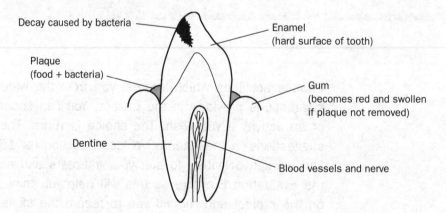

Decay caused by bacteria

Enamel
(hard surface of tooth)

Plaque
(food + bacteria)

Gum
(becomes red and swollen
if plaque not removed)

Dentine

Blood vessels and nerve

You need two substances in your diet for healthy teeth: calcium and fluoride. Calcium can help form and keep strong and healthy teeth. Fluoride also strengthens your teeth and seems to discourage the bacteria in plaque. It is commonly put in toothpaste.

As you eat food, especially sugary foods, the bacteria in the plaque, which is a colourless, sticky layer over the surface of your teeth, feed on the sugar and produce acid. The acid attacks the enamel covering your teeth and can cause decay. If you don't clean the plaque off properly it hardens to form tartar or calculus. This needs to be scraped off by your dentist as it is too hard for your toothbrush to cope with. Plaque can also cause gum disease. Gums can become swollen, painful, bleed easily and cause bad breath. Good mouth hygiene, which means a good teeth and gum care routine, helps keep your teeth and gums healthy.

Write a checklist which describes a good routine for caring for your teeth and gums which anyone could follow.

Find out what makes a good routine by using your own experiences and the information you have just read about teeth and gums. Add to your knowledge by finding books in the library about the care of teeth. Try the health section and books on child care which should give some good basic information on caring for teeth. Make notes and collect useful diagrams or pictures as you go along. Pick up leaflets about caring for teeth and gums from your local dentist. Write to a toothpaste manufacturer for some information.

Write out your care routine either as a list showing one step at a time, as a flow diagram or as a series of labelled diagrams. Show with line drawings how to brush teeth or use floss. Use photographs or diagrams to highlight the advice on your checklist. Select information from your notes and choose information to include in your final checklist. Use the worksheet provided to help with ideas on what to include in your checklist and how to present the information.

Read over your finished checklist for the care of teeth and gums and make sure you have included everything you planned to put in. Check it makes sense and is in a sensible order. Show your checklist to friends or people you work with and ask them for comments. Do they think your advice is practical and helpful?

(*See also* Worksheets: caring for teeth and gums)

	From this activity you may have evidence for:
Skills list	1, 3, 4, 6, 7, 8/9, 11, 13/14, 15, 16.
Core skills	Communication level 1 and 2.
Element	1.1/2.1 Take part in discussions.
Opportunities	Ask a dentist for advice on caring for teeth.
	Ask people to comment on the finished checklist.
Element	1.2/2.2 Produce written material.
Opportunities	Make notes on a variety of research activities.
	Write a letter to a toothpaste manufacturer for information.
	Write a checklist showing a good routine for the care of teeth and gums.
Element	1.3/2.3 Use images.

Opportunities	Show your checklist as a flow diagram.
	Use pictures, diagrams and photographs to highlight information in the checklist.
Element	1.4/2.4 Read and respond to written materials.
Opportunities	Read books, leaflets and labels for information to use in the checklist.

Activity 2 Carry out an investigation to find the best toothpaste

Most people use a toothpaste to help keep their teeth clean. There are many different brands for sale and a large variety of flavours. Some help to reduce the build-up of plaque and tartar, some help to whiten your teeth and some help to reduce gum disease. Other toothpastes promise to help you cope with sensitive teeth. Toothpaste packaging gives you information about how to prevent tooth decay and encourages you to clean your teeth every day after meals. Toothpastes come in a variety of colours. The most popular colour is white but blue or green gels are used and blue, white and red stripes are also popular. Flavours can vary to suit everyone's taste, from strong or fresh mint to mild mint or spearmint. With so many different choices available, how do you choose the best one? Carry out a short investigation to find out which, in your opinion, is the best brand of toothpaste.

Select a varied range of toothpastes and find out:

■ the price and size of the tube

■ the claims made on the box or tube

■ the taste

■ the texture

■ the smell

■ the colour

■ what the toothpaste is like to use (e.g. is it too foamy)

Choose six top selling brands of toothpaste. Ask an assistant in a supermarket about their best selling products or watch television adverts to see which brands appear to be the most popular. Ask your dentist which toothpaste they consider worth trying. Sample your chosen brands. Ask friends or family members who use your chosen brands for help. Explain to them exactly what you want to find out. Set a number of questions to be answered about each brand. The toothpaste which produces the most positive set of answers should then be the one you feel is the best. Use the worksheet to help you record the answers to your questions.

If it's not possible for you to actually sample the toothpastes, answer your questions by carefully reading the labels and packaging for information. Gather more information from adverts in magazines.

Record which brand of toothpaste you feel is the best. Give the reasons for your choice. Talk about your choice with other people and see if they agree with your reasons.

(*See also* Worksheets: toothpaste investigation)

From this activity you may have evidence for –

Skills list	1, 3, 4, 6, 7, 8, 10, 11, 12, 13, 15, 16.
Core skills	Communication level 1 and 2.
Element	1.1/2.1 Take part in discussions.
Opportunities	Ask friends to comment on toothpaste preferences.
	Ask a dentist or assistant for advice on choosing best selling toothpastes.
	Talk about your choice of best toothpaste with other people.
Element	1.2/2.2 Produce written material.
Opportunities	Write a list of questions.
	Record the results of your investigation.
	Evaluate your findings and record your choice of best toothpaste.
Element	1.4/2.4 Read and respond to written materials.
Opportunities	Read information about toothpaste from packaging and adverts.

Activity 3 Write a low sugar snack plan

Sugar in your diet, especially a sugary snack between meals, is a main cause of tooth decay. When you eat or drink sugary snacks such as biscuits, cakes, chocolate and fizzy drinks, the sugar starts off a reaction in your mouth. The bacteria in the plaque on your teeth use the sugar to produce acid. The acid attacks the hard enamel on the surface of your teeth. Your teeth can cope with quite a lot of these attacks, especially as your saliva can wash away some of the acid. However, your teeth will eventually begin to decay.

After a busy morning at work it's tempting to have a sugary snack to keep yourself going. Some people can get very grumpy when they are hungry and a quick burst of sugar seems to answer the problem. But does it really benefit you? Sugar contains only calories for energy, with no other nutrients for your body to use. You don't need sugar for energy, you can get all the energy you need from the other foods in your diet. Sugary snacks just cause a problem for your teeth. If you really need a snack to keep you going during the day pick one which is not packed with sugar.

Ask a friend or someone you work with, who you know likes sugary snacks, if they will try some low sugar alternatives. Write a low sugar snack plan which is practical, attractive and easy to use, with this person in mind.

Start by questioning your chosen person. Write a list of all the sugary snacks they like and might eat during an average week. Carry out some research to find out how to replace each sugary snack with a low sugar or sugar-free choice.

For example, you may have listed the names of favourite chocolate bars, biscuits, cakes, sweets and hot and cold drinks. What can you suggest your chosen person tries instead? Look for foods which have no sugar added or have sugar replacements. Look for the same snacks that are on the list but find a sugar-free version instead. Look for sugar-free mints, chocolate bars, chocolate drinks, squashes and sugar-free fizzy drinks. Look for fresh fruit, low sugar yoghurts, plain popcorn, fromage frais, or unsalted nuts.

Visit your local supermarket and health food shop for ideas. Read the labels on foods carefully to check what they contain, as sugar has a lot of different names. For example you may see cane sugar, muscovado sugar, brown sugar, honey, glucose, treacle, sucrose or syrup in a list of ingredients. Sugar-free sweets which contain sorbitol have a mild laxative effect on most people. It is best not to eat too many in one day. Choose a wide range of healthy snacks. Look through healthy eating magazines in your library or newsagent. Ask friends or people you work with for suggestions. Use the worksheet provided to help you record the details for your plan.

Write out your low sugar snack plan. Make your plan as interesting and practical as possible, so your chosen person will be prepared to try it. Use pictures from labels, magazines or leaflets to illustrate each snack you list.

Show your plan to the person you designed it for and ask them for comments. Do they think the plan looks attractive and easy to use? Are they surprised by the wide range of sugar-free snacks they can choose from? Are they prepared to try out the low sugar snack plan? If so, ask them to try the plan for a week and review their opinion of the plan. Record their comments on the worksheet provided. Amend your plan if there are selections which are not popular.

(*See also* Worksheets: low sugar plan)

	From this activity you may have evidence for:
Skills list	1, 3, 6, 8, 10, 11, 13/14, 15, 16.
Core skills	Communication level 1 and 2.
Element	1.1/2.1 Take part in discussions.
Opportunities	Question a chosen person about sugary snack choices.
	Ask people for ideas for low sugar snacks.
	Ask for feedback on your low sugar snack plan.
Element	1.2/2.2 Produce written material.
Opportunities	Write a list of sugary snack choices.
	Write a low sugar snack plan.
Element	1.3/2.3 Use images.

Opportunities	Use pictures to illustrate foods on the low sugar snack plan.
Element	1.4/2.4 Read and respond to written materials.
Opportunities	Read labels, leaflets, books and magazines for ideas for your low sugar snack plan.

Activity 4   Design a guide to good skin and nail care

Your skin is an important part of your body, protecting you against infection. It deserves to be well looked after. Your skin is tough, waterproof and full of blood vessels and nerve endings which can detect heat, cold, touch and pain.

The outer layer of your skin is called the epidermis and is made up of layers of cells. The cells die and flake off as new skin grows underneath. Under the epidermis is the dermis. This is fibrous tissue with fat cells which protect and insulate you. This is also the part of the skin which contains blood vessels, sweat glands, glands which release sebum to keep your skin supple, and hair follicles.

Do you look after your skin carefully? If you don't care for your skin and body properly, you can have all kinds of problems. For example, sweat evaporates from the surface of your skin, helping to keep you cool. If you don't wash away the sweat it will start to smell after a while as it reacts with the bacteria living on your skin's surface. Your skin may become dry and crack in cold weather if it is not moisturised. You may get skin rashes if you use harsh soaps on your skin.

As well as your skin, your nails are also worth looking after carefully. If you bite your nails or they split or the cuticle tears, they may become infected and painful. Your nails are made of a strong substance called keratin which is the same substance as your hair. The part of your nail which grows out of your skin is dead, that's why it doesn't hurt to cut it.

Design a fact file which explains good skin and nail care routines for people to follow. Recommend products to try out.

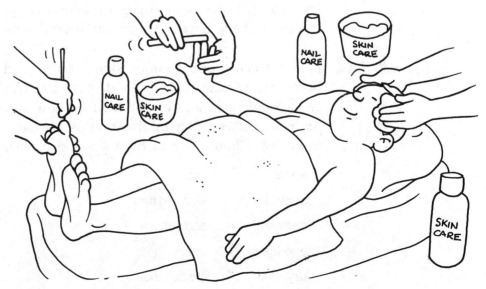

Collect information on good skin and nail care, including some useful products which you would recommend. Use your own experiences of skin and nail care for ideas. Consider these care routines:

■ cutting finger and toe nails properly

■ polishing and strengthening nails

■ removing hard skin from your feet

■ treating hard skin on your elbows and knees

■ safe shaving or hair removal methods

■ using moisturisers

■ removing make-up

■ skin cleansing and toning

■ safe self-tanning methods

Collect more information by asking about products in a supermarket or chemist. Ask for help and advice at the different beauty counters in a High Street chemist such as Boots. Read labels, pick up useful leaflets, and decide what kind of products you would suggest are best. Ask friends about their routines and the products they like to use. Look in magazines at the articles and adverts for information about different routines and products. Go to your local library to look at a variety of magazines. Borrow videos on the subject of skin and nail care. Make notes about your research as you go along.

 Present your fact file as a written guide or as a video tape, showing demonstrations of what to do and which products to use. Use diagrams and photographs to highlight important points in a written fact file. Recommend products and give information about how to use them, where to buy them and how much they may cost.

 Show your fact file or tape to friends or people you work with and ask for their comments. Is the advice easy to understand? Do they like the sound of the products you recommend? Would they use your fact file or tape if you gave them a copy? Make improvements to your fact file if you receive any useful ideas.

Optional task   Find out about one common skin problem and design a problem-buster action plan. Design a half page size (A5) handout which gives people help and information on how to deal with the problem. Present your information as a what to do and what not to do list. Choose one of the following problems:

spots	acne
cold sores	skin rashes
dermatitis	eczema
psoriasis	warts
dry skin	greasy skin

Question friends to find out which problems cause the most anxiety or pick a skin problem which you have some experience of yourself. Find out more information about your chosen skin problem from magazines, books, televisions programmes, product labels or leaflets.

For example, offer advice and information on spots. Explain briefly how they are caused – a hair follicle becomes blocked with a plug of sebum and turns a black colour when exposed to the air. If the blockage continues bacteria attack the trapped matter causing a red, painful area on the skin.

Show the problem as a labelled diagram. Give advice on what to do about the problem, such as a good skin care routine and a good anti-bacterial face wash. Reassure people that eating chocolate and chips doesn't cause spots! Give advice on what not to do, such as don't squeeze spots as the pressure on the skin can force the bacteria even deeper. Advise people not to panic, spots do go quite quickly if your skin is kept clean. There are some very good masking sticks on the market with anti-bacterial effects, so spots can be hidden while they heal and your self-confidence can be kept high!

(*See also* Worksheets: skin and nail care)

From this activity you may have evidence for:

Skills list	1, 4, 6, 7, 8/9, 10, 11, 12, 13/14, 15, 16.
Core skills	Communication level 1 and 2.
Element	1.1/2.1 Take part in discussions.
Opportunities	Ask friends, shop assistants and beauty consultants, for information on nail and skin care.
	Ask friends and other people for comments on the fact file or tape.
	Ask friends which type of skin problem they worry about (optional).
Element	1.2/2.2 Produce written material.
Opportunities	Write a fact file on skin and nail care.
	Make notes about research material.
	Write a problem-buster action plan about a common skin problem (optional).
Element	1.3/2.3 Use images.
Opportunities	Design a chart or tape on good nail and skin care, using diagrams or cartoons.
	Use diagrams to explain a skin problem in the problem-buster action plan (optional).
Element	1.4/2.4 Read and respond to written materials.
Opportunities	Collect information about how to care for skin and nails using leaflets, books, magazines, videos.
	Find out about skin problems using books, magazines (optional).

Activity 5   Investigate sun protection methods and products

Lying in the warm sun can feel wonderful, but too much sun too quickly can mean you are risking skin cancer. The sun is the main cause of skin cancer. Fortunately, most skin cancers are completely curable if treated promptly.

Skin cancer can be caused when your skin is exposed to short bursts of really strong sunlight, without any protection. This is just what many people do when they go on holiday. They rush out to enjoy the sunshine without stopping to protect their skin. Can you remember a time when your skin went really red after sitting in the sun for too long? One type of ray within sunlight is called UVA, and experts think it causes skin ageing, wrinkles, freckles and rashes. Another type of ray is UVB and this is the part of sunlight which causes sunburn.

Take care in the sun by covering your skin with loose clothing made from a close-weave fabric. Wear a hat with a brim to shade your face and neck and wear sunglasses. Use a sun cream which has a good level of sun protection from UVB and UVA rays and is suitable for your type of skin. Apply your sun cream often, especially after a swim. A child's skin is very delicate and is easily damaged by the sun so needs a high level of protection. Even some dark haired people have very fair skin. Buy fresh supplies of sun cream every year, as sun creams lose their effectiveness after a while. Never stay in the sun until your skin has turned red as all you are doing is burning your skin.

 Carry out a two-part investigation. Find out how people protect themselves in the sun and what sensible steps they should be following. Find out and recommend some good quality sun creams for dark, fair and sensitive skin.

 Ask friends and people you work with how they protect themselves in the sun. What equipment and sun barriers do they use? For example do they cover up their skin in the hot sun? Do they keep out of the sun around mid-day? Do they wear hats and sunglasses? Which types of sun cream do they prefer? Do they use creams which suit their age, skin type or holiday destination? Do they throw out old sun creams and buy fresh tubes each year?

Look for articles in magazines and leaflets about skin care in the sun at your local clinic or doctor's surgery for ideas about sun protection advice people should be following.

Look at a variety of sun creams and lotions on the market. Find out what kind of information and guidance you are given on the packaging. For example a sun cream for sensitive skin may say it is hypo-allergenic. This means it has been tested for reaction on skin and is likely to be perfume- and lanolin-free. These ingredients will often cause a rash on sensitive skins. It may explain how to apply the cream, and whether it is waterproof and has UVA and UVB screening. Without a good level of UVA protection some people suffer from a rash brought on by sunlight. It may say what skin types it is best for and list ingredients. By reading the information on the tubes, bottles or labels you should be able to carry out a really good investigation.

If the shops are not full of sun protection products because of the time of year, collect tubes and bottles from friends and family members to look at. Use adverts from back copies of magazines. Large High Street chemists should carry sun products all year round, or you could ask for leaflets on the subject. Read holiday brochures or ask in a travel agent's for information. Use the worksheet provided to help you plan your investigation.

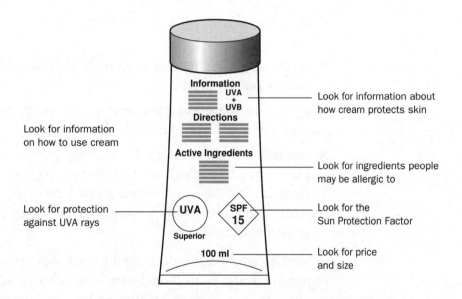

 When you have collected information from your two-part investigation, write a detailed account of your results.

- describe which methods of sun protection are the most popular

- describe which sun creams are most widely used

- describe whether you feel people are taking enough sensible steps to protect their skin

- describe what more they should be doing to protect themselves in the sun

- make some recommendations for good quality sun creams and explain the reasons for your choice

 Talk about your investigation results with other people. Do they agree with the sun protection methods you feel should be used? Do they like the sound of the sun creams you recommend? Would they carry out any of your advice?

Optional task Find out about and write a short checklist explaining how to choose a good pair of sun glasses.

Find information for your checklist by asking questions in shops which sell sun glasses. Telephone or visit your local optician for advice. Read the labels on sun glasses for information. Find out which British Standard is used for sun glasses and what it means. Your local Trading Standards Office may be able to give you some information. Their number will be in the telephone book. Look for useful articles in magazines.

Offer advice in your checklist about which types of glasses suit different shaped faces. For example, if you have a wide forehead and narrow chin, oval or aviator style glasses flatter your face. People with square faces, a broad jaw and sharp cheek bones should look good in round glasses.

Offer advice about:

■ checking glasses protect you from ultra-violet light and infra-red rays

■ checking glasses meet a current British Standard which should be shown on the label

■ trying out the glasses properly in the shop, checking to see if they feel too heavy or pinch the nose

■ reminding people not to wear cheap glasses with just darkened plastic or glass which do not protect your eyes at all from sunlight. (Children are often given very poor quality glasses to wear which are really a toy rather than sun glasses offering some protection.)

Present your checklist on a credit card sized piece of card. List the important features to look for in your chosen sun glasses. Put your mini-guide into a plastic wallet or have it laminated like a swipe card and carry it around in a wallet or purse for quick access. Make copies for friends and ask them to tell you how useful they find it.

(*See also* Worksheets: care in the sun)

	From this activity you may have evidence for:
Skills list	1, 3, 4, 6, 7, 8/9, 10, 11, 12, 13, 15, 16.
Core skills	Communication level 1 and 2.
Element	1.1/2.1 Take part in discussions.
Opportunities	Ask friends or chemists for information on sun protection routines and methods and products used.
	Ask for information about sun glasses in shops and opticians (optional).
	Telephone the Trading Standards for information on British Standards for sun glasses (optional).
Element	1.2/2.2 Produce written material.
Opportunities	Write an account of the investigation results.

Write a checklist for buying good quality sun glasses for sun protection (optional).

Element 1.3/2.3 Use images.

Opportunities Show examples of logos or symbols of quality for sun glasses on checklist (optional).

Element 1.4/2.4 Read and respond to written materials.

Opportunities Collect information about sun creams and sun protection methods from product labels, leaflets, brochures and magazines.

Read labels to find out about sun glasses (optional).

Activity 6 Write your opinion about body image

It's common to read in newspapers and magazines and to see on television stories about the way in which celebrities, models and actors look after their bodies. You may read about their exercise routines and diet and about the changes they make to their bodies through cosmetic surgery. Articles written about celebrities suggest that making changes to their bodies is commonplace. There is a very big market in diet and exercise books and videos written or presented by celebrities, which encourage you to change the way you look.

Write your opinion about the kind of ideal body image promoted by celebrities, models and actors in film, television, magazines and newspapers. Do you think it is a good or bad image for ordinary people to try to copy? Does it make people feel unhappy with the way their bodies look? Do you think this ideal body image may even lead people towards eating disorders? Do you think we should see more average-shaped people modelling designer clothes, for example?

Collect a selection of magazines and daily newspapers. Read through them carefully and select any stories, articles or photographs about the way people have altered their body image. They may have altered the way they look to be more slim, more muscled, more shapely or to look younger. Find out how people have gone about making changes and for what reasons.

Plan your written opinion carefully. Use examples in your written opinion from articles you have read or from experiences you have had yourself. Write down three important points you would like to make. Develop each point into several sentences to make a paragraph. Think of an example to explain each point and comment on why someone might have the opposite view point to yourself.

Read over your written work carefully and check it makes sense. Correct any spelling or punctuation mistakes you may have made. You may need to rewrite your work so you have a neat, readable copy. Give your written opinion to someone else to read and comment on. See if you share an opinion or whether you have different views about body image and the influence the media has on people.

Optional task   Interview several friends, other students or people you work with and find out if they are happy with their body image. Try to ask a mixed age group if you can. List some questions to ask and record the comments you receive by making notes or taping the interviews. For example, ask:

- if you could change any part of your body, which part would it be and why?
- do you try to alter your body with exercise or diet, and if so what do you do and what changes do you hope to make?
- would you ever consider cosmetic surgery, and if so why?
- is there a particular celebrity with a body image you admire and why?
- do you think the body image promoted by film, television and magazines can cause people to become unhappy with their own bodies?
- if you are happy now with your body image has this always been so?
- do you think people worry too much about body image?

Consider the answers you receive carefully and write a short summary of the results of your interviews. If possible from the information you obtained, write a general statement about whether people are happy with their own body image or not.

From this activity you may have evidence for:

Skills list	1, 3, 6, 8, 10, 13, 15, 16.
Core skills	Communication level 1 and 2.
Element	1.1/2.1 Take part in discussions.
Opportunities	Ask another person to read your opinion and discuss views on body image.
	Interview people about their body image (optional).

Element	1.2/2.2 Produce written material.
Opportunities	Plan and write an opinion about the influence of the media on body image.
	Make notes during interviews (optional).
	Write a summary of the results of the interviews on body image (optional).
Element	1.4/2.4 Read and respond to written materials.
Opportunities	Collect and read stories and articles from magazines and newspapers about celebrity body image to use for a written opinion.

 ## Evaluation exercise

What have you found out about teeth and how to care for them? Do you think you will follow a good care routine from now on or encourage someone else to do so? Have you found out about some new skin and nail care routines which you didn't know before? Do you feel more confident about protecting your skin in the sun? Do you feel encouraged by others to have a confident image of your own body from now on?

Do you feel your research skills have improved? Do you feel more confident about asking questions or presenting information in a variety of different ways? Do you feel more able to use pictures or diagrams to add information to your presentations?

Make sure you have recorded all the skills you have practised on the Skills Record Sheet. This sheet will be useful if you need to remind yourself about what you have achieved and what different resources you have used. Record in detail all evidence of competence you may have on your Skills Summary Record. Write down any links to an accreditation you may be working towards. Think about and record your progress and achievement. Write down which skills you plan to work on next.

Caring for teeth and gums

Use the ideas in this worksheet to help you write out a good checklist for caring for teeth and gums.

1. Start your checklist by suggesting what kind of diet is good for your teeth and gums

Can eating make a difference? Calcium in your diet can help form and keep teeth strong and healthy. Calcium can be found in foods such as cereals, vegetables, milk, cheese, meat and fish. Vitamin C is good for your gums. It can be found in foods such as citrus fruits and green vegetables.

2. Include information about fluoride in your checklist

Can fluoride make a difference? Fluoride is needed to strengthen the enamel on your teeth and help reduce bacteria. It is found in most tap water (but not everywhere), in toothpaste and in fish for example.

3. Give some advice in your checklist on how to brush your teeth

Can brushing make a difference? Brush carefully with a soft toothbrush over all the surfaces of your teeth. Finish with flossing. Gently work up and down the gaps between teeth and rinse well.

4. Suggest which toothpastes to use

Can toothpaste make a difference? It is sensible to use one which contains fluoride, especially if you live in an area where it is not put in tap water. Choose a toothpaste you like the taste of and which leaves your mouth feeling fresh.

5. Provide information about extra routines

Can disclosing tablets make a difference? Use disclosing tablets occasionally to check you are cleaning the plaque off your teeth. The tablets are chewed and then colour any plaque left on your teeth. The colour can be removed easily with a toothbrush.

6. Presenting the information

List your advice and provide tick boxes to fill in as each part of the routine is completed. Show the routine as a flow chart with steps to follow to complete it, or use pictures showing the routine step by step. Choose the method of presentation which appeals to you.

Toothpaste investigation

Use the following layout to record details of your selected brands of toothpaste.

Brands of toothpaste selected for investigation:

1   2

3   4

5   6

From the toothpastes you have selected which brand do you think:

has the most pleasant flavour/taste

leaves the freshest feeling in the mouth

has the most pleasant smell

has the most attractive colour

has the best texture (creamy/not gritty)

covers teeth well without too much foaming

leaves teeth feeling smooth and clean

is the best value (price and size of tube)

gives the most helpful advice about use

From the toothpastes you have selected, which manufacturers claim the product:

helps prevent tooth decay

helps prevent the build-up of plaque

helps prevent gum disease

helps keep breath fresh

reduces the pain of sensitive teeth

Is there one brand of toothpaste which is the best in most of the areas you have considered? If so, which brand is it and why do you think it is the best overall?

Brand

Reasons

Low sugar snack plan

Favourite sugary snacks

1.   2.

3.   4.

5.   6.

7.   8.

Comments on likes and dislikes from your chosen person to help with final selection of low sugar or sugar free selections:

Selected low sugar snacks   **Reason for selection**

1.

2.

3.

4.

5.

6.

7.

8.

Comments received about low sugar plan from chosen person:

Reactions to using the plan for a week:

Any changes to be made? If so, what?

Skin and nail care: fact file

Use the suggested layout below to help you collect and present information. One example has been completed to show you how the format can be used.

Part of body:

Problems if body part neglected:

A good care routine would be:

Daily

Weekly

Monthly

Useful products to try:

Product benefits:

Cost of products:

Part of body: Finger nails.

Problems if body part neglected: Dirty or bitten nails can become infected, a cuticle pushed back too far can be painful and sore, hangnails can be torn.

A good care routine would be:

Daily Wash hands and moisturise, working the cream or lotion into the nails. Trim nails as needed. Try not to bite nails.

Weekly Look carefully at nails for any problems and trim or buff as needed. Rub in a cuticle cream to keep the cuticle supple and healthy (can be done daily if preferred).

Monthly Give yourself a complete manicure. Wash, trim and moisturise nails and finish by buffing with a polisher or apply a nail polish. This can help to strengthen nails (can be completely colourless).

Useful products to try: Nail clippers, cuticle conditioner, nail protector with protein.

Product benefits: Nail clippers make trimming nails easy, cuticle conditioner keeps the cuticles supple so they are less likely to tear or split and nail protector strengthens nails.

Cost of products: Nail clippers £3.50, cuticle conditioner £2.50, nail protector £2.50.

Care in the sun

Investigate people's chosen methods of sun protection.

Clothes: do you wear loose, cool, close-woven fabrics in the sun to protect your skin?

People's choices:

Reasons:

Hats: do you wear a wide brim hat in the sun to protect your head, face and neck?

People's choices:

Reasons:

Sun glasses: do you wear a good quality pair of sun glasses?

People's choices:

Reasons:

Suncream: what kind of suncream do you use and why?

People's choices:

Reasons:

Investigate a good range of suncreams. Repeat the layout below for each suncream you look at. Recommend the best products.

Name of suncream:

Maker's name: Cost: £

Size: Is it a cream or a lotion?

What is the Sun Protection Factor (SPF)?

Does it have UVA and UVB screening?   Yes/No

Are you told what this means on the bottle or tube?   Yes/No

Are you given any advice on the care of skin in the sun on the
bottle or tube?   Yes/No

Is the suncream waterproof?   Yes/No

Are there any more claims made? (e.g. contains Vitamin E)   Yes/No

Is it suitable for all skin types?   Yes/No

Is there a full list of ingredients?   Yes/No

Do you think this product is good value?   Yes/No

Back to basics

Answers on pp. 311–12.

Missing words

Put back the missing words in the sentences below about caring for your teeth and body. Choose words from the box to help you or cover these words up if you would like to make the task a little more difficult.

enamel	barrier	clean	acne
epidermis	dental	fluoride	regular
sugar	healthy	germs	acid

a) A bad attack of spots is called _____.

b) The skin acts as a _____ to stop _____ getting in.

c) The top layer of your skin is called the _____.

d) _____ your teeth thoroughly as part of a _____ routine.

e) Use _____ toothpaste and _____ floss to keep your teeth and gums _____.

f) _____ left in your mouth after eating turns to _____ which can attack the hard _____ on your teeth.

Muddled words

Sort out these muddled-up words which are about teeth, skin and body care.

melnea   qualep   thastpoote   cadey

mesub   midres   niks reccan   slain

Reading for information

Read the following text about why your body sweats. Answer the questions which follow, looking in the text for the answers. Try to write your answers in complete sentences.

Sweat helps to cool your body. It stops your temperature from going up when you are working your body hard or sitting in the sun. There are about two million sweat glands spread over your skin. Sweat is mostly water with a little salt and body waste. People normally sweat between 500 and 700 cubic centilitres each day although you don't notice this amount of sweating. You sweat much more however when you are exercising or when you are frightened. At these times you may sweat a lot from the palms of your hands and the soles of your feet, where there a lot of sweat pores in the skin. Sweat, even underarm sweat, has a pleasant smell when it's fresh. However, if it remains for long on your skin, bacteria start to breed and an unpleasant smell can develop.

1. How many sweat glands do you have?

2. What is your sweat made up of?

3. If you are frightened, where on your body might you sweat the most and why?

4. Why does sweat start to smell unpleasant on your body?

Alternatives Other ideas for activities on personal care

Any activity from the group or individual projects can be replaced with an idea from the list below. Use the list to give you more choice of activities to do which suit your needs, interests and the amount of time you have available.

■ Make an audio or video tape of foot exercises which are good for your feet. For example circling ankles, stretching toes, raising your weight on to your toes and back down again or picking up a pencil with your bare toes. Exercises strengthen muscles and relax the foot.

■ Find out about and try a good aromatherapy oil to massage tired feet. Investigate and recommend the best buy in foot spas.

■ Find out and write a description or draw a diagram of how the foot develops from child to adult. Include examples of how a foot can become deformed by the wrong shoes or tight socks.

■ Find out about the training needed to become a chiropodist and what the job is like. Why do people choose a job which involves looking after feet? Speak to a local chiropodist about their work. Interview them, or write a letter asking questions.

■ Investigate reflexology. How does it work? Contact a reflexologist, speak to someone who has visited one, or write to an association for information. Write about your findings and draw a diagram of the regions of the foot.

■ What natural shampoos do people use? Find out about home made shampoos which really work. For example, adding lemon juice to your rinsing water is said to lighten blond hair. Beer and raw eggs are said to be good for hair. Find examples of natural shampoos in books on beauty or even herbal remedies. Ask members of your family or friends for some ideas. Write a guide to natural shampoos including instructions on how to make them.

■ Design a poster or chart which shows a good body care routine for children to follow. Choose an age range which interests you. If you choose the pre-school child for example, make sure your poster or chart shows the routine in pictures with very little text. A child in the age range of 5 to 8 would enjoy captions to read. Make your poster amusing and colourful.

■ Design a toothbrush which would encourage a young child to brush their teeth twice a day. Think about size, colour and shape. It could be in the shape of a favourite cartoon character for example. It could play a tune when it's picked up or change colour on contact with water.

■ Research and write a description of how people cared for their teeth in the past. Go back as far as medieval times if you wish. Dentistry was then carried out by a barber-surgeon. There was no such thing as anaesthetic! Decayed teeth were simply pulled out. Describe what it must have been like, perhaps putting yourself in the place of the person who is having the treatment.

Colour choices

INTRODUCTION

In this group project on *colour choices* you will be able to:

■ Discuss which colours you like to wear and how colours can influence mood.

■ Research the meanings of colours in clothes.

■ Interview people to find out about colour preferences.

■ Design a colour card to show colour meanings.

■ Research and find out about colour healing.

■ Design, test and discuss reactions to a colour board.

■ Discuss colour terms and make a colour wheel.

■ Design a questionnaire to find out about popular colours.

■ Write a descriptive passage about colour.

■ Follow a design process to design a household item in colour.

■ Research and present information about colour and festivals.

■ Survey the use of colour in danger and safety signs.

■ Write a report about the use of colour in warning and safety signs and equipment.

■ Design a poster using colour to warn of a local hazard.

■ Evaluate your work on the project.

Choose activities which interest you from the wide range of suggestions provided in the project. You can choose to do just part of an activity if you wish. The choice is yours. There are more suggestions in the Alternative Ideas section (p. 203), so you should find enough activities to suit your interests and needs. Finish with the Evaluation Exercise as this will help you think about your work on the project and remind you to record the skills you have covered.

For each activity you choose to do, use the information provided for you in the activity text and worksheets, as well as your own experiences and knowledge. If you need to look for more information consider resources such as books, newspapers and magazines as well as television, radio, video and CD-ROM. You can also use resources such as writing to an organisation or telephoning for information, talking to people you know and talking to other people who may be able to give you the information you need.

Optional task   If you have more time available and would like to try another task to develop the skills you have already used in an activity, you can look for the Optional Tasks which are linked to many of the project activities.

You will find the following worksheets useful:

Colour choices

Activity 1   **Find out about the meaning of colours you like to wear**

Look around at each other and notice what different colours you have all chosen to wear today. Is anyone wearing bright colours such as red, yellow, orange or lime green? Is anyone wearing dark colours such as grey, brown or black? How can the choice of a colour affect how you feel?

■ Wearing red might make you feel energetic and outgoing.

■ If you wear yellow it might encourage you to think positively about any problems you have.

■ Choosing to wear blue could bring a feeling of calm and peace. It might ease tension and help you feel more relaxed.

■ Wearing green could mean you need to feel secure and prefer not to stand out in a crowd.

■ Magenta is a very positive choice as it is said to encourage feelings of kindness in the person wearing it. It is also supposed to encourage other people to feel affection towards you!

Discuss what colour preferences you all have in the clothes you like to wear. Consider the following questions in your discussion:

■ What colours are in your wardrobe? Is it full of pale or dark or bright colours or a mixture of all of these?

■ Did you choose the colours you are wearing today by chance do you think? Were they the only items of clothing clean and ironed, or did you choose a colourful jumper or shirt because it suited your mood today?

■ Do you feel choosing a particular colour to wear can change your mood?

■ Are there some colours you never wear because you feel uncomfortable in them?

■ Are there any colours which you like to see on other people but wouldn't choose for yourself?

Present the results of your discussion by writing out a record of the colours you all like to wear and how they make you feel. List the colours and the feelings and moods you link to each one. Write down which situations or occasions you would choose to wear each colour and explain why. For example, one person may enjoy wearing black to a party or club as it makes them feel sophisticated and gives them the confidence to talk to new people. Use the worksheet provided to help you record your discussion and decisions about the colours you like to wear.

Carry out some research to find out more information on how the colours people wear can affect their emotions. Look for information in magazines and Sunday supplements. Look in your local library for books about colour. Look in the psychology section for books about the effects of wearing colour on people's moods. Look in the fashion section for a book called *Colour Me Beautiful* which offers advice about ranges of colours to suit each personality type. Watch fashion programmes on television where the effects of colours are commented on. Find out about red, blue, green, yellow, violet, orange, black and white. Allocate tasks to each other to get the research work done, taking a colour each or working in pairs on a colour. Make notes as you go along and get together as a group to share your research results.

Use your research information to prepare a few key questions. Find out which colours people choose to wear and the effects of their colour choices on mood and emotion. Use your prepared questions to interview friends, family members or people you work with. Agree how many people you will each try to interview and record the answers you get by making notes or taping the interviews. Find out:

■ what colours people like to wear and why

■ what colours people never wear and why

■ what moods or emotions people link to given colours

■ what situations they would choose to wear a particular colour for and why.

Share the results of your interviews and talk about the replies you all received. Can you make any general statements about how people feel colours affect them? Did you find that people have very similar feelings about their choice of colours? Did people give reasons which were similar or very different to the ones you recorded on your group record sheet? Can you identify the most popular colour people enjoy wearing and the least popular colour?

Optional task   Design a colour card which describes reactions to colours and gives reasons for wearing certain colours. Show a good range of colours. Next to each colour describe how you may feel when you wear it. List positive feelings as well as negative ones. Suggest situations which might be improved by each colour. For example, wearing turquoise is supposed to encourage people to show an interest in you so this might be a good colour for a party or even an interview!

Choose a practical size for the colour card. Use paint or cut up paint cards or magazines for the colour samples. Pin your copy of the card on your wardrobe door to help you make important colour choices for special events.

Show your card to other people and ask for comments on the group's choices and explanations. Would other people find it useful?

(*See also* Worksheets: group record of reactions to colour)

From this activity you may have evidence for:

Skills list	1, 2, 3, 4, 6, 8/9, 11, 12, 14, 15, 16.
Core skills	Communication level 1 and 2.
Element	1.1/2.1 Take part in discussions.
Opportunities	Discuss the effects of different colours in clothing choices.
	Interview a variety of people about their colour choices in clothing.
	Discuss and evaluate the results of the interviews.
	Ask for comments on the colour card (optional).
Element	1.2/2.2 Produce written material.
Opportunities	Record reactions to wearing different colours.
	Make notes about research on colours people wear.
	Design a colour card which describes reactions to colours and reasons for wearing them (optional).
Element	1.3/2.3 Use images.
Opportunities	Show samples of colours listed on a colour card (optional).
Element	1.4/2.4 Read and respond to written materials.
Opportunities	Read books and magazines for information about colours people wear to use in interview questions.

Activity 2   **Carry out research into colour healing**

Some people believe looking at colours and thinking about them can help with healing health problems you may have. For example:

■ **Blue** can make you feel at peace and relaxed. Blue is used in cardiac units to give a cool, airy feeling to the rooms. Handling a blue gemstone is supposed to soothe itchy eyes.

■ **Green** can bring a feeling of being in balance. It may also improve your appetite. Handling an emerald is supposed to soothe nerves and tension.

■ **Yellow** can improve your feelings of security, although too much yellow around you can be stressful. Many people feel looking at yellow gives them a boost and cheers them up.

■ **Red** can give you a feeling of alertness. Handling a pale pink rose quartz is supposed to calm anxiety and fears.

According to those who believe in colour healing, particular health problems may benefit from certain colours:

■ **acne** is said to be helped by turquoise

■ **cold sores** are said to be helped by blue

■ **colds** are said to be helped by red or orange

■ **cystitis** is said to be helped by magenta

■ **pre-menstrual tension** is said to be helped by blue

■ **emotional tiredness** is said to be helped by green

■ **depression** is said to be helped by orange

Discuss what you think about the healing changes colours are said to bring about. Do you think these changes can really happen by looking at or touching the colours? Does anyone have any personal experiences of colour healing they can share? Design a chart which describes the importance of each colour and how it is supposed to help with healing.

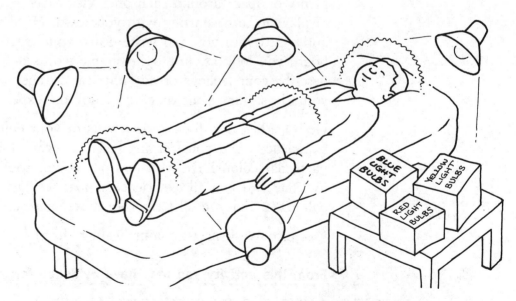

Research and find out more about colour healing. Visit your local library and look for books on colour therapy and colour healing. Look at the resource lists at the back of books for an address of a Colour Therapist Association and write for information. Look for information about the supposed effects of coloured gemstones. Ask for leaflets about colour healing in a health shop. Look in the Yellow Pages to see if there are any alternative therapy clinics in your area. Contact them for information on colour healing.

Allocate your research activities between yourselves to get the work done. Find out about one colour each or work in pairs.

Present your information as a chart. List the healing abilities claimed for each colour. Describe the positive feelings it can bring about. Describe the kind of problems each colour might help you with and how to use the colour. Use the worksheet provided to help you with your chart.

Discuss your finished chart. Would you try any of the colour healing ideas you have found out about? Do you think they sound practical and sensible? For example, blue is widely accepted as a calm, cooling colour. Make sure you all have a chance to say what you think about colour healing and listen to each other's views.

Optional task

Each choose a colour which appeals to you and which is said to have healing properties that meet your needs. For example, if you get quite a lot of headaches, blue may be a good colour to choose. Work in pairs if you prefer.

Make a colour board of your chosen colour. Select a good sized piece of strong card, or cut up a cardboard box. Cover your card with your chosen colour. Cut out shades of your colour from old magazines or use paints, pens or fabric pieces. Collect some objects of your colour which you can hold, such as stones, jewellery, china or articles of clothing.

Arrange each of your colour boards and objects in the room with plenty of space around each one. Visit several of the colour board displays in turn, starting with your own. Have a piece of paper and a pen with you and write down your reactions to each colour board you look at. Just write simple words or phrases which describe your feelings or any physical changes you notice in yourselves. Take your time and enjoy the experience!

Get together and discuss the results of your colour board experiences. Did you feel any reactions when looking at a particular colour? Did you find one colour soothing or exciting to look at? Did you all experience similar feelings towards some colours or did you all have very different reactions?

(*See also* Worksheets: colour healing chart)

From this activity you may have evidence for:

Skills list	1, 2, 3, 5, 6, 8, 10, 11, 13/14, 15, 16.
Core skills	Communication level 1 and 2.
Element	1.1/2.1 Take part in discussions.
Opportunities	Discuss views on colour healing.
	Ask people for information about colour healing.
	Discuss the results of your research.
	Discuss the results of colour board experiences (optional).

Element	1.2/2.2 Produce written material.
Opportunities	Write to a colour therapy organisation for information.
	Record information about colour healing on a chart.
Element	1.3/2.3 Use images.
Opportunities	Design a chart to record information about colour healing.
	Design a colour board (optional).
Element	1.4/2.4 Read and respond to written materials.
Opportunities	Read books, magazines, leaflets for information about colour healing to use in a chart.

Activity 3 — Discover colour preferences

Talk about the meaning of the different colour terms listed below. Check you all understand the terms and use a dictionary if you need more help. Add any more colour terms which you know about to the list:

- **Primary colours** are the three pure colours of blue, yellow and red.

- **Secondary colours** are two primary colours mixed together to make green, orange or purple.

- **Complementary colours** are colours which are opposite on a colour wheel. They have the effect of making each other seem more bright and vivid.

- **Harmonious colours** are colours which are next to each other on a colour wheel. They go well together without clashing.

- **Warm colours** are usually accepted to be yellows, oranges and reds. You tend to notice these colours easily.

- **Cool colours** are usually accepted to be greens and blues. In a picture these colours seem to be rather distant.

- **High key colours** could also be called bright.

- **Low key colours** could also be called dull.

- **Tone** is a very important term as it describes the lightness or darkness of a colour. Someone may have a preference for a dark toned orange but dislike a bright orange colour.

Make a colour wheel each using the labelled outline which is provided for you on the worksheet. Try to use as pure a colour as possible for your three primary colours. If you don't have access to much equipment you can make a very attractive colour wheel with felt pens, poster paint or by cutting up paint sample cards. Make a wheel each or work in pairs. Share resources as a group and help each other with ideas for how to mix each colour.

Use your colour wheels to identify the primary and secondary colours. Remind yourselves which colours are warm, cool, complementary or harmonious.

Discuss your personal colour preferences using your colour wheels. Each select your favourite colour and the one you most dislike. Explain your selections to each other. You may not like the exact colour used on your wheels but you may like a darker or lighter tone such as pale green or dark, golden yellow.

Discuss why you all have colour preferences. Why do you like one colour but not another? Talk about possible reasons for why people have colour preferences. Do you think you are influenced by memories of colours from events in your life? Do you think you could be influenced by the links people make with colours such as green with envy, purple with rage, white with shock or yellow with cowardice?

If you like a colour does this mean you wear it, or have a lot of things around you at home in this colour? Does it mean you like seeing it in shops, buildings or in the countryside? If you dislike a colour, does this mean you never wear it and don't like seeing it on other people or in things around you?

Present the results of your discussion as a list of the group's colour preferences. Write them on a board or large sheet of paper. Write down the colours you each like and dislike. Write down a reason for each of your colour choices and explain why you dislike a colour.

Compare the results you have written down as a group. Are there any colours which several people like? Does anyone have an unusual colour preference? Are all the colours which you dislike as a group different or do many people agree with each other? Does anyone have any unusual reasons for liking or disliking a colour?

Use the questions you have asked yourselves in discussing your colour preferences to design a simple questionnaire. Ask friends or people you work with to find out about other people's colour preferences. Use the worksheet to help you. Replace questions which you don't want to ask with ideas of your own. Agree to give the questionnaire to two or three people each or work in pairs. Meet up again to look at the results together.

Discuss the results of your short questionnaire. Write out a simple table showing which colours were liked and disliked. Count up the number of times people have chosen a particular colour as a favourite or as a least favourite colour. Are the results similar to your own earlier choices?

It is common for blue to be picked as a favourite. Did blue score the most responses or did another colour come out on top? Discuss any interesting reasons people may have given for liking or disliking a colour. Did most people make very similar colour associations? Write a short summary about your findings, describing which were the most and least popular colours and why.

Optional task Write a short poem (it doesn't have to rhyme) about a colour you either like or dislike. Don't name the colour. For example:

> This is my mood when I'm feeling low,
>
> The sky shows this on a sunny day,
>
> A favourite pair of jeans, though faded now,
>
> My ring once sparkled this soft glow.

Read your poems aloud to each other and see if you can guess the colours correctly!

(*See also* Worksheets: colour wheel outline. Questionnaire on colour preferences.)

From this activity you may have evidence for:

Skills list	1, 2, 3, 5, 8, 10, 11, 12, 13, 14, 15, 16.
Core skills	Communication level 1 and 2.
Element	1.1/2.1 Take part in discussions.
Opportunities	Discuss the meaning of colour terms and identify their use on a colour wheel.
	Discuss colour preferences.
	Discuss the results of the questionnaire.
	Respond to poems about colour (optional).
Element	1.2/2.2 Produce written material.
Opportunities	List colour preferences with reasons for choices.
	Design and distribute a questionnaire.
	Write a summary of the questionnaire results.
	Write a poem about a colour (optional).
Element	1.3/2.3 Use images.
Opportunities	Make a colour wheel.
Element	1.4/2.4 Read and respond to written materials.
Opportunities	Use dictionaries for meanings of colour terms.
	Read and evaluate completed questionnaires.

Activity 4 **Design new colours for a household item**

Design a new colour range for a household item, making colour the most important feature of the design. Work as a group to begin with, thinking of ideas together and finding out about the design process.

Choose one of the following ideas or think of other household items to re-design.

■ A breakfast set which wakes you up in the morning. Design the colour for a large cup, plate and cereal bowl with colours which will make you feel wide awake when you use them.

■ A beach towel. Pick a holiday destination and design colours to match the place you have in mind. It could be the colours of a sunset or the traditional colours of a culture.

■ A child's duvet cover. Show their favourite activities or people or toys. Use colours which will send them to sleep!

■ A tee shirt which cures a hangover. Design colours to soothe a thumping headache, upset stomach or swollen eyes.

■ A CD cover of a favourite singer or group. Use colours which represent all you like about the music and how it makes you feel when you listen to it.

■ A sheet of wrapping paper for a special event in your life or someone close to you. It may be an anniversary or an important birthday.

 Collect a good range of catalogues which show household items for some design ideas. Bring in catalogues from home or borrow from friends. Pick up catalogues from stores like Argos and Index or Ikea. Put all of your resources together and look carefully at the colours used in a range of household items. When you have chosen your household item, work in pairs or small groups to complete the design. All choose the same item or choose several different household items to work on.

 Discuss how to follow a simple design process. Read through the following instructions and talk about each one. Use the worksheet provided to help you remember the design process.

1. Add to your catalogue research by visiting shops and looking at the variety of colours used in household items. Look at items you have at home.

2. Write a design statement describing what you want to achieve with your new colour design. This will keep you on track. For example you might write 'We are going to design new colours for a pillowcase which will help ease the pain of migraine-type headaches'.

3. Think about the different combinations of colours you might use in your design and why. Sketch out any ideas as they come to you. Don't worry about how rough the drawings are at this stage.

4. Look carefully at your ideas and decide which ones are worth working on a little more.

5. Select your best design and improve it as much as possible. Work on it until you feel the choice of colours, the combination of colours and the amount of colour used is just right.

6. Draw out a good copy of your final design. Use a template or a grid to get a smooth shape or trace an outline. Use pens, paint, inks, crayons or magazine scraps to show the colours. Label your design to show the names of the colours used.

Get back together as a group to show each other your final designs and to give each other feedback. Question each other about the ideas which went into creating the colour choices. Comment on all of the designs. Keep your comments positive and helpful.

Write a short evaluation of another person's design. Describe what you like about the way colours have been used and what effect the colours may have on someone using the item.

(*See also* Worksheets: design wheel.)

	From this activity you may have evidence for:
Skills list	1, 2, 3, 5, 6, 9, 13, 14, 15, 16.
Core skills	Communication level 1 and 2.
Element	1.1/2.1 Take part in discussions.
Opportunities	Discuss choices of household items to redesign.
	Discuss how to follow a design process.
	Give feedback on colour designs.
Element	1.2/2.2 Produce written material.
Opportunities	Write a design statement.
	Write an evaluation of a colour design.
Element	1.3/2.3 Use images.
Opportunities	Draw the design of a new colour range for a household item.
Element	1.4/2.4 Read and respond to written materials.
Opportunities	Scan a variety of catalogues for design ideas for a household item.

Activity 5 Colour in festivals, ceremonies and celebrations

Colour plays an important part in many festivals, ceremonies and celebrations in different cultures all around the world. For example, part of the joyous Hindu festival of Holi is celebrated by throwing coloured powder and coloured water. Colour can symbolise many different meanings for people. For example:

■ **White** is a popular and important colour in weddings and christenings in western culture. It is a symbol of purity. White is used to paint the outside of houses in parts of Africa to ward off evil spirits. In Asia, white is a colour of mourning.

■ **Blue** is linked with the idea of heaven. It is the colour of the Virgin Mary in the Christian faith. It is a colour which symbolises faith and peace and loyalty.

■ **Green** represents harmony. It is a traditional colour in Ireland and a holy colour of Islam. In many cultures green represents the cycle of life and death. In the Christian faith green robes symbolise the hope of everlasting life.

■ **Yellow** is the Hindu marriage colour and symbolises life and truth. Saffron yellow is a holy colour in Buddhism. Yellow represents the sun in many cultures.

■ **Red** is the Chinese colour of luck and happiness. It is the marriage colour of India. In western culture it is linked with love and romance. For American Indians however, red, which is the colour of the desert, means disaster. In Celtic symbolism red can suggest death and many cultures use red to warn of fire and danger.

 Have a brainstorming session and write down all the festivals, ceremonies and celebrations you can think of which have colours associated with them. The colours may be used in decorations, face paints, flowers, costumes or foods for example. Talk about marriages, funerals, harvest, Christmas, Easter, May Day, Halloween, Japanese Star Festival, Chinese Dragon Boat Festival, Chinese New Year, Mardi Gras and Hannukkah for example. If you need more information write to The Festival Shop for a catalogue to give you some ideas, at 56, Poplar Road, Kings Heath, Birmingham.

Decide from the results of your brainstorming session which festivals or celebrations you are interested in finding out about. Find out the meaning and importance of the colours used in the festival or celebration and how they are used. Work in pairs or small groups so several festivals are researched, or decide on one colour as a group and find out how it is used in a large range of festivals and celebrations.

 Discuss how you will carry out your research activities. Talk about where to look for resources and use the worksheet provided for help. Add more ideas of your own. Make notes about your research as you go along. Choose from these methods:

■ Using the library for books, magazines and videos.

■ Writing to organisations, churches, museums or a country's embassy in London. Ask for leaflets, posters and information.

■ Interviewing people about their culture, religion or a festival they take part in. Look at the things they use. Photograph costumes if possible.

■ Visiting a number of different festivals and celebrations. Take photographs and notes or video what you see. Collect souvenirs.

When you have gathered enough material, talk about how you are going to present the information on colour in festivals and celebrations. Choose one of the following methods:

■ A series of shared spoken presentations given to each other or a small invited audience, explaining the use of colour. Use visual aids such as video, photographs, slides, foods, costumes, fabrics, flowers, etc.

■ Pool all the information you have found to create a large chart or colour wheel showing the festivals and meanings linked to each colour. Each be responsible for one part of it.

■ Make a video describing the use of colour in festivals, ceremonies and celebrations. Demonstrate the ways colours are used or video festivals you have witnessed. Write a script for the commentary. Allocate tasks to each other to produce the video.

Enjoy your presentations and ask each other questions. Give feedback on what you have heard or looked at.

Discuss what you have all found out about the use of colour in festivals, ceremonies and celebrations. Are you surprised at the importance or meaning of some colours?

(*See also* Worksheets: colour in festivals, ceremonies and celebrations.)

From this activity you may have evidence for:

Skills list	1, 2, 3, 4, 5, 6, 7, 8/9, 10, 11, 13/14, 15.
Core skills	Communication level 1 and 2.
Element	1.1/2.1 Take part in discussions.
Opportunities	Talk about and agree on the choice of colours to research.
	Discuss where to find resources and how to present information.
	Interview a variety of people about the use of colour in festivals, etc.
	Give a spoken presentation.
	Discuss the results of your research activities and presentations.
Element	1.2/2.2 Produce written material.
Opportunities	Make notes about your research activities.
	Write to organisations asking for information.
	Design a chart or wheel showing use of colour in festivals.
Element	1.3/2.3 Use images.
Opportunities	Use visual aids in a spoken presentation.
	Make a video on colour in festivals.
Element	1.4/2.4 Read and respond to written materials.

Opportunities   Look at books, travel guides, photographs and leaflets for information about colour for use in a presentation.

Activity 6   Collect information about warning and safety colours

Look around any large building such as a supermarket, office or college for example and you will notice signs warning you about dangers. You will also see signs or notices telling you where to find safety equipment. These signs and pieces of equipment all use colour to make you notice them or to remind you about safeguards. Fire exit signs in green direct you to the quickest route out of the building. Fire extinguishers in a variety of colours remind you they are there for different types of fires. For example:

- **black** extinguishers contain carbon dioxide for fires involving flammable liquids or electrical equipment

- **blue** extinguishers contain dry powder for fires involving flammable liquids or electrical equipment

- **red** extinguishers contain water and are suitable for most fires except those involving flammable liquids or live electrical equipment

- **cream** extinguishers contain foam for fires involving flammable liquids

- **green** extinguishers contain halon for fires involving flammable liquids or electrical equipment

A green sign tells you where First Aid equipment can be found in the building. A blue fire notice on a wall gives you information about what to do if you discover a fire. A yellow and black sign warns you about a hazard. The floor may be wet or repairs may be being carried out. Blue and white signs remind you to put on protective equipment before entering an area of the building.

Using different colours to warn of danger or remind you about safety is very helpful. You can get used to colour codes and understand the signs very quickly. Certain colours can also produce a physical reaction in your body. For example:

- red can produce an increase in your pulse rate and brain waves, so it's a useful colour to warn of danger

- green can encourage a purposeful mood which is useful if you are carrying out First Aid or getting out of a building quickly but calmly

- blue can slow your pulse and calm you, which is useful if you need to think carefully about putting on safety equipment

- yellow and black are a very intense combination of colours and so you are likely to notice them easily and be warned about a hazard

Carry out a survey and collect information on how colours have been used in warning and safety signs, in your building or another building you choose.

Walk around your chosen building slowly and record the colours you all see. Record how they have been used to warn you of danger or provide safety. Look for signs, notices, posters, stickers and equipment. Use the worksheet provided to help you with your survey. Amend it to suit your needs. Either carry out the survey together and video or take photographs as you go around, or work in pairs covering different parts of the building between you. One person may notice something another person misses.

Talk about and share your collected survey information. Discuss how colour has been used in the building. Make a few notes about your discussion as you go along to be used in a written report later. Use your survey information to answer these questions:

- ■ which colours did you find being used to warn of dangers or hazards?
- ■ do you think these colours are effective and if so, why?
- ■ which colours are most commonly used to show where safety equipment is stored or to remind you about safeguards?
- ■ do you think these colours are easily noticed?
- ■ do you think the colours used for danger and safety signs are the best choices?
- ■ why is fluorescent colour not used more, do you think?
- ■ what other colour combinations would be really noticeable?

Each write a report about your survey and discussion. Divide your report into colour sections, with the colour as a subheading. Report how you have seen the colour used and comment on the conclusions you all reached about the effectiveness of the colour. Finish your report by suggesting new colours which you feel would make effective warning signs or safety notices and explain why.

Optional task   Design a poster to warn about a hazard in your local area. Make colour the most important feature of your poster. You may be concerned about a busy road junction or a bad crossing outside a school. You may want to warn others about a piece of equipment at work which causes problems. You may want to warn others that car radios are constantly being stolen from cars parked in a local car park. Discuss and write down some ideas. Either take one idea each which interests you or pick the same idea and produce several different posters.

Look at the finished posters and give each other feedback on how successfully colour has been used. Display your posters near the danger areas and see if they have any effect on the hazard.

(*See also* **Worksheets:** survey of use of colour in warning and safety.)

From this activity you may have evidence for:

Skills list 1, 2, 3, 5, 6, 9, 11, 12, 13/14, 15, 16.

Core skills Communication level 1 and 2.

Element 1.1/2.1 Take part in discussions.

Opportunities Discuss how to carry out the survey.

Discuss survey information and answer questions.

Give feedback to each other about colour in posters (optional).

Element 1.2/2.2 Produce written material.

Opportunities Prepare a survey sheet to record use of colour around a building.

Carry out a survey and record the results.

Write a report about the use of colour for warning and safety.

Element 1.3/2.3 Use images.

Opportunities Design a poster about a hazard, using colour.

 ## Evaluation exercise

Discuss the work you have done together on this project. Will you think differently now about colours you choose to wear? Will you try colour healing? Will you feel more enjoyment of colours in a festival because you understand their meanings? Will you notice signs giving you information or warning you about a danger more easily?

Do you feel more confident about research activities? Do you feel more able to ask questions to obtain information from a variety of people? Do you feel confident about presenting information in a variety of different ways? Do you feel confident about explaining your point of view in a discussion?

Check your Skills Record Sheet is up to date. Record details of skills you have practised and how you went about it. Make sure you write down details of resources you have used. You may need to refer to this to find evidence of using a variety of different sources. Complete your Skills Summary Record. Write down all your progress and achievements. Note down evidence of competence you have collected for an accreditation you may be studying towards. Write down details of skills you wish to practise further and record realistic goal dates to aim for.

Group record of reactions to colour

Write your selected colours down the left hand side of the record sheet. Explain how each colour makes you feel and what emotions and moods you associate with it. Write down any situations or events where you would wear this colour and why.

Colour	Names of people who like this colour	How does this colour make you feel?	When would you wear this colour and why?

Colour healing chart

Fill in examples of colours and explain how they are supposed to heal. Some colours have been filled in as a guide to completing the chart. Add more information and amend the chart to suit yourselves. Include a sample of colour for each one you list.

Colour	Key word	Feelings	Healing claims	Healing gemstone
Blue	Relaxation	Peaceful Relaxed Calm	Anxiety Backache Insomnia	Sapphire Topaz
Magenta	Letting go	Let go of emotions Accept changes	Cystitis Fainting Morning sickness	Rock crystal Lapis lazuli
Green	Balance	Be at ease Feel home and work are in balance	Heart disease Gastric ulcer Heartburn	Emerald

Multi-use ■ *Use this worksheet for colour choices.*

Colour wheel outline

Complete this colour wheel by filling in the colours which have been labelled for you. Use coloured crayons, pastels, paints, inks, or pieces of fabric or cut up old magazines. Choose the best examples of each colour you can find.

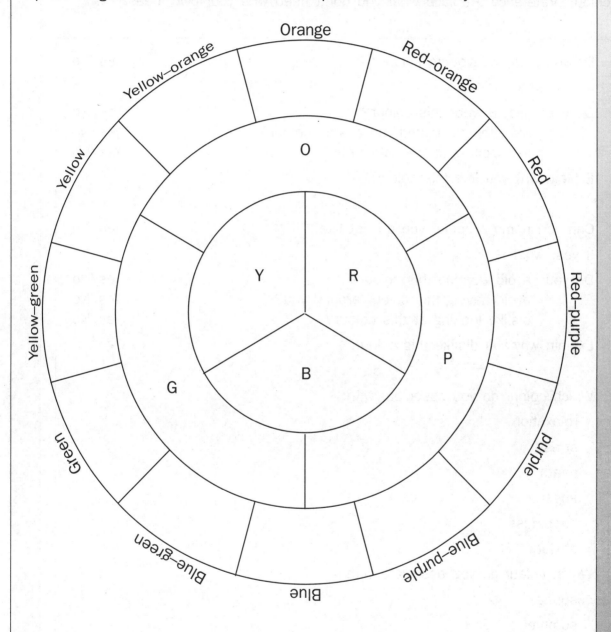

Questionnaire on colour preference

Use the ideas in this worksheet to help you design your questionnaire about colour preference. Replace what you don't need with your own ideas.

Do you have a favourite colour?	Yes/No
If yes, what is it?	
Do you: like to wear this colour?	Yes/No
have things around you of this colour?	Yes/No
like looking at the colour?	Yes/No
Explain why you like this colour:	

Can you name a colour you do not like?   Yes/No

If yes, what is it?

Do you: avoid wearing this colour?   Yes/No

        avoid having this colour around you?   Yes/No

        dislike looking at this colour?   Yes/No

Explain why you dislike this colour:

Which colour do you associate with:

relaxation

stress

death

anger

happiness

anxiety

Which colour do you associate with:

spring

summer

autumn

winter

Is colour important to you in your everyday life?   Yes/No

Give reasons

Multi-use ■ *Use this worksheet to follow a good design process.*

Design wheel

Cut out the circles and back them with card. Cut out the window in circle A. Place circle A on top of B. Hold in place with a split pin through the centre. Place the window by each number in turn and read information about the design process.

Colours in festivals, ceremonies and celebrations

Tick each suggestion for where to look for information, what to look for and what evidence to collect as you complete it.

Where to look for information

Library

- books (look for colour, costumes or traditions and folklore, religions, festival foods, or local history)
- video
- reference library
- back copies of local paper
- magazines, e.g. National Geographic   ☐ ☐ ☐ ☐ ☐

Museums

- visit a local museum and ask about local festivals or ceremonies.   ☐
  Ask for information on people to contact

☐

Embassies

- get address from library, write for information, leaflets or posters

People and places

- talk to friends, ask for souvenirs of local events or holidays, e.g. photos, costumes
- interview people who organise a local festival
- talk to a local florist about traditional colours   ☐ ☐ ☐ ☐ ☐
- ask about local events at the Tourist Information Centre
- visit a festival, ceremony or a celebration. Take photographs or video the colours

What to find out about the colours linked to an event

- symbolic meanings of the colours ☐

- how colours are used or shown, e.g. costumes, foods, banners, flowers, make-up or paints, powders ☐

- are the colours traditional? Are they always the same? Do the colours change every year? ☐

- are there any colours which are never used as they would be unlucky, for example? ☐

Collecting evidence of research

- make notes about facts, anecdotes, people's memories ☐
- collect brochures with photographs from travel agents ☐
- collect leaflets, posters, foods, postcards, flags ☐
- take photographs or video an event ☐
- tape people talking about colour in a festival ☐

Colour in warning and safety

Walk around your chosen building and look for signs, notices and equipment used to warn of danger or remind you about safety. Record how colour is used in everything you see.

Information: how is colour used in these signs?

	Colour used	Combination
Fire Exit signs		
Entry signs		
Lifts		
Stairs		
Ramps		

Warning: how is colour used in these signs?

	Colour used	Combination
Restricted access		
Toxic hazard		
No entry		
Caution		
No smoking		

Safeguards: how is colour used in these signs?

	Colour used	Combination
Eye protection		
Hearing protection		
Hand protection		
Head protection		

How is colour used in these pieces of equipment?

	Colour used	Combination
Protected fire alarm		
Fire extinguishers		
Fire hose reel		
First Aid equipment		

Back to basics

Answers on p. 312.

Mixed sentences

Rewrite these mixed-up sentences. Look for a capital letter or a full stop as this will help you find the start and finish of each sentence.

1. colour. cool is a Blue

2. danger red. is A colour to linked

3. red, yellow and blue. colours are The primary

4. opposite the colour wheel. on each other are colours Complementary

5. often linked Feelings are to colours, for example, envy. with green

Careful reading

Read this short text about the colour blue and answer the questions which follow. Try to write your answers in complete sentences.

In colour tests, blue is often chosen by people as their favourite colour. Although there are many shades of blue in nature it is always seen as a cool, peaceful colour. Blue is also a colour used to symbolise authority. The flag of the European Community has blue as its background colour. Blue has the effect of calming people and may even reduce their pulse rate. However, blue is not an easy colour for the eye to focus on. It is thought that very young babies cannot see blue at all. Blue is used in safety codes to remind people to wear protective equipment.

1. Which flag has a blue background?

2. What effects can be produced if you are exposed to the colour blue?

3. What are people reminded to do by the use of blue in safety codes?

4. In your opinion, why is blue often chosen as a favourite colour?

Missing punctuation

Put back the missing punctuation in this short text about the colour yellow. You need to replace capital letters, full stops and commas.

yellow brightens a room often used in kitchens it produces a feeling of welcome and friendliness yellow is just as useful in a small room which looks out over a dull city view it helps make a room seem light sunny and cheerful the painter monet's house in france has a famous yellow dining room

Seeing colour

INTRODUCTION

In this individual project on *seeing colour* you will be able to:

- Find out about the use of colour in interior decorating.
- Design a new colour scheme for a chosen room.
- Survey the colours people use on the outside of their houses.
- Research and draw out a plan for a colourful garden.
- Find out about descriptive colour words.
- Write an introduction to a holiday guide.
- Survey colours used in business signs.
- Design your own colour logo.
- Analyse how colour is used in product packaging.
- Write a letter to a manufacturer about use of colour.
- Redesign the use of colour in a chosen product.
- Design a questionnaire to find out about food colour choices.
- Find out about artificial colours in foods.

Choose activities which interest you from the wide range of suggestions provided in the project. You can choose to do just part of an activity if you wish. The choice is yours. There are more suggestions in the Alternative Ideas section (p. 203), so you should find enough activities to suit your interests and needs. Finish with the Evaluation Exercise as this will help you think about your work on the project and remind you to record the skills you have covered.

For each activity you choose to do, use the information provided for you in the activity text and worksheets, as well as your own experiences and knowledge. If you need to look for more information consider resources such as books, newspapers and magazines as well as television, radio, video and CD-ROM. You can also use resources such as writing to an organisation or telephoning for information, talking to people you know and talking to other people who may be able give you the information you need.

Optional task   If you have more time available and would like to try another task to develop the skills you have already used in an activity, you can look for the Optional Tasks which are linked to many of the project activities.

You will find the following worksheets useful:

Seeing colour

Activity 1   Using colour inside your home

What colours have you used to decorate the inside of your home or your own room? Do you like dark or bright colours? Do you prefer magnolia, cream or white? There are hundreds of different colours to choose from today. Sometimes it is difficult to decide which colours suit your needs.

The colours you use to decorate the inside of your own room or home are likely to affect your mood. The colours of floors, walls and ceilings will also have an effect on how big, cool or cosy a room feels. The effect you want to create in a room helps you decide on your choice of colour. Small rooms painted in pale, light colours tend to feel larger. Large rooms with high ceilings tend to feel more cosy if they are painted with rich colours.

Think about the effects which different colours may have on a room. For example:

- **Red** makes a room seem smaller. Red can also make you feel alert and awake. If it's toned down to pink the effects are milder. Red might be a good choice for a room where you want to chat to friends or watch television.

- **Blue** calms and relaxes you. Deep blue might help you to sleep. If it's toned down to a pale blue the effect will be pleasantly relaxing. It's a useful colour for a bedroom.

- **Yellow** is a warm and positive colour. A sunny yellow can cheer a room. Yellow can bring a feeling of summer for people affected by winter blues. It's useful in a kitchen where feelings of alertness are important! However, some people find too much yellow in a room rather stressful.

- **White** is a colour which can be used to tone down or calm the effect of a more vivid colour in a room. A lot of white by itself can seem rather cold and plain.

- **Turquoise** is a cool, refreshing colour which is said to be very good for your nerves. It is also said to improve your appetite, so a blue–green might be a good colour for an eating area in your home.

Design a completely new colour scheme for a room in your home where you spend quite a lot of your time. Think about the effect you would like to create in your chosen room. You may want a warm, cosy feel to the room, a quiet, calm feel or a lively room to eat in.

Find ideas for your colour plan by visiting a large DIY store. Collect paint cards, look at wallpaper samples and make notes about any colours you like. Look at tiles, carpets, furnishing fabrics and lampshades. Ask for brochures or leaflets to take away. If you can't find all you need in one store, look in catalogues for ideas or visit several smaller shops. Look in magazines and Sunday supplements for ideas of colour schemes. Look in your local library for books on interior decorating for ideas about putting colours together. Ask friends, family members and people you work with for ideas about colour selections. What colours have they used to decorate their homes? Make notes about colour ideas as you go along.

Draw out a simple plan of your chosen room. Select and label colour choices for the flooring, walls, ceiling and main pieces of furniture. Make colour selections for a few accessories in your room such as cushions, curtains, rugs or pictures. Cut up paint sample cards and arrange colours next to each other to see what you like and don't like before making your final selections. Use the worksheet provided for ideas on how to draw out your plan, note down choices or use the given room plan.

Write detailed labelling for each colour featured in your design. Name the colour and say how it is used, for example, Cornflower blue paint, Whisper grey wallpaper, Country Clover tiling or Wild Sage fabric. Give a brief reason for each colour choice and include a sample. Stick the samples onto your plan. Use paint cards, pieces of fabric or wallpaper pieces.

When the colour plan for your chosen room is complete, check the labelling is clear. Have you given reasons for your choices? Have you put in the names of the colours and how they are used in the room? Have you created the effect you wanted for the room?

Show your room plan to a friend or someone you work with and ask them for their comments. Would they enjoy living in a room with your chosen colours? Do they feel you have achieved the effect you wanted?

(*See also* Worksheets: colour room plan)

From this activity you may have evidence for:

Skills list   1, 3, 4, 6, 7, 8/9, 10, 11, 13, 14, 15, 16.

Core skills   Communication level 1 and 2.

Element	1.1/2.1 Take part in discussions.
Opportunities	Ask friends about colour schemes they have used at home.
	Ask an assistant for help in a DIY store.
	Ask friends for feedback on the colour plan.
Element	1.2/2.2 Produce written material.
Opportunities	Make notes about your colour choice research.
	Write detailed labelling and reasons for choices on the colour plan.
Element	1.3/2.3 Use images.
Opportunities	Draw a colour plan of a room.
Element	1.4/2.4 Read and respond to written materials.
Opportunities	Read information about colours in a DIY store to use in the colour plan.
	Read books and magazines for information about using colour in interior decorating.

Activity 2   Street colours

How colourful is the area where you live? Are you surrounded by red brick houses with painted front doors? Do you live in an area where most of the houses or flats are built of grey stone or concrete slabs? Do you live in a rural area where people paint their whole houses pink, yellow or white? Find a street which interests you in your local area and survey the colours people like to put on the outside of their homes.

Write out a survey sheet for yourself so you can easily record what you see when you are walking down your chosen street. Record the colours of walls, doors, window frames, gates and garages. Record what type of houses you look at, for example note down if it is a terraced house, a flat, a bungalow or a mobile home. Record on your survey sheet evidence of neighbours getting together over colour schemes for their houses. Record also evidence of neighbours using colours which go badly together. Take photographs of any interesting colour combinations you see or colours you think look awful. Use the worksheet provided to help you carry out your survey.

When you have completed your survey on the colours people use on the outside of their homes, look carefully at the results. Use the information you have recorded to answer the following questions:

- which colours are the most commonly used?
- why do you think these colours are so popular?
- what is the most unusual colour combination you recorded?
- which colour is the least used?
- can you say why you think this colour is not popular?

■ which parts of the outside of a house are most commonly painted?

■ do some types of houses have more colour than others, and if so, which ones? can you say why?

■ which colours looked the most attractive on the outside of a house in your opinion, and why?

■ which was the least attractive colour scheme? why didn't you like it?

Write a description of the most attractive colour scheme you saw on your survey and explain why you like it. Does this colour scheme use the most popular colours? Describe the most unattractive colour scheme you recorded and explain why you don't like it. Does this colour scheme use the most unpopular colours? Finish your written presentation by explaining why, in your opinion, people like to decorate the outside of their homes with colour. Do you think it's for the simple reason of protecting wood or metal doors and window frames? If this is so, why don't people pick wood or metal coloured paint for the job? Do you think people choose colours which say something about themselves? Use any photographs you took to illustrate your written description.

Talk about your survey results with a friend or people you work with. Ask them which colours they think sound the most attractive from the survey results and why. Do they agree with your choices? Ask them why they think people like to paint their houses with different colours. Do they agree with your reasons or do they have a different opinion?

Optional task Draw out a simple outline of your garden or a friend's garden. Draw in and label a selection of plants and flowers for a really colourful garden. Decide on a colour theme such as blue and white or a variety of yellows or just go for a mass of colour!

Find ideas and the names of plants and flowers for your garden plan by visiting a local garden centre. Ask for advice and read the labels on plants or seed packets carefully. Make a note of any helpful information. Watch or listen to gardening programmes on television or the radio for ideas. Go to your local library and look for books on gardening or look through gardening magazines. Ask friends or family members who are keen gardeners for ideas.

Mark in your chosen plants on your garden plan. Label to show the name of the plant and its colour. Put in sample colours or cut up magazines or old seed packets.

Show your garden plan to someone you work with. Would they enjoy having such a colourful garden? What do they like about your plan?

(*See also* Worksheets: survey a street)

From this activity you may have evidence for:

Skills list	1, 3, 4, 6, 7, 8, 9, 10, 11, 12, 13, 14, 15, 16.
Core skills	Communication level 1 and 2.
Element	1.1/2.1 Take part in discussions.
Opportunities	Ask people for ideas and opinions about the use of colour on houses.
	Ask people for ideas and information about colourful plants (optional).
	Ask someone for an opinion on the colourful garden plan (optional).
Element	1.2/2.2 Produce written material.
Opportunities	Plan and write a survey sheet.
	Record survey results.
	Evaluate survey results and write a description of the use of colour on houses.
	Make notes about colourful plants for a garden plan (optional).
Element	1.3/2.3 Use images.
Opportunities	Take photographs of house colours to use in a written description.
	Draw and label a plan for a colourful garden (optional).
Element	1.4/2.4 Read and respond to written materials.
Opportunities	Read labels, seed packets, books and magazines for information about colourful plants for use in a garden plan (optional).

Activity 3   Write a description for a holiday guide

Add a descriptive word to a colour name and you can paint a picture in the mind of someone reading your description. Read the examples listed below of descriptive colour words. Add more examples of your own. Use a dictionary or thesaurus for ideas.

Yellow	*White*	*Red*	*Orange*
buttercup	cream	rosy	old gold
primrose	pearl	crimson	marigold
lemon	marble	flame	apricot
honey	ivory	wine	marmalade

Brown	*Green*	*Blue*	*Purple*
copper	moss	azure	amethyst
rust	jade	sapphire	plum
cinnamon	apple	aquamarine	heather
coffee	olive	indigo	lavender

Write a short introduction to a guide for your favourite holiday place. Choose somewhere you have already been or somewhere you have always wanted to go. Include in your introduction a description of the colours a visitor to the place will see and experience.

Collect information about your chosen holiday place. Visit your local library and look for holiday guides. Ask for information at a travel agent's or the Tourist Information Centre and collect brochures. Search for photographs you may have at home showing your chosen place or ask friends or family members for holiday snaps. Watch any helpful holiday programmes on television.

Read through the information you have collected. Find out about the attractions on offer at your chosen holiday place. Find out which colours are linked with the place. They may be traditional colours seen on houses or in local costumes or festivals. They may be colours seen in the landscape, sea, sky or beaches. They may be colours seen in plants and flowers or used in local foods.

Write out your introduction to a guide for your chosen holiday place. Read a few introductions to holiday guides and brochures to get an idea of how they are written. They are usually a general description of a place or area, making all the sights and attractions sound exciting and enjoyable. Write your introduction in a similar style. Use a photograph or picture to show the colours and attractions you are describing.

Check your finished introduction describes the holiday place accurately. Have you included descriptions of the colours linked with the place? Give your introduction to someone else to read and ask them if they can see a picture in their mind's eye of what you have described. Can they see the colours you have written about? Have you made your chosen holiday destination so colourful and attractive that they would like to go there?

From this activity you may have evidence for:

Skills list	1, 3, 6, 7, 8/9, 10, 13, 15, 16.
Core skills	Communication level 1 and 2.
Element	1.1/2.1 Take part in discussions.
Opportunities	Ask friends for holiday photographs.

Ask for information at a travel agent's or Tourist Information Centre.

Ask someone to read and comment on your written introduction.

Element   1.2/2.2 Produce written material.

Opportunities   Add to the list of descriptive words for colours.

Write an introduction to a holiday guide.

Element   1.4/2.4 Read and respond to written materials.

Opportunities   Read holiday brochures, guides, books and leaflets and look at photographs to find out about the attractions and colours at a holiday destination.

Read holiday brochures to find out what kind of information is included in an introduction.

Use a dictionary or thesaurus to find descriptive words.

Activity 4   Find out how colour is used in High Street signs

Many shops, banks, building societies and businesses use colour to advertise themselves. They have coloured logos or name boards above their premises. They use the same colours inside, for furniture and staff uniforms. As a customer you learn the familiar colours of a business. You would probably have no trouble recognising a branch of the same business if you saw it in another town.

Colour is used as a message to customers. Companies would like you to remember them, so they choose colours carefully which say something about what they have to offer. It might be colours which remind you of the fast service they offer. It might be colours which tell you a shop sells high quality goods. As a customer you learn to look for these colour clues. For example:

- **Red** is a food colour and when it's mixed with yellow it means fast food. MacDonalds and Wimpy use it to remind you of fast service. It might also be used in discount stores which sell goods very cheaply. They make money by selling a lot of goods quickly and rely on people popping in to see what bargains are on offer.

- **Green** is a safe, healthy colour. The famous store Harrods uses the colour to suggest quality. It is also used by health food shops. Mixed with gold it reminds the customer that good, reliable items can be bought in the shop.

- **Blue** is a reliable colour and is used a lot by banks and insurance companies. It is popular with some travel agents. It suggests that a calm, well thought-out service will be on offer to you.

Carry out a survey to find out which colours are linked to the shops banks and businesses you find on your local shopping High Street.

Before you start your survey, think about which colours you expect to find. Write down a few predictions. You can check how accurate your predictions are when your survey is finished. For example, which colours do you think you will find linked to:

- banks
- chemists or discount drug stores
- fast food outlets
- clothes shops
- travel agents

Discuss your predictions with a friend or someone you work with and write down your final choices. Choose a combination of colours if you wish.

Design a simple record sheet to record your survey. Make sure it's easy to use while you are walking about. Use the worksheet provided for help. Walk along your High Street and record each shop or business you see. Note down how they are using colour in their signs or logos.

When your survey is finished, take a careful look at the results. Did you find any popular colours, often used for a particular type of shop or business? Use your results to answer the following questions.

- Which range of colours are most commonly used by banks? Did you find any unexpected colours being used? You might have expected to find the safe, secure colours of blue or green, perhaps highlighted with some gold, white, or red. Did you find any unusual colours?

- Which colours did you find being used most often by fast food outlets? You might have expected to find red, orange or yellow. Did you find any unusual colours?

- Which colours did you find being used by chemists or similar types of shops? You might have expected to find blue and white. Did you find any unusual colours?

Look back at your written predictions. How accurate did they turn out to be? Were you successful in guessing some of the colour combinations for a business?

Use the information from your survey to write a short report on how colour is used in shop and business signs. Break your report up into two sections. In the first section describe some of the popular colour combinations you recorded. Describe which businesses use them and explain why, in your opinion, these colours may have been chosen.

In the second section of your report describe some unusual colour combinations you recorded on your survey. Describe which businesses use them and explain why, in your opinion, these colours may have been chosen.

Finish your report by explaining how useful you feel colour logos and signs are to the customer. Is it helpful to be able to recognise shops and businesses easily? Do the colours used give you a good clue about the business or shop, or can they be confusing? Use the worksheet provided to help check your report is complete.

Ask a friend or someone you work with to read your report. Are they surprised that colour is used in shop and business signs in this way? Have they ever noticed these colour clues for themselves? Do they agree with your opinions about why a colour may have been used?

Optional task   Design a graphic symbol or logo about yourself, using colour. Choose colours which you feel say something about the type of person you are or your name, the work you do or your hobbies. Imagine the logo is going to be printed on a tee shirt or a bag or folder. Use a computer paint program if you have access to one.

Show your colour logo to a friend or someone you work with who knows you well. Do they think your chosen colours show what you are really like or the work you do? Improve your logo if you get any helpful comments.

(*See also* **Worksheets: survey of High Street signs. Report writing prompt list.**)

	From this activity you may have evidence for:
Skills list	1, 3, 6, 7, 9, 10, 11, 12, 13/14, 15, 16.
Core skills	Communication level 1 and 2.
Element	1.1/2.1 Take part in discussions.
Opportunities	Discuss colour predictions with a friend.
	Ask someone for comments about your written report.
	Ask someone for feedback on your colour logo (optional).
Element	1.2/2.2 Produce written material.
Opportunities	Write down colour predictions.
	Design a survey record sheet.
	Carry out and record a survey on colour in the High Street.
	Write a report about the use of colour in business signs.
Element	1.3/2.3 Use images.
Opportunities	Design and draw out a colour logo (optional).
Element	1.4/2.4 Read and respond to written materials.
Opportunities	Read High Street signs and logos to record use of colour.

Activity 5 **Find out how colour is used in product packaging**

Advertisers know that you as a customer are likely to link certain colours with certain kinds of products. A large supermarket will display goods in blocks of colour, so you can scan the shelves quickly and find your favourites. You will look for familiar colours to find the products you like to buy. Advertisers also think that you can be attracted to a new product if you see a big splash of colour.

Blue or blue–green is often used, for example, on the packaging for foods such as salt and vinegar crisps. Although the wrappers may have other bits of colour on them in the writing or brand names, the main colour remains blue. You can get so used to colour codes that if a company changed the colour you would probably pick up the wrong flavour crisps!

The link with colour and taste is very important in packaging. A customer expects a jar of coffee packaged in blue will have a milder taste than a coffee packaged in red, for example. If you buy a lemon scented toilet cleaner you expect it to be yellow. If you chose a pine scented one you would probably be surprised if it wasn't green! Product makers spend a lot of time and money finding out which colours you are likely to find the most attractive for each item you buy. A product must make a good 'shelf impact' so customers see it easily, pick it up and buy it.

 Choose three well-known products which you buy regularly at the supermarket. Collect the product packaging. Choose a cleaner, a cereal, a box of tea, a tub of butter or a shampoo bottle, for example. Investigate the way colour has been used in the packaging for each of your chosen products.

 Find out a little more about colour and packaging by visiting your local library. Ask the librarian for help to look for books about colour, packaging, advertising, marketing or even photography. You may find the information you need is just a small section in a book. Read some more about how colours are used to attract people to buy products. Ask friends or people you work with what colours they link with well-known products. Find out the following for each of your three products:

■ **List all the colours that have been used.** You should find there are one or two main colours. Other colours used may be less important.

■ **How does the colour link to the use of the product?** For example, look at a spread. The deep yellow colour of the tub is there to remind the customer that the spread tastes like butter and can be used to replace butter.

■ **What links do you make with the main colours used?** For example, look at a baby shampoo. The main colour may be pink. As a customer you will easily link pink with mildness and gentleness.

■ **Is the use of the main colour successful?** Do you think the colour of the packaging would persuade you to buy this product rather than another similar one? Perhaps you already have? If so, can you say why?

■ **What is the purpose of the secondary, less important colours on the packaging?** Are other colours used on the packaging to give a contrast to the main colour? Are they there so printed information can be seen clearly? For example, an oven cleaner which has green as a main colour suggests cleanliness. Orange may be a secondary colour and is being used to suggest the power of the cleaning product and to contrast with the green.

Use the worksheet provided to help you record the results of your investigation into the colours used in your three products.

Check how accurate your results are. Write to one of the product makers. Explain what you have been doing. Ask for some information about the colours used on the product packaging. How were the colours chosen and why?

When you receive a reply you can compare the information to the investigation results you recorded about product colours. Did you make some sensible guesses?

Optional task Choose one of the products you have been investigating and redesign the packaging colour scheme. Draw out your product as accurately as you can, showing size, shape and brand name. Use colours you feel are really unexpected. Choose colours which wouldn't normally be linked to such a product by a supermarket customer.

Show your finished drawing to friends or people you work with. Don't say anything about the colours, just ask people to comment honestly on their reaction to your colour scheme. Do they like it? Would it attract them if they saw the product on the supermarket shelf? Do they think the colours link with the use of the product?

Listen to and note down comments you receive or tape replies. Evaluate the replies you received. Did people feel a little unhappy about the colours? Did they feel they wouldn't easily recognise the use of the product? Or did you get some surprising results and find people liked having a new, unexpected colour scheme? Write a short summary of the reaction you got to your redesigned product. In your opinion, do people prefer the colours they are used to, or do they enjoy and accept new colour schemes?

(*See also* Worksheets: product colours)

From this activity you may have evidence for:

Skills list	1, 3, 6, 7, 8/9, 10, 11, 12, 13, 14, 15, 16.
Core skills	Communication level 1 and 2.
Element	1.1/2.1 Take part in discussions.
Opportunities	Ask the librarian for help to find information on colour.
	Ask people for ideas about colour links to products.
	Ask people to comment about a redesigned product (optional).
Element	1.2/2.2 Produce written material.
Opportunities	Record information about use of colour in product packaging. Write to a product maker for information about colour in packaging.
	Record people's comments about a redesigned product (optional).
	Write a summary of responses to a redesigned product (optional).
Element	1.3/2.3 Use images.
Opportunities	Draw out a well-known product using a new colour scheme (optional).
Element	1.4/2.4 Read and respond to written materials.
Opportunities	Read selected books about colour in packaging.
	Read the reply to your letter and compare colour information with your own ideas.

Activity 6 Write a questionnaire to find out about the importance of colour in food

If you can't see the food you are eating, for example if you are blind-folded for a food test, you can become quite confused about the taste. You use colour to help recognise taste. By the time food reaches your mouth, you have already looked at it and been given a colour clue about its taste. For example, when you east a red sweet you are likely to expect it to taste of strawberry, raspberry or cherry. If it tastes of lemon, you may not even realise it for a while, because your link to colour and taste is very strong.

Oddly coloured food can confuse you so you become uncertain about the taste. You may feel rather sick just looking at the food. You may not be willing to try an oddly coloured food as its unusual look may suggest it will taste unpleasant. Children are usually an exception. Most children happily accept strangely coloured foods and don't feel confused about the taste. Children's sweets often use colours which don't match up with the taste at all. Ice lollies in bright blue will taste of strawberry, which a child happily accepts. Do you think this may be because a child has not had time to learn and get used to food colour clues?

Design a two-part questionnaire to find out how people respond to food colours.

In Part One describe some ordinary foods but give them an odd colour. Ask about the following foods and think of more ideas for yourself:

■ a plate of green potatoes

■ pie and purple mushy peas

■ sliced blue carrots

■ grey baked beans on toast

■ turquoise apple pie

■ magenta bananas

■ bright yellow mushrooms

■ black tomatoes

Choose ten oddly coloured foods for your questionnaire. Ask people for their reactions to each food listed. Find out if people expect foods to have a different taste if the colour is unusual. Ask:

■ would you eat this food?

■ what do you think it would taste like?

■ if you wouldn't try the food can you explain why not?

In Part Two of your questionnaire, choose five basic foods and find out about the ordinary colours people like their foods to be. Ask about peas, bread, ice cream and orange squash for example. Find out if people have a strong idea of the colour they prefer. For example, ask people to:

■ circle which colour they prefer tinned peas to be:
dark green / bright green / dull green / grey–green

■ circle which colour they prefer vanilla ice cream to be:
brilliant white / pale cream / deep cream / yellow–cream

Make sure your questions are clear. Check you have provided enough room for people to write their replies. Remember to include a thank you at the end of your questionnaire.

When your questionnaire has been completed by a variety of people have a careful look at the results. Do most people seem to be unhappy about eating foods which are oddly coloured? Do most people have a clear idea about the colour they prefer ordinary foods to be?

Add to the information you are gathering about people's response to food and colour by organising a short taste test. Find out if people can guess a flavour correctly without getting any colour clues. Give a few volunteer tasters a fruit sweet to taste, but don't allow them to see the colour. Record what flavour they say the sweet is. Use the worksheet provided for help to prepare and run your taste test and record the replies you receive.

When your taste tests are finished have a careful look at the results you recorded. Do most people seem to need a colour clue to guess a flavour accurately?

Write a short report explaining the results of your questionnaire and taste tests about the way people respond to colour in food. Divide your report into three parts.

Start by describing how people responded to oddly coloured foods. What strange colours were people most unhappy about and what reasons did they give? Were there any oddly coloured foods which people felt they would try?

In part two of your report explain what colours people seem to prefer for ordinary, basic foods. Did most people have a clear idea of what colours they like foods to be?

In the final part of your report describe the results of your taste tests. Do most people need to be able to see the colour of a food to guess the flavour correctly?

Optional task   Pick up a packet of sweets in your local supermarket and you may find E102 has been added. This is an artificial yellow colour which has been added to the food because the makers feel that is what the customer wants. E102 is tartrazine. It is an artificial colour which some people are sensitive to, especially some people who have asthma. It is used in cakes, fish batters, sweets, squashes and fizzy drinks for example. Artificial food colours are added to foods to make them a more attractive colour. E124 or ponceau is an artificial red. It is added to trifle, cake mixes and tinned red fruits for example. It can produce reactions in some people, especially people sensitive to aspirin. Food can be coloured by natural colours as well. E160(b) is annatto, which gives a yellow colour and is used in margarines, butter and cheese for example. It has no known harmful effects. E162 is Beetroot Red. It is used to colour oxtail soup for example and has no known harmful effects. All the additives, even natural ones, have an E number. This means they have been approved as safe to go into food.

Find out about common artificial and natural colours which are added to your favourite foods. Visit your library and look for books about food colouring. Ask the librarian for help. One very useful book is called *E is for Additives*. Look at bottles of food colourings in the supermarket and find artificial colours listed. Read the labels on foods which say they have no artificial colours added and find out which natural colours have been used. Visit a local health food store and find out about natural food colours.

Design a hit list for yourself, listing some common artificial colours you would like to avoid and the natural colours you are happy to eat. Make your hit list credit card size and have it laminated or put it into a plastic wallet to make it durable.

Show your hit list to friends or people you work with and ask them if they would find it useful. Make copies for people who would also like to use your hit list.

(*See also* **Worksheets**: taste test)

From this activity you may have evidence for:

Skills list	1, 3, 4, 6, 7, 8, 10, 11, 12, 13, 15, 16.
Core skills	Communication level 1 and 2.
Element	1.1/2.1 Take part in discussions.
Opportunities	Ask people to complete a questionnaire.
	Ask people to take part in a taste test.
	Ask for help to find information about artificial colours (optional).
	Ask people for comments about the hit list of food colours (optional).
Element	1.2/2.2 Produce written material.
Opportunities	Design a questionnaire on colour and food.
	Record the results of a taste test.
	Write a short report on the questionnaire and taste test results.
	Design a hit list of food colourings (optional).
Element	1.4/2.4 Read and respond to written materials.
Opportunities	Read and evaluate the results of the questionnaire and taste tests.
	Read books, leaflets or labels for information about food colourings (optional).

Evaluation exercise

Will you think differently now about the colours you use in your home? Do you think you will be more aware of how you are persuaded to buy products because of the colours used? Will you be more aware of the colourings used in food?

Do you feel more confident about carrying out an investigation or a survey? Do you feel you have gained competence in questioning a variety of people? Do you think your presentation skills have improved?

Check you have recorded the work you have done and the skills you have covered on your Skills Record Sheet. You will find this very useful if you have to look back and remember how you practised various skills on the project. Write down the variety of resources you have used.

Complete your Skills Summary Sheet. Write down details of the evidence of competence you have collected during the project. Write down the skills you need to practise a little more and the date you will aim to complete the work by. Evaluate and write down your achievements. Write down the progress you have made towards an accreditation you may be working for.

Colour room plan

Look carefully at the example plan and room contents. Choose colours for the walls, flooring, doors, windows, ceiling and accessories. Use coloured pencils, pastels, paints, fabrics, paper samples or paint cards. Use the mini-chart to list colours you are showing on your drawing.

Feature	Colour	Reasons	Sample
Floor			
Walls			
Door			
Window frame			
Rug			
Bed covers			
Curtains			
Desk			
Window seat			

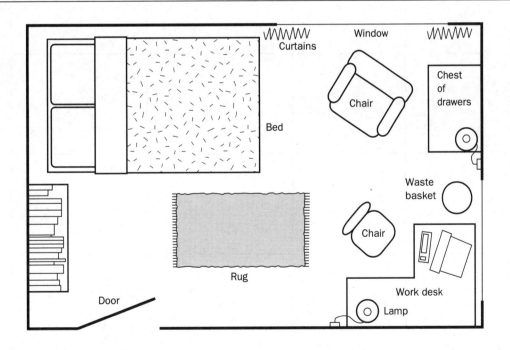

Survey a street

Write down each type of house you see. Write down which colours have been used and where they have been put, e.g. door, window frame. Comment on the colours. Are they bright, dull, attractive, unusual?

Type of house	Colours	Where used	Comments

Survey of High Street Signs

Write down each business you survey on your local shopping High Street. Write down the background colour of the name sign, the colour of the words and any logo used.

Business details	Colour details		
Name and type of business	Background colour	Word colour	Logo colour

Multi-use ■ *Use this worksheet to help with report writing.*

Report writing prompt list

Use this worksheet to help plan and check your report. Tick each prompt as you go through the writing process. The prompt list refers to your survey of colour in High Street signs. The prompt titles can be used to help with any report you write.

Give your report a title which explains clearly what it is about. Underline the title to highlight it. ☐

Start with a short introduction which explains simply what the report is about. ☐

In this case, your report is about the results of carrying out a survey on colour in High Street signs.

Divide your report into sections and give each section a sub-heading. Underline the headings so they can be seen. Provide information and examples in each section. ☐

In this case, divide your report into two sections. In section one, write about popular colours and colour combinations. Describe the colours and which businesses use them. Give some examples. Comment on the effect these colours have on customers.

In section two, describe some of the unusual or unexpected colours and colour combinations. Give some examples. Comment on the effect these colours have on customers.

Finish with a summary or conclusion. You may either repeat the main points you have made in your report or make some recommendations. These could be changes you think should be made or actions you think people should take. ☐

In this case comment on how helpful the colour messages are for customers seeing signs and logos above a High Street business.

Check through your report. Make sure the sentences make sense. Check for any spelling or punctuation mistakes and put them right. ☐

Give your report to someone else to read. Can they understand your ideas easily? Do they think the report is interesting and informative? ☐

Product colours

Use this worksheet to record the results of your investigation into the use of colour in packaging. Repeat this format for each product you look at.

Product: One / Two / Three

Name of product:

Type of product:

Main colour(s) used:

Possible reasons for each main colour:

Is the use of the main colour successful?

Secondary colour(s) used:

Purpose of secondary colours, e.g. provide a contrast, show print clearly, link product with others in the maker's range?

Other colours used:

Purpose of other colours?

Overall: Do the colours used show the use of the product or the reason why people might buy it?

Yes/No

Do the colours used persuade you to buy the product?

Yes/No

If yes, why?

Taste test

You will need a blindfold and two packets of Fruit Pastilles or Opal Fruits. This should give you enough sweets to test six people. Repeat the layout below for volunteers 5, 6 and 7.

Explain carefully to the person taking part in your taste test what you are going to ask them to do. They shouldn't be at all worried about what you are going to ask them to taste. Tell your taster you will be giving them sweets but don't give any details about what make or flavour sweet it is.

Find a quiet place for the taste test, with no onlookers.

Blindfold the person ready to give them the sweets to taste. Don't let them see the sweets at any stage of the test.

Explain: 'I am going to give you three fruit sweets to taste, one at a time. After each tasting I will ask you what flavour you think the sweet is.'

Repeat these preparations for everyone who takes part in your taste test. Thank each taster when their test is complete.

Taster 1	Actual flavour	Guessed flavour	Correct?
Sweet one			
Sweet two			
Sweet three			

Taster 2	Actual flavour	Guessed flavour	Correct?
Sweet one			
Sweet two			
Sweet three			

Taster 3	Actual flavour	Guessed flavour	Correct?
Sweet one			
Sweet two			
Sweet three			

Back to basics

Answers on p. 313.

Match up

Write out the two lists below so the colour names in list one match up with two descriptive words in list two.

List one	List two
Blue	tan
	foxglove
Green	chocolate
	apricot
Yellow	mustard
	sapphire
Red	leaf
	ruby
Purple	golden
	amber
Brown	lime
	scarlet
Orange	plum
	turquoise

Proof-reading

Fill in the missing punctuation in the following short text about colour in advertising. You need to put back capital letters, commas and full stops.

the customer judges the quality of a product by its colour pink is used in hand creams as it is a colour which suggests a soft tender mildness green is used successfully on toilet cleaner containers as it suggests a clean natural freshness if the customer wants a mild coffee they look for a blue labelled jar coffee jars with red labels suggest a stronger flavour

Careful reading

Read the following text about the eye carefully and answer the questions which follow. Try to write your answers in complete sentences.

The eye works very much like a camera. Just like a camera you have a lens which works to focus the rays of light. Like a camera, your eye has control over the amount of light which is allowed to enter. The iris, the coloured part of your eye, widens or narrows to alter the size of your pupil and so control the amount of light getting in. The pupil is the hole in the middle of the iris which looks like a black circle. The information received by your eye is sent to your brain. The physical action of the eye can be affected by your emotions. Experiments have shown that the pupils of your eyes open wider and let in more light when you see something or someone you like. The opposite happens when you see something you don't like!

1. What part of the eye focuses the light?
2. What does the iris of your eye control?
3. What happens to your eyes when you see something you like?
4. What happens to your eyes when you see something you don't like?

Alternatives Other ideas for activities on colour

Any activity from the group or individual projects can be replaced with an idea from the list below. Use the list to give you more choice of activities to do which suit your needs, interests and the amount of time you have available.

■ Find out how colours are used to warn or attract in nature. Consider insects, plants, birds and animals. What colour signals do they send out to others? How do they use colour to warn others they are poisonous? How do they use colour to attract a mate? Write a description of your research or design a colour wheel showing how colours are used in a variety of ways.

■ Find out about the fashion changes in colour in make-up. Think about seasonal changes, and differences between cultures. Design a new make-up colour range.

■ Design a questionnaire to find out which colours people feel are the most suitable for a range of occasions such as a formal interview, a wedding, a funeral, a first date, etc. Write a mini-guide to the best colours to impress!

■ Find out about colour meditation. Try out some meditation exercises using colour. Write a description of the changes or feelings you observed.

■ Design the colour scheme for a special event. It could be a wedding, a child's party, an important anniversary, a graduation dinner, etc. Plan the whole use of colour including room decorations, invitations or posters, flowers, banners and balloons, etc.

■ Carry out a survey to find out the ten most popular car colours. Observe cars on a busy road and tally the colours which pass you by or interview friends or a car dealer for the information. Write the top ten most popular car colours with the reasons for each colour's popularity and its position on the list.

■ Consider which colours are associated with each season in the year. Think about seasonal foods, celebrations and clothes. Write a poem about seasonal colours.

■ Find out about the problems of being colour blind. Find out about glasses which can be prescribed by an optician to help correct the problem. Write a diary about a day in your life as if you were one of the very rare group of people who can only see in black and white. Describe what your world is like.

■ Collect and display a range of black and white photographs. Look in books, newspapers and family albums. Ask people to look at the display and record their comments. Write a description of why black and white photographs can produce such powerful images.

■ Carry out a survey to find out how colour is used in public places. What colours are used, and do they have an effect on people's moods and behaviour? For example, look at the colours of waiting rooms, hospitals, railway stations and restaurants. Write a short report about your survey results.

■ Design a complete menu for a celebration meal with a colour theme. Research and find dishes which fit in with your chosen colour.

Pollution and noise

INTRODUCTION

In this group project on *pollution and noise* you will be able to:

■ Discuss what noise pollution means to you.

■ Write a top five noise list.

■ Write a description of noise at home.

■ Carry out a survey of noise pollution in your local area.

■ Find out how to be a quiet neighbour.

■ Find out how to complain about noise pollution.

■ Consider a case study about a noisy neighbour.

■ Write an article about noise pollution for a local paper.

■ Find out about noise at work and hearing protection.

■ Design a questionnaire to find out about noise at work.

■ Design a poster to warn about the dangers of noise at work.

■ Investigate car alarms.

■ Write a letter to a local paper about car alarms.

■ Evaluate your work on the project.

Choose activities which interest you from the wide range of suggestions provided in the project. You can choose to do just part of an activity if you wish. The choice is yours. There are more suggestions in the Alternative Ideas section (p. 253), so you should find enough activities to suit your interests and needs. Finish with the Evaluation Exercise as this will help you think about your work on the project and remind you to record the skills you have covered.

For each activity you choose to do, use the information provided for you in the activity text and worksheets, as well as your own experiences and knowledge. If you need to look for more information consider resources such as books, newspapers and magazines as well as television, radio, video and CD-ROM. You can also use resources such as writing to an organisation or telephoning for information, talking to people you know and talking to other people who may be able to give you the information you need.

Optional task   If you have more time available and would like to try another task to develop the skills you have already used in an activity, you can look for the Optional Tasks which are linked to many of the project activities.

You will find the following worksheets useful:

Pollution and noise

Activity 1   **Find out about noise pollution**

What is noise pollution and how does it affect you? The everyday sounds you enjoy can upset another person's life and cause them distress and misery. Everyone makes some noise, but loud music late at night, shouting, car alarms, noisy traffic, drilling or barking dogs can all become too much. Neighbours may get angry and start to complain. New regulations will allow your local council to fine householders on the spot for making an unreasonable amount of noise. You must control the amount of noise you make between 11 pm and 7.30 am. Noise Officers can take away equipment such as hi-fis if you are using it too loudly and causing a noise nuisance.

People today are becoming more aware of noise and are more upset by the amount of noise around them. It is very difficult to shut out noise. The amount of complaints about noise made to the police and to local councils is increasing. Many houses have poor sound insulation. You may be able to hear your neighbours quite easily and find this disturbing. This is not such a problem in Scotland where there are tougher regulations for sound insulation when houses are built.

Talk about and list the everyday sounds you can think of which irritate and annoy you and which you would call noise pollution. Write down all of your ideas on a large piece of paper or a board, or make notes. Keep going until you can't think of any more. Don't discuss your ideas too much at this stage, just write them all down.

Write down irritating noise from home or work situations. You may be annoyed by noisy dogs, equipment which hums, road works or a family member who is learning to play the drums! You may have a partner who snores or neighbours with a faulty car alarm. Tape some different noises which bother you and listen to them together and decide if you would all call them noise pollution. Loud, quarrelling neighbours, blaring televisions or late-night parties might be obvious noise pollution. However, people find all kinds of noise irritating. Neighbours have even been known to fall out over the sound of running water in a garden waterfall!

Talk about what noise pollution means to you. Decide together which are the five most irritating noises on your list. Discuss your reasons for calling these sounds noise pollution. How does this type of noise pollution affect your lives? Discuss and answer the following questions:

- does this noise pollution ever make you feel helpless, tired or tearful, and if so, why?

- do any of these noises make you feel really angry, and if so, why?

- have you ever felt violent towards the people making the noise, and if so, why?

- have you ever complained to the council about this noise pollution?

 Present your top five as a table or chart and write the reasons for your choices. Use the worksheet provided to help you record your top five and ideas on noise pollution.

 Consider your discussion, list and ideas about noise pollution. Are there any big differences in the kind of noise which upsets some people but doesn't bother others? Have you found most people will enjoy noise in certain situations such as a party, concert or street fair for example, but will want peace and quiet at other times? Do you think some people seem to be able to cope with more noise than others?

Optional task Each write a short description of how much noise there is in your own home. Do you enjoy the noise or does it get on your nerves? Do you live with other people who like a lot of noise or do they think you are noisy? Are there times when you like noise and other times when even little sounds can distract you?

Compare your different accounts. Does anyone match up, liking or disliking the same amount of noise?

(*See also* Worksheets: noise pollution top five)

From this activity you may have evidence for:

Skills list 1, 2, 3, 11, 12, 13, 15, 16.

Core skills Communication level 1 and 2.

Element	1.1/2.1 Take part in discussions.
Opportunities	Discuss which sounds irritate and annoy.
	Discuss the meaning of noise pollution.
	Compare accounts of noise at home (optional).
Element	1.2/2.2 Produce written material.
Opportunities	Write a list of irritating sounds.
	Write a top five.
	Write a description of noise at home (optional).

Activity 2 Carry out a survey on local noise pollution

Is your home noisy? You may like to have your television and radio turned right up. You may have the washing machine working all the time. Many homes are full of noisy equipment and DIY tools. Some families do a lot of shouting and arguing with each other. If you are trying to study, or sleep because you've been on a night shift, or just relax with the paper, a lot of noise can be very irritating.

Some people can hear their neighbours very easily through the walls of their homes. Old terraced houses can have thin inside walls because at the time of building them, people were less concerned about noise. You may live on an open plan estate and hear a lot of noise from other gardens. There may be few walls, fences or hedges to block off the sound. You may live in a block of flats and have noise both above and below you.

Is there a noisy estate, road or street in your local area? Carry out a survey to find out if any of your local areas suffer from a lot of noise pollution.

Work in pairs or small groups and survey a different local area each. Decide which areas to visit. Choose a street of terraced houses, a new estate, some flats or a row of houses with large gardens. Listen for any sounds which are irritating or which may spoil people's enjoyment of their daily life. Record details of each type of noise pollution you hear and comment on how irritating it is. Listen for the sounds listed below and add more ideas of your own.

- car engine being revved up continually
- car or house alarm
- noisy DIY
- road works
- gas/water company repairing pipes
- people arguing or shouting
- heavy traffic
- loud radio or television
- a dog barking or howling

Use the worksheet provided to help you plan and record your survey on noise pollution.

Share and discuss the results of your survey on noise pollution in your local area. Look carefully at the evidence of noise pollution you have recorded. Use your survey results to answer the following questions:

- which was the most common noise recorded?

- which was the least common noise recorded?

- can you say why you got these results?

- which type of noise seemed the most irritating and disturbing to daily life?

- can you link any particular noise pollution with a type of housing? For example, did areas of open plan estates seem to suffer more from DIY noise, lawn mowers or dogs barking?

- can you explain some of the sources of noise pollution? For example, is it a holiday area or busy shopping area?

- did you record more noise pollution than you had expected or less?

Use your survey results and discussion to each present a written opinion on how much noise people put up with in your local area.

Start by describing any noisy areas you found and explain reasons for the noise. Do some local areas have a lot more background noise than others? Go on to describe a quiet local area and explain why you think there is less noise. Explain any links you found between types of housing and noise pollution. Finish your writing by saying whether in your opinion your local area suffers from a lot of noise pollution.

(*See also* Worksheets: survey of noise pollution)

	From this activity you may have evidence for:
Skills list	1, 2, 3, 5, 6, 8, 10, 11, 12, 13, 15, 16.
Core skills	Communication level 1 and 2.
Element	1.1/2.1 Take part in discussions.
Opportunities	Discuss what to include in a survey on noise pollution.
	Discuss the results of the survey on noise pollution.
Element	1.2/2.2 Produce written material.
Opportunities	Write and carry out a survey on noise pollution.
	Write your opinion on noise pollution in your local area.
Element	1.4/2.4 Read and respond to written materials.
Opportunities	Read and evaluate the survey results.

Activity 3   Write a checklist on how to be a noise-free neighbour

If you are surrounded by noise in your daily life such as road works and noisy traffic, you may be very glad of some peace and quiet at home. Sound is measured in decibels. If silence is zero decibels and the threshold of pain for your hearing is around 120 decibels, you can imagine a vacuum cleaner at 70 decibels is quite irritating. Noisy traffic from a busy road outside your home can build up to 90 decibels of sound. If a neighbour's loud stereo is blasting away at over 100 decibels the noise can make you feel very angry.

Collect and discuss ideas and information about how to keep noise levels down in the home. Write a checklist on how to be a noise-free neighbour.

Contact your local council's Environmental Health Department for information on how to cut down on noise. The Citizens' Advice Bureau (CAB) may be able to help you as well. Look in your local library for leaflets or books about noise pollution for more ideas. Write to the Noise Abatement Society, a registered charity, for information. Their address is PO Box 518, Eynsford, Dartford, Kent, DA4 0LL. Ask for a helpful booklet called *Bothered by Noise*. You need to include a large stamped, self-addressed envelope when you write.

Find out how much noise ordinary household equipment can make. Find out how much noise you are allowed to make between 11 pm and 7.30 am in your local area. Use your own experiences of noisy neighbours for ideas for your checklist. Interview friends and people you work with who have had experience of a noisy neighbour or have been noisy neighbours themselves! Ask about the kind of noise involved and how the situation was sorted out. Allocate the tasks between you to get the research done.

Present your checklist on how to be a noise-free neighbour as a leaflet, flyer or an audio-tape. Use pictures, photographs, drawings or cartoons to illustrate each important point you make on your written checklist. Use sound effects to explain important points on your tape. Allocate tasks to each other to complete your presentation. Include the following advice:

- Make sure your dog doesn't bark constantly. Dogs may bark quite often when they are lonely or bored.

- Warn your neighbour if you are going to do any noisy DIY and how long it is likely to take.

- Tell your neighbour about a party you are planning. Invite them if possible.

- Think about the time of day before you start household jobs. Just because you enjoy getting up early and vacuuming the whole house or mowing the lawn doesn't mean your neighbours are early risers as well! Some people enjoy a long lie in, especially at the weekend.

- Keep the volume on the television at a reasonable level or move the set away from a connecting wall.

- Make sure house alarms or car alarms are working properly.

Go over your checklist together or listen to your tape. Have you included all the important points you planned to make? Check your advice is sensible. Discuss how practical your checklist really is. Everyone makes some noise. Is it possible to be, if not noise-free, then a quiet neighbour at least? Show your checklist or tape to other people and ask for their comments. Would they carry out any of your suggestions?

(*See also* Worksheets: noise-free neighbours)

From this activity you may have evidence for:

Skills list	1, 2, 3, 4, 5, 6, 7, 8/9, 13/14, 15, 16.
Core skills	Communication level 1 and 2.
Element	1.1/2.1 Take part in discussions.
Opportunities	Discuss how to be a quiet neighbour.
	Telephone local organisations for information.
	Record the checklist as an audio-tape.
	Discuss and evaluate the checklist.
	Ask people for comments on the checklist.
Element	1.2/2.2 Produce written material.
Opportunities	Write to organisations for information.
	Write a leaflet on how to be a noise-free neighbour.
Element	1.3/2.3 Use images.
Opportunities	Use pictures or cartoons to illustrate a checklist.

Element 1.4/2.4 Read and respond to written materials.

Opportunities Read information about being a quiet neighbour.

Activity 4 Find out how to complain about noise pollution

A problem for many local authorities today is dealing with the noise nuisance often caused by the anti-social behaviour of people towards each other. This noise problem may involve shouting, abuse, smashed windows or loud arguing and fighting. Some local authorities would like to be able to put tenants on probation. Before being allowed to stay long-term on a housing estate, people would have to prove they are good neighbours and not too noisy. Some housing charities are worried that these powers will be used to get rid of unpopular families. Some people think there should be special courts, where specially trained judges deal just with noise nuisance complaints. Victims of noise nuisance can sometimes be so scared of the people causing the noise that they don't complain about it. Special courts would be more caring towards people's worries.

What do you think? Talk about your views. Make sure everyone has a chance to speak. Share any experiences you have had of trying to complain about noise. Find out how to complain about noise pollution in your local area.

Contact your local council for information on how to complain about noise pollution or noise nuisance. Find the telephone number or address in your local telephone book. You may find it is listed as Environmental Health or Environmental Services, or you may have a Noise Team in your area who deal with noise pollution problems.

Prepare some questions to ask on how to complain about noise. Find out if someone is prepared to visit the group and answer all of your questions. Use the worksheet provided to help you plan questions to ask by telephone or in person and to record the answers.

If you complain about noise pollution you will probably get a form to fill in, asking you for details about the noise. You may be asked to keep a detailed record of when the noise starts and finishes and the days and times. You may be asked what the noise is like and how it affects you, for example, whether it keeps you awake.

Once your record is complete your local Noise Team may arrange to visit you or talk to your neighbour or whoever is causing the noise problem. They may take measurements of the level of noise.

Read the following case study carefully. Use the information you have discovered on how to complain about noise pollution to complete the tasks which follow the case study.

Mr and Mrs Brent are a retired couple who have lived in their terraced house for thirty-two years. A few months ago a young couple, Sue and Dave and their two small children, moved in next door. At first there was a lot of hammering and banging as the house was altered to suit the new family. Mrs Brent tried to be friendly with her new neighbours but didn't see a lot of them. Dave went out to work early and Sue was either at her part-time job or meeting friends who also had young children. As the weeks went by Mr and Mrs Brent expected the noise to get less. Unfortunately it got worse.

Dave started repairing motorbikes in the back yard in his spare time. He worked every evening until 11.30 pm or later, with the radio blaring to keep him company. He and Sue didn't seem to be getting on very well and had constant loud arguments. Sue shouted at Dave and he shouted back or turned his radio up so he couldn't hear her. Mr and Mrs Brent put up with the noise day after day.

Mrs Brent tried to chat to Sue, to ask her to try and do something about the noise. Sue said she would try to get the family to be more quiet, but nothing improved. Mr and Mrs Brent felt the only time they had any quiet was for a few hours in the morning while Dave was on an early shift, Sue out at work and the children being looked after by a friend.

They both felt very tired and upset about the situation. Finally, they rang the Environmental Health Department at their local council and explained the problem to a Noise Officer. They received a Noise Complaint Record through the post. They completed the form and returned it to the Noise Team.

 Discuss together exactly what you would record on the Noise Complaint Record over a ten day period, as if you are Mr and Mrs Brent. Use the worksheet provided as an example of a form, or one you have obtained yourselves from your own council. Make up suitable details of dates and times for yourselves.

 Discuss in detail what you think may happen next to Mr and Mrs Brent and their neighbours Sue and Dave. Use information you have received from your council about how noise pollution is controlled in your area. Try a role play of what you think may happen, exploring how all the people involved feel. Act out some possible solutions to the problem.

Write a summary of the events which are likely to follow after Mr and Mrs Brent's complaint about noisy neighbours.

Optional task Look through as many local newspapers as you can and collect stories about noise pollution. Look at back copies of a local newspaper at your local library. Read and discuss the stories you find. Comment on how the articles have been written. Each write an article as if it is for your local paper, about a noise pollution problem. Use the stories you have collected for ideas or write about an experience of your own. Write your article in a similar style to the ones you have discussed. It should also be of a similar length.

(*See also* Worksheets: questions on noise pollution. Noise complaint record)

From this activity you may have evidence for:

Skills list   1, 2, 3, 4, 6, 7, 8, 10, 12, 13, 15, 16.

Core skills   Communication level 1 and 2.

Element   1.1/2.1 Take part in discussions.

Opportunities   Telephone the local council for information.

Ask prepared questions about noise pollution.

Discuss case study.

Take part in role plays.

Element   1.2/2.2 Produce written material.

Opportunities   Fill in a noise complaint record.

Write a summary of events based on the case study.

Write a newspaper article about noise pollution (optional).

Element   1.4/2.4 Read and respond to written materials.

Opportunities   Read information on complaining and controlling noise pollution.

Read the case study.

Collect and read newspaper stories on noise pollution (optional).

Activity 5   Find out about noise at work and ear protection

While you are working as a group you may be able to hear:

■ noisy traffic outside

■ people talking, shouting or laughing

■ someone coughing

■ people walking or running past the room you are in

■ the hum of lifts, machines or other equipment

■ scraping chairs or tables

List all of the noises you can hear. Discuss what kind of noise you can put up with and still carry on with your work. Talk about the kind of noise which would distract or annoy you. Are some people more easily put off work by noise than other people?

The Noise at Work Regulations control what must be done at work to protect people's hearing. Very noisy jobs can damage your hearing. Your hearing can be damaged if you work in a noisy place for a long time. It can also be damaged if you are exposed to very loud noise for a short time. An employer must check noise levels. They must take action when the level of noise is 85 decibels, and more action still if the noise reaches 90 decibels. If you have to shout to talk to someone just a few feet away, ask for the noise levels to be checked. If your ears buzz or ring after you have finished work, ask for the noise levels to be checked.

A lot can be done in the workplace to reduce noise levels. Equipment can be designed to run quietly, can be insulated to reduce noise, or can be serviced to reduce noisy faults. People can be moved around on jobs so they are not exposed to loud noise for too long, or they can wear ear protection correctly and protect their hearing.

Discuss the noisiest jobs you have ever done or the noisiest workplace you have ever been in. You may have had part-time or full-time jobs, or temporary or voluntary jobs in noisy places. List the kind of noise you had to cope with at work. Talk about how the noise affected you and your ability to work.

Use your experiences of noisy jobs and ideas from your discussion to design and write a questionnaire. Find out how much noise people put up with at work and how it affects them. Ask:

■ do people work in a noisy place?

■ are people aware of the importance of protecting their hearing at work?

■ how do people protect their hearing?

■ can people describe the noise they have to work with and how loud it is?

■ can people explain what causes the noise in their workplace?

■ how does working in a noisy place affect people?

■ what kind of noise do people find the most irritating? (even humming machinery can be tiring to work with and leave you with a headache at the end of the day)

If you need more information to help with ideas for questions, contact your nearest Health and Safety Executive. Ask about the Noise at Work Regulations and for information on noise control. The address will be in your telephone book.

Use the worksheet provided to help you present your questionnaire. Write a range of questions and put them into a sensible order. Check you are all satisfied with your questionnaire before asking other people to complete it. Agree how many friends, family members or people you work with you will each ask. Meet up again to read and compare the questionnaire results.

Look at your completed questionnaires and discuss them together. Use the information you have gathered to answer the following questions about noise at work:

- have many people worked in a noisy job?

- what different jobs are listed as being noisy?

- are these the kind of jobs you expect to be noisy?

- what kind of noise most commonly irritated people at work?

- what problems did noise have for people at work? (e.g. they had to shout to be heard, they had a headache most days, they went home with ringing ears most days)

- did most people know their hearing could be damaged by a noisy job?

- did most people protect their hearing at work?

- how did people protect their hearing in a noisy job?

Discuss how well you think your questionnaire worked. Did you ask the right questions to get the information you wanted? Did you miss anything out which you should have put in? Did you find out some interesting information about noise at work and the effects it has on how people feel and work?

Optional task Design a poster which warns people to take care of their hearing in a noisy workplace. Work in pairs or design a poster each and evaluate the finished work together. Either make the poster general to fit in with most noisy jobs or design it for one kind of job you are interested in.

Ear protection only works if you use ear plugs and muffs properly. Once your hearing is damaged it is permanent. The danger to your hearing depends on how loud the noise is and how long you are working in the noisy environment. Show a picture or cartoon of a noisy job and label the dangers. Offer advice on hearing protection. For example, show a DJ at work in a disco or a noisy workroom.

Display your posters and comment on the impact they all make. Would your posters persuade someone to protect their hearing at work?

(*See also* Worksheets: noise at work)

From this activity you may have evidence for:

Skills list 1, 2, 3, 4, 5, 6, 7, 8, 11, 12, 13/14, 15, 16.

Core skills Communication level 1 and 2.

Element 1.1/2.1 Take part in discussions.

Opportunities Discuss noisy jobs and the effects of noise.

Ask people to fill in a questionnaire.

Discuss the results of the questionnaire and answer questions.

Discuss and evaluate posters (optional).

Element 1.2/2.2 Produce written material.

Opportunities	Write a list of noises around you.
	Design and write a questionnaire.
	Write to the Health and Safety Executive for information.
Element	1.3/2.3 Use images.
Opportunities	Design a poster warning about noise at work (optional).
Element	1.4/2.4 Read and respond to written materials.
Opportunities	Read information about the problems of noise at work.

Activity 6 Investigate car alarms

Even though car alarms protect a car from being stolen they are a large source of noise pollution. Car alarms which are faulty and don't stop after a few minutes are a special nuisance. Car alarms make a very loud and disturbing noise. Some are so loud you can't hear yourself speak when you are standing nearby. If people report being disturbed by a faulty car alarm, an Environmental Health Officer, with the help of the Police, can break into the car and disable the alarm. The car may even be towed away. Before action can be taken however, the owner is allowed a reasonable time to return to their car. As the local Noise Team will not be able to react at once to a complaint, the faulty alarm will probably have disturbed a lot of people by the time it is turned off.

Investigate the uses and problems of car alarms.

Do you think car alarms are a good idea? Do you have an alarm on your car? Describe and discuss any experiences you have had with car alarms. For example, have you ever found you cannot turn one off? Have you ever set one off just by walking past a car? Have you ever been woken up in the early hours of the morning because of a car alarm? Have you ever seen a car alarm put off a thief?

Find out about the cost of having an alarm fitted, and the type of noise and level of sound the alarm makes (how many decibels). Find out how the alarm is activated and how long it will go on for if it isn't turned off by the car owner. What claims are made about the alarms by the makers? Allocate tasks to each other to carry out your investigation.

Find information about car alarms from car and motoring magazines in your local library. Contact car dealers or car organisations and ask for information. Talk to friends, family members or people you work with who have a car alarm. Find out what common problems people have with car alarms. Look through the Yellow Pages for Car Alarms and Security and contact car alarm fitters. Ask for information. Prepare your questions so you don't take up much of their time. Note down any information you receive.

 Use the worksheet provided to help you record and present the results of your investigation.

 When you have completed your investigation discuss what you have found out and decide if your opinion about car alarms has changed at all.

- do you think they are good value for money?
- do you think people have the right to protect their car and other people should put up with the noise?
- do you think the length of time an alarm is allowed to go on for should be controlled?
- do you think people who have faulty car alarms should be fined on the spot or given a set amount of time to have the alarm repaired?

Optional task Plan and write a letter as if you were writing to your local paper. Either defend car alarms as an important form of security or criticise them as a source of noise pollution. Look at the letters page of your local paper and discuss the style and length of letters the paper publishes. Write your letter in a similar way. Swap letters with each other. Read another letter and decide if the opinion expressed seems clear and reasonable.

(*See also* Worksheets: car alarm investigation)

From this activity you may have evidence for:

Skills list	1, 2, 3, 4, 5, 6, 7, 8, 11, 13, 15, 16.
Core skills	Communication level 1 and 2.
Element	1.1/2.1 Take part in discussions.
Opportunities	Discuss your experiences and opinion about car alarms.

Ask questions to gather information on car alarms.

Discuss the results of the investigation on car alarms.

Discuss the style and length of letters in a local paper (optional).

Element 1.2/2.2 Produce written material.

Opportunities Record the results of the car alarm investigation.

Write a letter to a local paper about car alarms (optional).

Element 1.4/2.4 Read and respond to written materials.

Opportunities Read information about car alarms in magazines.

Read the Yellow Pages for information on car alarm fitters.

Read the letters page in your local paper to find out about style and length (optional).

 ## Evaluation exercise

Discuss what you have learned about noise pollution. Do you think you'll be a quieter neighbour from now on? Do you feel more confident about dealing with noisy neighbours? Will you remember to protect your hearing from loud music or a noisy workplace?

Do you feel you have improved your speaking and listening skills? Are you more confident about asking questions to find out information? Have you collected some useful evidence in presentation or research skills?

Check your Skills Record Sheet is up to date so you can refer back to the skills you have covered. Record the resources you have used. Complete the Skills Summary Record making sure you write down all your progress and achievements. Record the evidence of competence you have for any accreditation you are working towards. Record details of skills you wish to practise further and decide on sensible goal dates.

Noise pollution top five

List your top five irritating sounds. Give each one a rating for how much it disturbs your daily life. For example:

*   = not very disturbing

**   = fairly disturbing

***   = very disturbing

**** = extremely disturbing

For each noise you list write down the main reasons why you feel it is noise pollution and how it affects you. For example, does the noise stop you sleeping, stop you working, make you feel angry or distressed, or give you a headache?

	Type of noise	Rating	Main reasons
1.			
2.			
3.			
4.			
5.			

Does noise pollution affect you?

Do some people seem to notice noise very easily?	Yes/No
Do some people seem to be able to ignore noise easily?	Yes/No
Do some people live in noisy homes and enjoy the noise?	Yes/No
Do some people live in quiet homes and enjoy the quiet?	Yes/No

Survey of noise pollution

Write down the different noises you hear as you survey your chosen area. Note down the type of housing. Some examples are listed for you. Add more to the list as you carry out the survey.

Keep a tally of how many times you hear each type of noise. Try to describe the typical situation, e.g. children playing in street. Describe the typical volume of the noise using a simple rating, e.g.

* = loud   ** = very loud   *** = extremely loud.

Noise	Tally	Level	Housing	Situation
Radio playing				
Heavy traffic				
Roadworks				
Gas repairs				
Water repairs				
Dog barking				
Car alarm				
House alarm				
Shop alarm				
DIY				
House building				
Television				
People arguing				
Children playing				
Pub or club				

Noise-free neighbours

Use this worksheet to help with the design of a leaflet or an audio tape.

Leaflet/flyer

Describe the problem and suggest some different solutions to try. Add a cartoon, photograph or drawing to each problem.

Problem	Solution
Loud television	Turn the volume down. Get a set of headphones. Move the TV away from a joining wall.
Doing some noisy DIY	Warn your neighbours. Tell them how long you will take. Don't start very early in the morning or carry on to really late in the evening. Be helpful if your neighbour works night shifts.
Loud radio/music	Don't turn your radio up so you can hear it in another room, take it with you. Remember, open windows in the summer will let more sound be heard by others.

Audio tape

Record different noises, for example, a dog barking constantly. Record interviews with people explaining how the noise makes them feel or how it disturbs them. Follow this with some sensible advice on how to reduce noise.

Include general advice to remind people to keep noise down and think about their neighbours.

Record your tape as if the situations and people are real, or record real situations, or do the whole tape as a comedy sketch but with a serious meaning.

Questions on noise pollution

Use these questions when you telephone the Environmental Health Service about noise pollution. Choose the questions which interest you and add more of your own. Decide who will be responsible for finding out each answer. Use this sheet to record the information.

If you have been able to arrange for someone from the Noise Team to visit your group choose which questions you would like to ask and decide who is going to ask each one. Record the answers you receive.

1. Can you give us some examples of how loud everyday noises are? For example, how many decibels is ordinary conversation or someone shouting?

2. What kind of noise do people complain about the most?

3. When someone contacts you to complain about noise pollution, what information do you need to deal with the complaint?

4. Do you think noise pollution is becoming a greater problem than ever before? If so, why?

5. Are noise levels permitted by law at work very different from the amount of noise householders are allowed to make?

6. What training do you need to become an Environmental Health Officer or a part of the Noise Team?

7. Do you have the power to enter private or business premises to deal with noise such as an alarm going off?

8. How much can people be fined for continually making a lot of noise?

Noise complaint record

Noise complaint record

To help the Noise Team investigate your complaint please keep a record of the noise which is causing you a problem. Fill in the dates when the noise arises and the time it starts and finishes. Describe how the noise makes you feel and any physical problems, such as loss of sleep for example.

As any steps taken by the Noise Team could result in court action you must make sure your record is as accurate as possible. Try to avoid general descriptions such as 'the noise goes on all the time'.

Your details:　　　　　　　　　　　　**Source of the noise problem:**

Name　　　　　　　　　　　　　　　　　Name

Address　　　　　　　　　　　　　　　　Address

Date	Start	Finish	Detail of noise	How it makes you feel

I declare that the above record is an accurate and true account of the noise I am complaining about

Signed　　　　　　　　　　　　　　　Date

Noise at work

Add to the following questions and layout to design your own questionnaire on noise at work.

1. Do you work in a noisy place?   Yes/No

If yes, what job do you do?

How loud do you think the noise levels are at work?

extremely loud / very loud / loud / fairly loud / not loud

2. Can you suggest any ways in which you think noise levels at work can be controlled?

3. What kind of noise would irritate you at work and why?

4. Tick which problems you think noise at work can cause:
   a. having to shout to be heard
   b. headaches
   c. ringing or buzzing ears
   d. tiredness
   e. feelings of irritation
   f. feelings of depression

Which of the problems listed, if any, have you experienced in a noisy workplace?

Any other problems?

5. Have you ever been warned about hearing protection at work? Yes/No

6. Have you ever protected your hearing at work?   Yes/No

If yes, describe which method of hearing protection you used and how useful you found it.

Car alarm investigation

Find out as much detail as you can about a range of car alarms. Visit car show rooms and shops, use the Yellow Pages, or write to alarm makers or the AA or RAC for information. Use your own knowledge or the experience of friends, family or other people you work with who have alarms fitted to their cars.

Make	Cost	Level of noise	Duration of noise	Claims by makers

What are the most common problems linked with car alarms?

1.

2.

3.

4.

Back to basics

Answers on p. 314.

Missing words

Fill in the missing words in this short text about noise pollution. Choose the words from the box below, or cover this up if you want to make the task a little harder.

harm	risk	protection	delicate
loud	tinnitus	exposed	long
permanent	level	noise	damage

Noise is a part of our daily lives. If _____ is at a reasonable _____ it can do you no _____, but if noise is very loud it may cause _____ to your hearing which can be _____. The _____ of damage depends on how _____ you are _____ to the noise and how _____ the noise level is.

After a time listening to very loud music can damage the _____ workings of your ear. Working with noisy machinery without any ear _____ can also cause you harm. Sometimes people who have damaged hearing may suffer from _____, which is a constant ringing or buzzing in their ears.

Careful reading

Read the following extract from an article in a local newspaper about a noisy neighbour and then answer the questions below. Try to write your answers in complete sentences.

> Residents of Quarry Road are up in arms over their noisy neighbour Mrs Alice Robinson. Mrs Robinson has a hobby which she really enjoys. Unfortunately her neighbours don't share her enthusiasm. They have got together to complain to the council, asking the Noise Team to sort things out. Her neighbours say they can't hold a conversation in the street because of Mrs Robinson's noise. The reason for the noise is her collection of 59 drums, which she keeps in her front room and plays every morning and evening. 'I always enjoy having a really good bash! It's a wonderful way to get rid of stress', says Alice.

1. Why are the residents of Quarry Street so upset?

2. How many drums does Mrs Robinson own and where does she keep them?

3. What time of day does Alice play her drum collection?

4. Who have the residents of Quarry Street turned to for help?

5. Do you think Mrs Robinson's neighbours have a reasonable complaint and why?

Matching up

Rewrite the following two lists. Each word in the first list must be opposite a word in the second list which has a very similar meaning.

List one	List two
damage	sound
delicate	guard
loudness	lifelong
noise	impair
danger	high volume
permanent	hazard
protect	fragile

Pollution and waste

INTRODUCTION

In this individual project on *pollution and waste* you will be able to:

- Carry out a survey to find out how much litter is dropped in your local area.

- Design a questionnaire to find out why people drop litter.

- Design a new type of litter bin.

- Design a poster to persuade people not to drop litter.

- Read a case study on a litter problem and decide what action should be taken.

- Find out how to recycle ordinary household items.

- Write a guide to easy recycling.

- Find out how to be a scrimper.

- Write a plan on how to make money from recycling.

- Carry out a survey on packaging.

- Design packaging and a label for a product.

- Write a letter to find out about the packaging policy of a High Street store.

Choose activities which interest you from the wide range of suggestions provided in the project. You can choose to do just part of an activity if you wish. The choice is yours. There are more suggestions in the Alternative Ideas section (p. 253), so you should find enough activities to suit your interests and needs. Finish with the Evaluation Exercise as this will help you think about your work on the project and remind you to record the skills you have covered.

For each activity you choose to do, use the information provided for you in the activity text and worksheets, as well as your own experiences and knowledge. If you need to look for more information consider resources such as books, newspapers and magazines as well as television, radio, video and CD-ROM. You can also use resources such as writing to an organisation or telephoning for information, talking to people you know or talking to other people who may be able to give you the information you need.

Optional task If you have more time available and would like to try another task to develop the skills you have already used in an activity, you can look for the Optional Tasks which are linked to many of the project activities.

You will find the following worksheets useful:

Pollution and waste

Activity 1   A survey on litter in your local area

Dumping litter and waste is a serious offence. If you drop litter or dump rubbish you can be fined up to £2500. Your Local Authority can apply to the Home Office to bring in bye laws to keep special areas free of litter and waste. These bye laws will be different in every part of the UK, as each Local Authority will have different concerns. For example, you may live in a holiday resort. Your Local Authority will be concerned about keeping popular areas clean and tidy to attract tourists. They may have a poop scoop bye law which means people must clean up after their pets in certain local areas.

If a litter problem can be traced to a local business, shop or take-away for example, the council can issue a Street Litter Control Notice. This means the owner of the take-away must keep the area in front of the shop, as well as either side, free from litter.

Carry out a survey to find out how much litter and rubbish is dumped in your local area. Survey either an area around your home, where you work, or a local park or shopping area.

Use a local street plan to choose an area to survey. Decide what you are going to look for while you are out and about. Write to an organisation such as the Tidy Britain Group for more ideas and information about litter and the law. Write to them at Tidy Britain Group, The Pier, Wigan, WN3 4EX and ask for the leaflet *Litter and the Law*. Enclose a stamped, self-addressed envelope with your letter.

Read through the following suggestions for your survey. Add more ideas of your own:

■ Decide which part of your local area seems to have a litter problem and carry out your survey there.

■ Look for hot spots for litter such as cafés, take-aways, the corners of streets, empty buildings, etc. List the hot spots and explain why they are litter traps.

■ Count the litter bins in the area you are surveying. Decide if there are enough and if they have been put in the best places.

■ What different kinds of litter can you find, e.g. paper, food, glass, cans, carrier bags, pizza boxes, dog waste, etc? Which is the worst kind of litter in your opinion?

■ Are there any signs in the area you survey which explain that dropping litter is an offence?

 Present your survey sheet as a series of questions for yourself, with yes or no answers to tick. Make sure it is easy to complete while you are out and about. Decide on a simple rating scale for some questions, such as 1 = a lot of litter about, up to 5 = no litter at all. Use the worksheet provided to help you set out your survey and record your results.

Take photographs of hot spots while you are carrying out your survey. Video part of your litter survey if you have access to the equipment. Photograph or video examples of bad litter areas and areas where litter is being cleared up.

 When your litter survey is complete, use the results to write a description of your local area.

■ Describe how much and what kind of litter you found.

■ Describe if you found litter everywhere or just in certain hot spots. Explain possible reasons for this.

■ Describe any signs of litter being cleared up.

■ Describe how people are encouraged to throw litter away safely, for example, notices or litter bins.

Use photographs to illustrate your description. Highlight on a street plan the worst litter areas and where the cleanest places can be found.

If you were able to video the survey use your description to record a spoken commentary on the survey results.

Optional task   Draw a design for a completely new type of litter bin which encourages and rewards people who throw away their litter safely. Cut out the pieces you need for your design from old magazines or use graph paper to help plan the outline. Be as creative as you can and have fun thinking up an unusual litter bin which could really work. For example, your design may work like a pin-ball machine or arcade game or have a mechanical grabber which takes the litter from your hand! Consider how to make your litter bin vandal proof.

Show your finished design to friends or people you work with. Ask them if your design would encourage them to throw away their litter safely. Do people who are parents feel it would help them teach their child to care for the environment by making throwing away litter a fun thing to do? Improve your design if you receive any helpful feedback.

(*See also* Worksheets: litter survey)

From this activity you may have evidence for:

Skills list	1, 3, 4, 6, 10, 11, 12, 13/14, 15, 16.
Core skills	Communication level 1 and 2.
Element	1.1/2.1 Take part in discussions.
Opportunities	Record a commentary for your litter video.
	Ask people for feedback on your litter bin design (optional).
Element	1.2/2.2 Produce written material.
Opportunities	Write to the Tidy Britain Group for information.
	Write and carry out a survey on litter.
	Write a description of survey results.
Element	1.3/2.3 Use images.
Opportunities	Use photographs, street plan or video images to illustrate a description of litter.
	Use a street plan to select the survey area.
	Draw a design of a new type of litter bin (optional).
Element	1.4/2.4 Read and respond to written materials.
Opportunities	Read information about litter laws for ideas for survey questions.

Activity 2   Design a questionnaire to find out about litter habits

Litter is always unpleasant to see on the streets, in parks, in play areas and in the countryside. Have you ever been to a lovely place and thought it looked a mess because there was so much litter about? Even when rubbish is put in a bin it can still be a problem. Bins soon fill up and if they aren't emptied regularly the rubbish overflows. The council collects the waste, much of which could have been recycled, and puts it in a land fill site. Many sites are well planned and eventually landscaped with grass and trees. However, some are unpleasant to look at and cause a nuisance by attracting rats and seagulls.

Design a questionnaire and ask friends, family members and people you work with about their litter habits.

For example, ask:

- do they drop litter?
- is there any kind of litter they wouldn't drop?
- do they feel guilty about dropping litter?
- do they ever try to dispose of litter safely?
- do they notice litter around them and think it looks unpleasant?
- would they change their litter habits if they were fined on the spot by a Litter Warden?
- do they know it is an offence to drop litter?

Present your questionnaire so yes or no answers can be recorded. Provide space for longer replies to be written where appropriate. Either explain the questionnaire and tape the answers, or leave people with a copy of the questionnaire to fill in for themselves. Use the worksheet provided to help you write your questionnaire.

Read through the answers you have collected from your questionnaire. Do most people have some good litter habits and some bad habits? Decide if there are more good or more bad habits overall. Write a short report about the main litter habits people seem to have. Decide if, in your opinion, people could be persuaded to change any bad habits for better ones and if so can you suggest how this may be achieved?

Optional task Design a poster to try and persuade people to stop dropping litter. You could target a local area which is very dirty, or a well-known beauty spot which gets a lot of visitors and a lot of litter! Use the worksheet provided to give you some ideas for your poster design. Copy your poster and put it up where people will see it. Visit the area a few days later and see if your poster has had any effect on the amount of litter dropped.

(*See also* Worksheets: questionnaire about litter. Ideas for poster design)

From this activity you may have evidence for:

Skills list 1, 3, 4, 6, 8, 10, 11, 12, 13/14, 15, 16.

Core skills Communication level 1 and 2.

Element	1.1/2.1 Take part in discussions.
Opportunities	Ask people to complete a questionnaire about litter habits.
	Record answers on tape.
Element	1.2/2.2 Produce written material.
Opportunities	Design and write a questionnaire about people's litter habits.
	Write a short report on questionnaire results.
Element	1.3/2.3 Use images.
Opportunities	Design a poster to persuade people not to drop litter.
Element	1.4/2.4 Read and respond to written materials.
Opportunities	Read and assess questionnaire information.

Activity 3 — Consider a case study about a litter problem

Read through the following case study carefully and decide on what action could be taken to improve the problem.

Tony lives just around the corner from a fish and chip shop. He is fed up with the amount of litter dropped outside the shop which gets blown or trampled about and ends up in his front garden. There is a waste bin outside the shop but it's usually overflowing with rubbish. It never seems to be emptied. Tony has been into the shop to have a chat with the owner and to ask if anything can be done to prevent the large amount of litter. The owner says that he provides a litter bin and it is not his problem if people choose not to use it. He says there is nothing more he can do. Tony did persuade the owner to empty the bin more often, which he did for a while, but it was soon overflowing again.

What can Tony do next? Find out how this irritating litter problem can be sorted out. Write down a summary of the action Tony should take.

Telephone your local council's Environmental Health Department and ask for information to help with your answer. Find the number in your telephone book. Describe the problem and ask what they would advise someone like Tony to do. Ask for information about a Litter Control Notice which can be issued to a business. This obliges the owner to keep their shop premises free of litter. Use the worksheet provided for some tips on asking for information on the telephone.

Contact the Tidy Britain Group (01942 824620) which is a registered charity interested in litter control and the siting of litter bins. Contact your local Citizens' Advice Bureau for information about dealing with litter nuisance.

Present your suggestions for the action Tony should take as a short summary, listing each step.

Talk about the case study with a friend or someone you work with. Ask them if they feel the actions you have suggested seem sensible and effective.

(*See also* **Worksheets: telephone tips**)

From this activity you may have evidence for:

Skills list	1, 3, 4, 6, 7, 8, 10, 13, 15, 16.
Core skills	Communication level 1 and 2.
Element	1.1/2.1 Take part in discussions.
Opportunities	Telephone the local council or Tidy Britain Group for information.
	Discuss your summary of action with another person.
Element	1.2/2.2 Produce written material.
Opportunities	Write a summary of action for the case study problem.
Element	1.4/2.4 Read and respond to written materials.
Opportunities	Read the case study carefully.
	Read information about litter control.

Activity 4 Find out about easy recycling

These are some of the easiest items to recycle:

- **Aluminium cans** are worth recycling as aluminium is a useful metal. It's used in window frames, saucepans and foil as well as drinks cans. It's an expensive metal to produce, so it's sensible to recycle it and not just dump it in a land fill site.

- **Glass** is worth recycling. It is easy to deposit it in bottle banks found in many supermarket car parks today. The glass can be melted down and new bottles made. This saves a lot of energy which would have been used in processing raw materials. Recycling your glass bottles safely also cuts down on the amount of dangerous litter which ends up in gutters, parks and beaches.

- **Paper** can be recycled easily. If more people bought envelopes, writing paper, toilet rolls and kitchen towels made from recycled paper there would be a bigger demand for these products.

- **Plastic** can be recycled. You can easily re-use plastic bags but there may be only so many plastic ice cream cartons or squash bottles you can make use of at home! Many recycling centres now take plastics. Items such as squash bottles and detergent bottles can be marked with a code so they are easier to sort. Once sorted they can be flattened down into bales and sent to a variety of industries around the country who recycle plastics into new products.

Find out how easily you can recycle everyday household items in your area. Write *The Lazy Guide to Recycling* for yourself, friends and family members to use. Make recycling sound easy to do!

 Find information for your guide to easy recycling by contacting your council and asking about their services. They may operate a system of delivering several different waste bags to a household. Waste can then be sorted at home into different types, such as garden waste, food, paper, glass, etc. Find out about recycling opportunities by going around your local area and looking out for facilities. Telephone local businesses or charities and ask them how they collect items they need. Use your telephone book or Yellow Pages. The Citizens' Advice Bureau may be able to give you some more ideas. Ask people you know who already do some recycling. Ask for their tips on easy recycling. Record their replies on tape so you can replay the information to use in your own time.

 Present clear instructions in your guide on how to recycle as many ordinary household items as possible, with the least amount of effort.

■ give information about the nearest bottle, paper and can banks

■ give information about clothing banks – the Salvation Army may have one in your area – or local charity shops which take clothing

■ give information about book banks, or centres which are glad to receive old magazines

■ show where these recycling facilities are by use of simple plans or maps marked with the locations

■ provide a telephone number for any local businesses who will collect paper, for example, from your home

■ list information about any charities who will collect clothing, small electrical items or bric-à-brac from your home

Show a picture or photograph of each type of item to be recycled and give instructions for how easy it is to dispose of. If you prefer, put *The Lazy Guide to Recycling* onto an audio tape. Design an attractive cover and an insert leaflet or card showing plans or maps.

Show your finished guide to friends, family members or people you work with and ask for their comments. Would they be encouraged to recycle more household items by using your guide? Does the guide make recycling sound easy to do? Use any worthwhile feedback you receive to improve your guide.

Optional task A scrimper is someone who enjoys and is good at finding a use for everyday items which would normally be thrown away. Be a scrimper for a day.

Look at all the things you would have thrown away in a day and try to think of another use for everything.

For example:

- put out the day's food scraps for the birds, or start a compost heap
- re-use envelopes from the day's post by sticking a label over the address
- cut up any reasonable paper for a shopping list pad
- shred old paper for bedding for a hamster or rabbit
- decorate plastic ice-cream tubs to make storage boxes or use for bath toys for children
- re-use old shoes as unusual planters for the garden – hang them up by the laces with trailing plants inside for a novel hanging basket!

Write about your scrimping experiences by listing the new uses you have found for each item you would normally have thrown in the bin. Try out some of your ideas. Write down what worked and what didn't. Talk about your scrimping with a friend. Decide if you will carry on with a little scrimping in the future.

(*See also* Worksheets: easy recycling)

From this activity you may have evidence for:

Skills list 1, 4, 6, 7, 8/9, 10, 11, 13/14, 15, 16.

Core skills Communication level 1 and 2.

Element 1.1/2.1 Take part in discussions.

Opportunities Ask friends and other people for ideas on easy recycling.

Telephone the local council for information on recycling.

Telephone local businesses and charities for information.

Ask people for comments on your guide.

Produce an audio tape version of your guide.

Element 1.2/2.2 Produce written material.

Opportunities Write a guide to easy recycling.

Write a scrimping list (optional).

Element   1.3/2.3 Use Images.

Opportunities   Use maps, plans and pictures in the recycling guide.

Design a cover and insert for audio guide.

Element   1.4/2.4 Read and respond to written materials.

Opportunities   Read information about easy recycling.

Read the Yellow Pages for information on recycling facilities.

Activity 5   Write a plan for making money from recycling

You can make money from recycling, but it does take some imagination, energy and time! For example, on average we get through 100 aluminium cans per person each year. That is a lot of cans, but only a small number of them are recycled even though there are can banks provided in most local areas. The makers of drink cans can save up to 95% of the energy they would use to make a can from raw materials by recycling old cans. They will buy back the cans from people who collect them. Collect cans from family members, friends and people you work with and sell them back to the makers for a profit! Read the ideas below for making money from recycling. Think of more ideas to add to the list.

Car boot sale   Rent a table at a car boot or table top sale and sell all the things you were going to throw out anyway. By planning ahead you sell well and make some money. Choose which sale you go to carefully. Look around for one which attracts a lot of customers. Arrange your stall so the items can be seen clearly and look attractive. Make it easy for customers to pick things up. Group the same kind of items together, such as clothes, books, tapes, children's toys, shoes, jewellery, games, bundles of magazines and kitchen items. Decide how much you hope to get for each item. Be prepared to bargain! Don't accept low offers at the beginning of the day. Reduce your prices when the sale is beginning to close down. Be cautious if you find you have a lot of customers just as you are setting up your stall or putting away at the end. These will often be dealers who offer you next to nothing and then re-sell the item for twice the price on their own stall!

Dress agency   Find a dress agency in your area. You can take all sorts of clothing to them so long as it is neat and clean. They will try to sell it for you and charge a small commission. Check how much they take for the service and how long you can leave your clothing there before you must collect what has not been sold.

Rags   Collect jumble clothing and cut up into small strips. Sort into bags of colours and make some simple rag rugs. Design the pattern on a computer paint program. Sell your rag rugs at craft fairs or visit a craft shop and see if they will take your rugs on a sale or return basis. Get orders from friends or family who would like a rug for themselves.

Metal Visit your local tip and see what you can recover to repair and sell. Look for bicycles. They are often thrown away because of a broken chain or twisted handle bar. Get a book from your library about how to repair and maintain a bike. Sell the bikes you repair.

Chairs Learn how to upholster chairs or repair rush seating by going on a short course at your local college. Get a book or video from your local library on repairing chairs. Recover chairs from the tip, repair them and resell them.

Glass Collect some nicely shaped glass bottles. Clean them thoroughly inside and out. Fill them with a good vegetable oil, add herbs and spices and seal the bottle. Leave for several days while the oil takes on the flavour of the herbs. Find ideas for flavoured oils from cookery books in your local library. Sell your flavoured oils. Rent a table at a local craft fair and sell your crafts.

Cardboard Make A4 files and box files for storing paper or magazines from old cardboard cartons from your supermarket. Make storage holders for tapes and CDs. Paint and varnish them or cover them in fabric, or layer them with magazine cut-outs. Design the covers to meet people's special requests.

Newspaper Make egg shapes or heart shapes from papier-mâché using old newspapers. Paint and varnish them and sell as attractive containers for soaps, pot pourri or chocolates.

Plants Collect petals and flower heads, leaves and seed heads from your garden and turn them into pot pourri. Get a book from the library to find out how to make different varieties. Pack bundles with cellophane and ribbon and sell them.

Cards Recycle old greetings cards to make new ones. Make pop-up cards and 3D cards. Make cards to order featuring the person's favourite things. Collect old cards from family and friends.

Choose a product which interests you from the ideas you have read about. Carry out a careful investigation to find out if you can make money from recycling.

■ Find out if you can collect the recycled materials easily. Check what would be easy and what might cause you problems.

■ Work out exactly what your expenses would be. Do you have to buy any equipment?

■ Find books, magazines or videos for information on how to make your recycled product. Is it easy to make? How much time would the product take to produce?

■ Find out by asking friends or people you work with if there is a market for your recycled products. Are people interested in buying your products?

Write down a plan on how to go about your money-making idea. Use the worksheet to help you. Compile a good, detailed plan and have a go!

Review the progress of your recycled products. Are the materials easy to collect? Are you spending a reasonable amount of time on the product for the money you make? Is it worth continuing with your money-making plan?

(*See also* Worksheets: making money from recycling)

From this activity you may have evidence for:

Skills list   1, 4, 6, 7, 8, 10, 12, 13, 15, 16.

Core skills   Communication level 1 and 2.

Element   1.1/2.1 Take part in discussions.

Opportunities   Ask people for recycling ideas.

Talk to people about your product idea.

Element   1.2/2.2 Produce written material.

Opportunities   Write a detailed plan for making money from recycling.

Element   1.4/2.4 Read and respond to written materials.

Opportunities   Read information about making money from recycling.

Read information in books and magazines about skills for making a chosen product.

Activity 6   Carry out a survey on the use of packaging

Many ordinary products on the supermarket shelves have just too much packaging. Some products can cost twice as much because of all the expensive packaging. Buying fruit, apples for example, in a plastic tray and wrapped in more plastic can cost twice as much as apples sold loose. This can happen with other fruits and vegetables sold in your local supermarket. You pay a lot of money for the wrapped product because it looks nice and it's quick to pick up when you're in a hurry, and then you throw all the packaging away when you get home. You have spent extra money and created more rubbish to fill your bin. A large amount of household waste comes from packaging, most of which will end up in the nearest land fill site. Buy goods which are not pre-packed or over-packaged, or have reuseable packaging.

Some items, foods in particular, need to be packed to keep them clean and fresh and away from contact with other foods so bacteria cannot be spread. Some packaging is there for safety reasons, especially to protect children from dangerous substances. Packaging can also provide a place for important information to be printed about the product. This might tell the shopper how to use it or what the ingredients are, for example. Packaging can also protect the product and stop it from getting broken or squashed.

There is a need for some packaging. However, there are still many items which have been over-packaged to persuade the shopper to buy them or to make them into a nice, easily stackable shape!

Carry out a survey on four ordinary household items which you buy weekly and four luxury items which you might buy just for a treat or a celebration. Make a list of the items.

Visit a few local shops or one large supermarket where you can look at several different brands of your chosen items. Write down the details of the most over-packaged example you can find of each item on your list. Write down details of the least packaged example you can find of each item. Note down the cost of each item. Pick examples which are the same size or weight so you can compare their packaging fairly. Use the worksheet provided to help you record your findings.

Look at the results of your short survey and use them to answer the following questions:

■ are there any products from your list which seem to use a lot of packaging?

■ can you provide any reason for the packaging or is it being used only to persuade a customer to buy the product?

■ is there a similar product which uses much less packaging?

■ are luxury items usually over-packaged or do some basic items also use too much packaging?

■ if you bought all the over-wrapped items you saw, what kind of packaging would you be throwing away?

■ would you save much money if you always chose the least wrapped choices? Do you think it is worth doing?

Choose one item from your survey which uses a lot of unwanted packaging. This must be any packaging which is not needed to protect the item from damage or provide the customer with information. Draw a diagram of the packaging, labelling all the unwanted parts.

Draw a second diagram showing how you would package the item. Label how your packaging protects the product, gives information or can be recycled. Design a simple label or logo which could be put on products which use the minimum amount of packaging, so the shopper can spot these items easily. Your label could also contain some suggestions on recycling the packaging.

Less packaging would mean less weight to carry home and a lot less rubbish to fill up the bin. Show your diagrams to friends or people you work with and explain what you have tried to achieve. Which packaging do they prefer and why? Do they think it is a good idea to choose products with the least amount of unwanted packaging? Would they choose products with the least amount of packaging if there was a label to help them spot these items easily?

Optional task   Choose a large, well-known High Street store. Find out if they have a policy for trying to reduce the amount of packaging they use. For example, Sainsbury encourages the recycling of carrier bags by giving a small amount of money back for every carrier a customer reuses. Boots and Our Price both ask customers if they would like a bag. If you are only buying a couple of small items you can manage quite well without a bag and so have less rubbish to put in your bin. The Body Shop will refill containers for you rather than using new containers every time.

Find out about your chosen store's policy by writing a letter to ask for the information. If you prefer, telephone and ask for the information. Ask:

■ is the customer left to decide if they need a bag?

■ do they offer unwrapped choices of products rather than all pre-packed?

■ do they refill containers or ask customers to return bottles or containers?

■ do they try to keep their packaging to the least amount needed?

■ do they have any recycling facilities on site?

(*See also* **Worksheets: survey of packaging**)

From this activity you may have evidence for:

Skills list	1, 3, 4, 6, 8/9, 10, 11, 12, 13/14, 15, 16.
Core skills	Communication level 1 and 2.
Element	1.1/2.1 Take part in discussions.
Opportunities	Ask friends for comments on diagrams of your packaging and label.
	Telephone a High Street store and ask questions about their packaging policy (optional).
Element	1.2/2.2 Produce written material.
Opportunities	List items for survey.
	Write and carry out a survey on packaging.
	Write a letter to a High Street store to find out about their packaging policy (optional).
Element	1.3/2.3 Use images.
Opportunities	Draw a diagram to show how packaging can be reduced.
	Design a label or logo to show a product has the least amount of packaging.
Element	1.4/2.4 Read and respond to written materials.
Opportunities	Read information on packaging to find out why it has been used.
	Read information about packaging policies (optional).

Evaluation exercise

Think about what you have achieved during this project on pollution and waste. Do you think you will be more careful about disposing of litter from now on? Do you think you will try to recycle more household items? Will you try making some money from recycling? Do you think you will try to buy products which haven't been over-packaged?

Do you feel more confident about carrying out a survey and recording the results? Do you feel your skills in finding information have improved? Do you feel more able to speak to a variety of people or telephone for information?

Check your Skills Record Sheet is up to date. Use this to remind yourself about the evidence you have to show your ability in skills you have practised. Complete your Skills Summary Record. Write down the details of all you have achieved. Evaluate your progress and write down details of evidence you have for an accreditation or award you may be working towards. Make a note of skills you need to practise further and set yourself a date to complete the work.

Litter survey

Use some of these questions in your survey on litter. Add more so you get a clear picture of the litter situation in the area you survey. Take photographs or video evidence of litter or evidence of litter being cleared away.

Is there litter about?	Yes/No
A lot / quite a lot / very little	
Does the litter look unpleasant?	Yes/No
Does it spoil the area?	Yes/No

What kind of litter and rubbish has been dumped?

(circle choice)   paper   household waste

                            food   dog waste

                            glass   other litter

                            cans

Which is the most common type of litter?

Can you see any reason for this? Explain.

Are there any hot spots for litter?	Yes/No

If yes, explain what they are.

Do you think there are enough litter bins around?	Yes/No
Have they been put in the right places?	Yes/No
Is there evidence the bins are being emptied regularly?	Yes/No
Have you seen anyone drop any litter?	Yes/No

Are there any signs that litter is cleared up, e.g.

someone employed to pick up litter?	Yes/No
local business clearing up, sweeping up?	Yes/No
signs telling people not to drop litter?	Yes/No

Questionnaire about litter

Use some of these questions for your own questionnaire. Add more ideas of your own.

Check you have asked questions which are going to give you the kind of information you need, and that all of your questions are clear. Check you have provided enough space for people to write their answers. Thank people for taking the time to complete your questionnaire.

1. Do you drop litter? Never / Sometimes / Often

2. If you don't drop litter, do you Take it home / Put it in a bin

3. Do you notice litter around you? Yes/No

4. Do you think litter looks unpleasant? Yes/No

5. Do you think people are more likely to drop litter if there is already a lot of litter about? Yes/No

6. Which of the following do you feel is the most serious?

Litter on local streets

Litter in a local play area

Litter in a local beauty spot

Litter blown into your front garden

Explain the reason for your choice:

7. If a friend dropped some litter would you suggest they pick it up? Yes/No

8. If a child dropped some litter would you suggest they pick it up? Yes/No

9. Do you think there are enough litter bins provided in public places? Yes/No

10. Why do people drop litter in your opinion?

11. What is the worst litter you see in your local area?

Ideas for poster design

Use this worksheet for presentation ideas. Choose one of the messages for your poster design. Keep your poster bold and striking so people will notice it. Put it up in an area where there is litter. Return a few days later to see if your poster has had any effect on people's litter habits.

Messages

- Give examples of how litter has harmed wildlife.

- Warn people about the law, e.g. you can be fined for dumping litter and waste. Find out more about new regulations and put some facts on your poster.

- Ask local businesses to provide more litter bins outside their premises.

- Tell people about the large amount of money spent on cleaning up litter. Suggest some things which the money could be better spent on in your local area.

Presentation

- Use pictures from old magazines, line drawings, cartoons or photographs of litter in your local area.

- Cover your poster with words which describe litter.
  For example:

  muck, rubbish, waste, debris, refuse,
  garbage, trash, junk, scrap

  Use a thesaurus to find more words.

  Use different kinds of print to write the words. Print out different sizes and styles on a computer. Present all the words in a heap, like a pile of litter.

- Show a dirty, littered scene and label all the dangers to people, animals and the environment from litter. Warn people about the dangers of disease caused by contaminated waste.

- Show an overflowing litter bin in the middle of a local beauty spot with scavenging birds and rats picking at the rubbish.

Multi-use ■ *Use this worksheet for help on asking for information by telephone.*

Telephone tips

■ Check you have the correct telephone number before you dial. Write down the name of the person you want to speak to or department, so if you get a little flustered you won't forget who you want to contact.

■ Think carefully before you begin your call about the questions you would like to ask or what information you need to find out. Write them down so you can't forget. Practise them before you telephone if you wish.

■ You may get through to a switchboard first of all. Don't waste time explaining why you are calling to the operator or receptionist, just ask to be put through to the named person or department.

■ When you have been connected to the right person or department, explain briefly why you are telephoning. This checks you are speaking to a person who can help you before you launch into your questions or requests.

■ Speak as clearly and politely as you can. Give the other person time to think about your questions or requests before you rush on to the next one.

■ Explain or ask your questions in a sensible order.

■ Make sure you listen carefully to any information you are given. Ask the person to repeat anything you didn't hear or understand. Ask for more information if you are not clear about anything.

■ Make notes to help you remember the information you are given either while you are speaking on the telephone or immediately afterwards.

■ Make sure you have plenty of change if you are in a pay phone.

■ Finish the conversation and remember to say thank you!

Easy recycling

Use this worksheet to help you design your guide, showing how easy it is to recycle ordinary household items.

What do I recycle?　　**Where do I take**　　**Why bother?**
　　　　　　　　　　　　　　each item?

1.

2.

3.

4.

What other household items　　　**Where do I take each item?**
can I recycle easily?

1.

2.

3.

4.

5.

Which items can be collected from my home?

Who collects them and how often? (the council, a charity?)

What kind of recycling banks do I have within walking distance of my home?

Where are they located? (Include a plan or map of location)

If I use my car to go to a recycling centre, who can I share the trip with to make it worthwhile?

If I only go monthly to a recycling centre, how can I store items for recycling safely?

　　stack newspapers in bales
　　flatten drinks cans carefully and store in a bag
　　wash plastic bottles and flatten, store in a bag
　　pack bottles in a box or carton
　　fold clothes and store in bin liner

Any other ideas:

Making money from recycling

Use this worksheet to help you record your plans for making money from recycling.

Outline of money-making idea:

What item will be recycled?

Will I collect enough from my own home or do I need to collect from friends?

What information do I need to collect? (circle choice)
   where to go for a selling outlet
   how to book a space for a stall
   how to advertise
   who to ask for advice or tips

What I need:

Do I need to learn any new skills?   Yes / No

If yes, how? (Circle choice)
   a friend could show me   a book from the library
   a short college course   a television programme
   an instruction video   a club or organisation

Do I need to spend any money on tools, equipment, advertising to get started on my idea?   Yes / No

If so, what do I need and how much will it cost?

Items   Cost

Who do I think my customers will be and how can I make sure I reach them?

I will begin my plan for making money by recycling on
I will review my progress on   and decide if it is worth the time and effort spent.

What is a realistic profit to expect?

Survey on packaging

Ordinary household goods chosen for survey	Luxury household goods chosen for survey
1.	5.
2.	6.
3.	7.
4.	8.

Details of least packaged goods found on survey
(brand name, cost and type of packaging)

1. £ packaging
2. £ packaging
3. £ packaging
4. £ packaging
5. £ packaging
6. £ packaging
7. £ packaging
8. £ packaging

Details of most over-packaged goods found on survey
(brand name, cost and type of packaging)

1. £ packaging
2. £ packaging
3. £ packaging
4. £ packaging
5. £ packaging
6. £ packaging
7. £ packaging
8. £ packaging

Choose the most over-packaged item you found in your survey. List the unwanted packaging:

Product   Cost £

Wasted packaging

Give details of how much money and packaging could be saved if a similar product which uses the least packaging is chosen:

Product   Money saved £

Packaging saved

Back to basics

Answers on p. 315.

Missing punctuation

The text below, which is about packaging, has no punctuation. Rewrite the text, replacing capital letters, full stops and commas.

packaging is important to protect preserve and keep products fresh when the customer buys goods they expect them to be in good condition safe packaging on medicines can help keep dangerous drugs away from children most packaging is thrown away as soon as the goods are brought home from the shops we can help to protect our environment by choosing products which use the least amount of packaging wherever possible packaging removed from products should be recycled by taking it to a local recycling centre

Jumbled sentences

Sort out these jumbled-up sentences. The capital letters and full stops give you a clue about where the sentence begins and ends.

1. reduces the waste of materials. raw Recycling

2. can be recycled. which items Choose

3. litter. Don't drop

4. dropping litter. can You for fined be

5. litter can people harm and Dangerous wildlife.

6. recycle items household to Try such as glass, paper drinks cans. and

Scan and read

A Mother and Toddler group have organised a meeting to find out about the dangers of infection from dog waste. This infection, called toxocariasis, can cause serious illness in young children. Answer the questions which follow by looking at the notice for the information. Try to write your answers in complete sentences.

Woolton Mother and Toddler Group
invite you to hear Dr Andrew White
talk about the dangers to our children
of dog waste on streets and play areas.
Meeting begins 2 PM
on Friday
In Woolton Community Centre
Everyone Welcome!
* Free Crèche facilities * Free refreshments

1. Who has organised the meeting?

2. What is the name of the speaker?

3. What is the speaker going to talk about?

4. Where is the meeting going to take place?

5. What facilities have been arranged to help mothers come to the meeting?

6. Explain the meaning of the logo on the notice.

Alternatives **Other ideas for activities on pollution**

Any activity from the suggested group and individual projects can be replaced with an idea from the list below. Use the list to give you more choice of activities to do which suit your needs, interests and the amount of time you have available.

■ Follow the progress of one household item as it is recycled. For example, find out how glass is reused, or how plastic drinks bottles are recycled. Research using your library, or write to the Department of the Environment or to a company which recycles the item you are interested in.

■ Make a video of how much litter is dropped in your local area. Use the video to try and persuade people to be tidier in a play area or park or sea front for example. Question people after they have watched your video to see if they feel their opinions about litter have changed.

■ Design a fact pack about recycling for use in a local school. Decide on the age group you wish to target. Design activities, quizzes, experiments and surveys for the children to carry out. Provide a review sheet and ask for comments about your fact pack.

■ Find out how to recycle large household items in your local area. Design a recycling passport. Include details of where to take items such as old sofas, a mattress, garden waste, hard core or top soil, tyres and refrigerators, for example. Provide space in the passport for people to mark off each time they recycle a large item.

■ Write to an organisation such as Friends of the Earth and ask them about their work. You may know of a project they might be interested in in your local area. Ask for their suggestions about the project. It could be anything from saving a small piece of woodland to clearing up a local play area.

■ Carry out a survey in your local supermarket or shopping High Street. Find out what products you buy which have been made from or packaged using recycled materials. Write a directory for other people to use who wish to buy goods made from recycled materials or packaged with recycled materials.

■ Select a group of friends or people you work with and carry out an investigation into how loudly they like to play their personal stereo. Produce a poster or leaflet which warns people about hearing damage from loud equipment. Find out how irritating people find noise leakage from others' personal stereos. Ask people to complete an agreement to try to cut down on noise.

■ Arrange to visit a noisy workplace. Write a detailed description of how the noise made you feel.

■ Collect information about one aspect of pollution such as noise nuisance or energy wasting and have a debate about whether the efforts of just one person can make a difference to the environment. Collect newspaper articles and examples to argue your case.

Living with animals: pets and people

INTRODUCTION

In this group project on *living with animals: pets and people* you will be able to:

■ Discuss and list the responsibilities of being a pet owner.

■ Design and write a guide for pet owners.

■ Discuss why people enjoy keeping exotic or dangerous pets.

■ Write a checklist for giving a good talk.

■ Give a talk, using visual aids, about a pet.

■ Organise a fun quiz about pets.

■ Carry out an investigation into the cost of pets.

■ Discuss how the death of a pet affects the owner.

■ Write a letter to an animal charity for information or arrange for a speaker to visit.

■ Organise a fund raising event for a local charity.

■ Discuss the dangers of dog litter in public places.

■ Review television adverts and discuss the use of animals in advertising.

■ Evaluate your work on the project.

Choose activities which interest you from the wide range of suggestions provided in the project. You can choose to do just part of an activity if you wish. The choice is yours. There are more suggestions in the Alternative Ideas section (p. 304), so you should find enough activities to suit your interests and needs. Finish with the Evaluation Exercise as this will help you think about your work on the project and remind you to record the skills you have covered.

For each activity you choose to do use the information provided for you in the activity text and worksheets, as well as your own experiences and knowledge. If you need to look for more information consider resources such as books, newspapers and magazines as well as television, radio, video and CD-ROM. You can also use resources such as writing to an organisation or telephoning for information, talking to people you know and talking to other people who may be able to give you the information you need.

Optional task   If you have more time available and would like to try another task to develop the skills you have already used in an activity, you can look for the Optional Tasks which are linked to many of the project activities.

You will find the following worksheets useful:

Living with animals: pets and people

Activity 1   ## Write a guide to being a pet owner

Being a pet owner can bring many benefits. For example, a pet:

- offers an excuse to have some exercise
- brings fun, enjoyment and company
- may offer some security at home
- can offer chances to meet other people, e.g. pet shows
- can offer chances to make money, e.g. breeding animals
- can give children a chance to learn how to be caring

Being a pet owner can also bring many responsibilities. Add more ideas to the list below:

- **Money**   Pets can be very expensive, needing food, equipment, and care when they are ill. They may live for a long time so this expense can be a long term commitment.
- **Time**   You must have enough time to give to your pet. Even a small animal such as a rabbit needs time and attention. If you have a busy life and are out and about a lot, you may not really have time for a pet.
- **Space**   Think about how big your pet will become. A very small snake can become a huge adult snake. Do you have enough space in your house for your chosen pet? An animal can become stressed and aggressive if it doesn't have enough space.
- **Training**   Are you prepared to train your pet properly? For example, people who are not dog lovers do not enjoy having a badly behaved dog jumping up at them. Untrained or badly trained animals can harm people or damage their surroundings. Training takes time and effort and may cost money if you have to ask for help.

■ **The law**   Do you need a licence for your pet? Have you chosen a pet which it is illegal to own? Some animals are protected species and shouldn't become pets.

■ **Disease**   Are you allergic to your pet's fur, hair or the dust from its body? Check you are careful about hygiene around your pet. It's easy to catch disease but also to spread disease to your pet. For example, a hamster can catch your cold!

■ **Holidays**   What you will do with your pet if you go on holiday? It could be expensive if you have to pay for it to be looked after. It can be difficult to find a friend to help if you have an unusual pet. If you take your pet on holiday, will it restrict where you can go?

■ **Family**   Have you chosen a pet which is suitable for the age range and people in your family? Iguanas make interesting pets but a male iguana may not always react well to women in the household. By confusing them with the scent of another male iguana your pet may spend a lot of time in display behaviour. Who will be in charge of the pet? If you are sharing make sure everyone is clear about the tasks they have to do.

■ **Care**   Consider how much love and attention your pet will need. Are you prepared to play with your pet, and keep it stimulated and exercised? Are you prepared to care for it when your pet is no longer a cute baby?

 Discuss why so many people choose to have a pet. Talk about the responsibilities a pet owner must accept. Design and write a guide for people who would like to become pet owners.

 Make a list of the things you think people should be aware of before becoming pet owners. Make notes or write down your ideas on a board or large sheet of paper. Find out more about the problems of being a pet owner by interviewing some pet owners you know. Ask them if there are things they wish they had thought about before getting their pet.

Write to the RSPCA for information and advice about being a pet owner. Go into local pet shops and ask for ideas. Listen to a phone-in on the radio or look out for useful television programmes on pets. Allocate tasks to each other to get the research work done. Work in pairs on each part of your guide.

Present your guide as a fact pack or a set of cards linked together, each dealing with one part of your guide. Offer sensible and practical advice on what to find out about before getting a pet. Use the worksheet provided to help you with ideas for how to present your guide. Share out the tasks of producing your guide with each other.

Discuss your finished guide. Are you all happy with how it is presented? Show your guide to other people and ask for their comments. Do they feel your guide would be useful if they were considering getting a pet? Revise your guide if you get any helpful comments and feedback. Make copies of your updated guide and give them to people considering getting a pet.

Optional task   Discuss why people enjoy having dangerous or exotic pets which are difficult to keep. People keep exotic reptiles, insects and birds. Dogs which are part wolf, a mixture of German Shepherd and wolf called wolf-hybrids, are becoming popular. These dogs are not covered by the Dangerous Dogs Act and yet owned by a poor handler, they could easily harm someone. Children would be in danger from the wolf-dog's hunting instinct.

Discuss your opinions about why people keep unusual, exotic or dangerous animals as pets. Make sure everyone has a chance to put their point of view. Do you know anyone who keeps an unusual pet? Have they had any problems? Summarise your opinions and decide who is for and against people keeping dangerous or exotic pets.

(*See also* Worksheets: a guide for pet owners)

	From this activity you may have evidence for:
Skills list	1, 2, 3, 4, 5, 6, 7, 10, 11, 12, 13/14, 15, 16.
Core skills	Communication level 1 and 2.
Element	1.1/2.1 Take part in discussions.
Opportunities	Discuss why people own pets.
	Discuss what people should consider before becoming pet owners.
	Ask a variety of people questions to find out information about being a pet owner.
	Ask for comments on the finished guide.
	Discuss keeping dangerous or exotic pets (optional).
Element	1.2/2.2 Produce written material.
Opportunities	Write to the RSPCA for information about being a pet owner.
	Design and write a guide for pet owners.

Element	1.3/2.3 Use images.
Opportunities	Illustrate the guide using diagrams, photographs and pictures.
Element	1.4/2.4 Read and respond to written materials.
Opportunities	Read the reply from RSPCA and use the information in the guide.
	Read books and magazines for information about being a pet owner to use in the guide.

Activity 2 Give a planned talk about a pet

Give a talk to each other or a small, invited audience, about a pet you have or once owned. If you prefer, talk about a pet which is owned by a friend. Work in pairs on a joint talk if you wish.

Discuss how the information can be delivered in an interesting way. Help each other with ideas for all of the talks. Find out as much about your pet as you can. Offer information about the animal as well as personal comments.

For example, suppose one of the talks is about a parrot.

- **Do some research**: add background information. Find out about the different colours, names and countries of origin for parrots and how long they can live, for example.

- **Use visual aids**: collect photographs, or a tape recording of a parrot's call or one talking with its owner.

- **Talk about common problems**: describe the illnesses a parrot can suffer and common treatments needed. For example, overgrown bill or claws, feather loss.

- **Talk about the benefits**: describe the funny habits and intelligence of the bird which make it an enjoyable pet.

Use the worksheet provided for more planning ideas for your talks.

Discuss how to present a good talk. Write a checklist for how to plan and present a talk. Use your checklist as a guide for presenting your own talks to each other.

Include some of the following ideas in your checklist and add more of your own:

- **Plan your talk** carefully. Give it a simple structure so it is easy to understand. Start with an introduction. The middle part will contain most of the information you wish to talk about. Sum up at the end and answer any questions.

- **Make some notes** on what you plan to talk about. Write these as a clear list on a piece of paper, or on pieces of card with one point on each piece. Put these aside as you cover each point. Notes help you to deal with nerves. If you forget what you were going to say you can glance at your notes for help.

■ **Use body language**: your facial expressions, gestures, body position and eyes can all show how enthusiastic you are about your talk. Good body language can help keep your audience interested. Poor body language such as lack of eye contact, a wooden face or nervous habits can irritate people trying to listen to your talk.

■ **Use your voice** with care. Make sure you can be heard by your audience. Speak clearly and at a reasonable pace, not too slowly and not too quickly. If you are feeling nervous it is tempting to speak quickly and get your talk over and done with! Try to slow down if you feel this is happening. Change the tone of your voice to make it sound interesting. Imagine you are just telling a story to a good friend.

■ **Listen** to the person speaking. Make an effort to be a good audience for each other. Listening doesn't mean just sitting doing nothing, it is an active role. Look at your speaker, nod and use facial expressions to show you are listening. Make 'agreeing' sounds or laugh or smile at a joke. Make notes about the talk or about questions you would like to ask when the talk is over.

When you have presented all of the talks to each other, give some feedback about the talks. Discuss how useful you found your group checklist on presentation. Comment in a positive way on what was enjoyable about each talk. Write a short review each about one of the talks you listened to.

Optional task

Organise a fun quiz about pets. Make up a large chart showing pets belonging to yourselves and to celebrities. Provide a list of names of the owners. Ask people to successfully match as many pets to their owners as they can. People sometimes say that owners look a little like their pets. Find out if this is true!

Research in magazines and newspapers to find pictures of the pets owned by sports stars, pop and film stars and other famous people.

Have fun with your quiz and discuss why people pick surprising pets. You may find a film star with a tough-guy image owns a toy dog or fluffy cat or cuddly rabbit! You may think someone is a dog lover and find out they collect spiders.

(*See also* Worksheets: plan a talk)

From this activity you may have evidence for:

Skills list	1, 2, 3, 4, 5, 6, 7, 8, 9, 10, 11, 12, 13/14, 15, 16.
Core skills	Communication level 1 and 2.
Element	1.1/2.1 Take part in discussions.
Opportunities	Discuss what to include in a talk and how to present the information.
	Present a talk to the group.
	Discuss the talks and offer feedback.
	Discuss celebrities and their pets (optional).

Element	1.2/2.2 Produce written material.
Opportunities	Write a checklist for giving a good talk.
	Write a plan for a talk.
	Make notes about a talk.
	Write a review of a talk.
Element	1.3/2.3 Use images.
Opportunities	Use visual aids in a talk.
	Produce a chart showing pets to be matched to their owners for a fun quiz (optional).
Element	1.4/2.4 Read and respond to written materials.
Opportunities	Read and use information to plan a talk.
	Read newspapers and magazines for information about famous people's pets (optional).

Activity 3   Carry out an investigation into pet costs

Pets can be expensive to keep. Tropical fish are popular pets and often become an interesting hobby for their owners. What costs are involved? For example:

- buying and replacing different varieties of fish
- buying equipment to house the fish
    - a large tank with a lid and stand
    - a heater
    - a light
    - a spare tank for cleaning or for young fish
    - gravel, tank ornaments, weed
    - tank cleaning tools
    - gravel filter system
    - a water aeration system
- buying medicines for sick fish
- buying dried and fresh fish food

Some of these costs may be small or equipment may not need to be replaced very often. However, fish can live for a long time if properly cared for and some varieties can be expensive. Tanks may need to be replaced with larger versions if the pet owner becomes very keen on fish!

Carry out an investigation to find out just how much a pet can cost its owner. Discuss and agree on five popular pets you would like to find out about. Pick some small and some large pets.

List all of the costs you can think of which the owner would have to be prepared to pay for the lifetime of the pet. Costs can vary a great deal depending on your chosen pet. There would be a big difference between the cost of keeping a hamster which lives for around two years to keeping a large dog for around fifteen years, for example.

Find out about costs by asking friends how much they spend caring for their pets. Visit pet shops and ask for information. Write down the cost of food and equipment. Find out about the cost of insurance for your chosen pets. It may cover vet's bills if the animal needs an operation or expensive treatment.

Visit a local vet's surgery and pick up leaflets about the cost of common treatments such as clipping claws or overgrown teeth, vaccinations and flea treatment. Find a local club for the type of pets on your list, they may be able to give you information about possible expenses. Visit your local library for books or magazines about your selected pets for ideas about possible costs.

Compare the costs of keeping each of your chosen pets for a week with some common household expenses. For example, is one of your chosen pets as expensive as feeding a family of four for three days or running a car for a day?

Allocate the research tasks between you. Meet up again and pool your collected information. Use the worksheet provided to help you with your research.

Present the information about the costs of keeping a pet as a poster. Feature each pet, showing a photograph of the animal with its typical costs labelled around it. If you prefer, present the information as a chart using colour to show which pets are the most expensive to keep.

Discuss the results of your investigations. Are you surprised at some of the hidden expenses you discovered? Do people bother to think carefully about cost before choosing a pet do you think? Will you think more carefully about pet expenses before committing yourself to keeping an animal? Put your poster or chart where people can read it. Ask people you work with if they are surprised at the costs involved in owning a pet.

Optional task   A further expense for a pet owner can be when your pet dies. This may not be a big problem when your pet is a hamster or a gold fish but is much more expensive if your pet is a large dog. If you have a friendly vet they will take your pet for disposal for a small charge.

Many people prefer to arrange for a beloved pet to be buried at a special pet cemetery. A pet may have been part of the family for a long time and its unexpected death from an accident or even death from old age can be very upsetting. Pet owners can be helped by being able to bury their pet in beautiful surroundings.

Find out where your nearest pet cemetery is and the costs involved in having a pet cremated or buried in the cemetery. Discuss the costs and facilities and decide if you think pet cemeteries offer a useful service.

Ask a local vet for information. Contact your local council for advice or the Citizens' Advice Bureau. Write to the RSPCA who might be able to help you with some information about regulations concerning pet burial and where pet cemeteries are located in the country. Look in the Yellow Pages. Ask friends and people you work with about the kind of arrangements they have made for pets who have died.

Use the information you have collected to either write an advert for a pet cemetery for the classified section in a newspaper, or record a message which someone would hear if they telephone the cemetery for information. Describe the facilities on offer at an ideal pet cemetery.

Discuss how to word your advert or message. A distressed pet owner must be made to feel their pet is going to be put to rest in a pleasant and sympathetic way. For example, you may offer a plaque, a shrub or tree planted in memory of the pet, or an entry in a book which is opened to view on the anniversary of the pet's death. Put the information in your advert or telephone message.

(*See also* Worksheets: record of pet costs)

From this activity you may have evidence for:	
Skills list	1, 3, 4, 5, 6, 8, 10, 11, 12, 13/14, 15, 16.
Core skills	Communication level 1 and 2.
Element	1.1/2.1 Take part in discussions.
Opportunities	Ask a variety of people for information on pet costs.
	Discuss the results of your investigation.
	Record a telephone advert for a pet cemetery (optional).
	Ask a variety of people for information about pet cemeteries and costs (optional).
Element	1.2/2.2 Produce written material.
Opportunities	Write a list of possible pet costs to investigate.
	Record your findings on pet costs.

Write to the RSPCA for information (optional).

Write an advert for a pet cemetery (optional).

Element   1.3/2.3 Use images.

Opportunities   Present the results of your investigation as a chart or poster.

Element   1.4/2.4 Read and respond to written materials.

Opportunities   Read leaflets, books and magazines for information on pet costs.

Read and use information from the RSPCA (optional).

Activity 4   Find out about the work of an animal charity

The RSPCA began when a group of men met in a London coffee house to discuss the cruel way in which animals were treated. This was the 19th century, when it was common for people to beat animals almost to death to make them work harder. The aims of the RSPCA remain ones which try to prevent cruelty and encourage people to act with kindness towards their animals and pets.

Find out about the work the RSPCA does with pet animals, or a local charity in your area which helps abandoned or ill-treated pets. The RSPCA also tries to find new homes for pets which people can no longer keep because of money difficulties or because someone in the family is allergic to the pet. You may know of a local charity which specialises in a particular kind of service, for example, releasing captive birds of prey back into the wild or rescuing exotic pets which people cannot cope with any longer.

Agree on your choice of charity and research and collect information about it. Discuss what you would like to find out about the work of your chosen charity. List the questions which you could ask in a letter or in a discussion with a representative from a charity.

Select and ask some of the following questions:

- when was the charity set up and who by?

- are all the people who help run it volunteers?

- do people bring animals to you?

- do you go out and rescue animals which people have reported are in trouble?

- what kind of prosecution can you bring against people who have abandoned or ill-treated a pet?

- what kind of care do you give animals you take in?

- what is the worst case of ill-treatment you have seen?

- how many animals do you find new homes for each year?

- how much does the charity cost to run each year?

- how do you raise money?

Find out information by inviting someone to come and speak to the group and answer your questions in person. Check you make proper arrangements, such as booking a room, sorting out seating and arranging for refreshments. Allocate tasks to each other to arrange for a visiting speaker. Prepare any equipment your speaker needs such as an OHP or video player for example.

If a visit is not possible write a detailed letter asking a range of questions to your chosen charity. Write to several charities and compare the work they do. Plan your letters carefully together. Select the questions you ask so you find out what you would like to know. Make sure the letters you send are clear and enclose a stamped and addressed envelope.

When you have met and questioned a charity representative or received a reply to letters, discuss what you have found out about one or several charities. Do you think they do some useful work? Why do you think people ill-treat pets so that there is a need for the charities' work?

Optional task   Organise an event to raise some money for a chosen animal charity. Organise a coffee morning where you charge people for entry or a large raffle or tombola. Organise a sponsored event such as a walk, swim, trampoline bounce or how long a team of people can keep a shuttlecock in the air. Discuss how you can raise money for your chosen charity.

Discuss in detail what you want to do, and who is responsible for each task. Make a list so everyone can remember the jobs they are responsible for. If you are well organised you can enjoy the event yourselves. Use the worksheet provided to help check all the important details have been organised for the event.

Design an attractive poster advertising your event. Give details of why you want to raise money, the time, date, place and cost of the event. Do plenty of advertising by putting up posters and by telling people about the event. Advertise your event on local radio.

(*See also* Worksheets: organise a fund-raising event)

From this activity you may have evidence for:

Skills list	1, 2, 3, 4, 5, 6, 7, 8, 10, 11, 13/14, 15, 16.
Core skills	Communication level 1 and 2.
Element	1.1/2.1 Take part in discussions.
Opportunities	Discuss questions to find out about an animal charity.
	Question and respond to a visiting speaker.
	Discuss the arrangements for a fund-raising event (optional).
Element	1.2/2.2 Produce written material.
Opportunities	Write a list of questions to ask an animal charity.

Write a letter to an animal charity asking for a variety of information.

Record and allocate tasks to run a fund-raising event (optional).

Element   1.3/2.3 Use images.

Opportunities Design a poster to advertise a fund-raising event (optional).

Element   1.4/2.4 Read and respond to written materials.

Opportunities Read responses to written questions from a chosen animal charity.

Activity 5 Find out about the dangers of dog litter

One problem for pet owners is how to cope with the waste products their pets produce. This is not a big problem if your pet is small, although you should always remember to wear rubber gloves when you clean cages and tanks out. It is easy to pass on infection to your pets or catch diseases from them yourselves.

Dogs cause a different problem because so many owners allow their dogs to foul pavements, play areas, canal footpaths and public parks. Dog litter is a serious problem, more than just an unpleasant sight and smell and a messed-up shoe! The problem is also Toxocara, a round-worm carried by puppies and some adult dogs. The round-worm's eggs are passed on by dog waste. Dog owners are not obliged to have their dogs 'wormed' and so the disease can be spread.

The toxocariasis disease can cause fevers and coughs in people. More seriously, it can also cause asthma, epilepsy or blindness. Children are the most at risk because they play in public areas. They touch all kinds of things and may put their hands in their mouth or suck their thumb. If they have accidentally touched some dog waste they can spread the disease to themselves. The eggs can survive in the earth for up to three years!

'Poop-scooping' is a safe and sensible thing for all dog owners to do. Poop Scoops can be bought easily in pet shops, or an old plastic bag would do just as well. Many councils are now providing plenty of dog litter bins so owners can dispose of their dog's litter safely.

Design and print a flyer about the dangers of dog litter. Imagine you are a parents' group, campaigning for streets and parks in your area to be clean of dog waste. Design the flyer as if it is going to be put through everyone's door in your town. What could you say which would persuade dog owners to be more concerned and more careful?

Discuss ideas for your flyer. What do you all think about the problem of dog litter in public places? What do you think dog owners should do about the problem? Do you think there should be on-the-spot fines for owners of dogs who foul public places? Should there be more dog-free zones in the centres of towns and in parks?

Find out more about the problem from your local vet. Visit your local library and look for articles in magazines about the infections passed on by dogs. Ask your local council for information on local policies for fining owners of dogs who foul the pavements. Adults can avoid dog litter as they walk about but children find it harder to do so and need to be protected. Discuss your views together, making sure everyone has a chance to speak. If someone in the group has visited another country where different rules are enforced about dog litter, talk about those as well.

Discuss how to present the information on your flyer. Your flyer must be attractive and easily readable. Collect and look at a range of flyers to see how other people have tackled the problem. Find a selection at your local library or at a Tourist Information Centre, or collect flyers from home. They are often put through the door or inside the pages of free newspapers. Collect some examples between you and assess how they work. Include a logo on your flyer which represents or explains what your campaign is about. The two examples below give you ideas which you could use or adapt.

Draw out a variety of design ideas for your flyer. Look at all of the designs. Take the best elements from each one and combine them into one agreed design.

Evaluate your final flyer design. Does the design work? Have you given enough information for people to take the problem seriously? Show your flyer to a range of friends and people you work with. Ask dog owners, people who don't own a pet and people with young children. Ask them to comment on your flyer. Does it influence a dog owner who up to now has not been bothered about their pet's waste? How many people have never heard of the problem?

Discuss the feedback on your flyer. If you really were a group of people campaigning against dog litter in public places, would your flyer have helped the campaign?

From this activity you may have evidence for:

Skills list   1, 2, 3, 4, 5, 6, 7, 8/9, 11, 12, 13/14, 15, 16.

Core skills   Communication level 1 and 2.

Element	1.1/2.1 Take part in discussions.
Opportunities	Discuss different views on the nuisance of dog litter. Ask a variety of people for information on toxocariasis.
	Discuss the design for a flyer.
	Ask people for reactions to the flyer design.
	Discuss the feedback on your flyer.
Element	1.2/2.2 Produce written material.
Opportunities	Write out a design for a flyer with text giving information.
Element	1.3/2.3 Use images.
Opportunities	Design a logo for use on the flyer.
Element	1.4/2.4 Read and respond to written materials.
Opportunities	Read information on toxocariasis infection to use on a flyer.
	Collect and read various flyers and assess designs.

Activity 6   Review the use of pets in advertising

The use of pets and other tame animals to sell products in television advertising is popular. The advertisers know their customers enjoy the 'ah' factor produced by the cuddly or amusing little animals. This helps to sell the products. Another popular method is to put human thoughts and words into the mouths of the animals, as if they think like you do. Do you think watching a puppy play with toilet paper makes you choose that brand when you are looking at a shelf full of similar products in your local supermarket?

Agree to watch as many adverts as possible on television which feature pets or other tame animals. Track the showing of your chosen adverts for an agreed time or number of days, noting down when they are shown. If you prefer, video a selection of adverts using pets and watch them together.

Use the worksheet provided to help you record information about the adverts. Use the information you collect about a variety of adverts to discuss why you think advertisers use animals to sell products. Make some notes about your ideas as you discuss them.

Ask yourselves:

■ are all the adverts which use pets advertising products for pet care or pet food?

■ how are the pets used in the adverts? are they seen doing natural activities?

■ which different animals have you seen used in adverts and is it a wide range?

■ are the pets shown in adverts given human thoughts and voices and if so, why?

- which group of consumers is likely to be influenced by the use of animals in each advert?

- which kind of pets do you never see used in adverts and why do you think this is so?

- have you ever been persuaded to buy a product because of a cute pet you saw in an advert?

Collect more information about the use of pets in advertising. Write to a commercial television station or the makers of the product used in an advert. Ask about the guidelines they have for the care of animals used in commercials. The RSPCA may be able to give you information about regulations concerning the use of animals.

Use the information you have collected from your reviews, replies to letters and discussion to write a range of questions about the use of pets in advertising. Agree to interview two or three people each and use the questions you have written together. Record the replies you receive on tape or make notes. Report back to the group to pool the results of your interviews. For example, ask:

- can you think of any adverts you see on television which use pets?

- which adverts using pets do you enjoy watching and why?

- which do you find the most entertaining – animals involved in natural activities in adverts or copying human behaviour?

- have you ever been persuaded to buy a product because of an advert you have seen which uses a pet?

- are there any animals currently used in adverts which you think shouldn't be used?

- are you a pet owner?

- would you offer the services of your pet for an advert?

Share the results of your short interviews. Did you find evidence that people liked watching adverts which used familiar pets? Did you find any evidence that using pets in adverts persuaded people to buy products?

(*See also* Worksheets: record of advert information)

From this activity you may have evidence for:

Skills list   1, 2, 3, 4, 6, 7, 8, 10, 11, 12, 13, 15, 16.

Core skills   Communication level 1 and 2.

Element   1.1/2.1 Take part in discussions.

Opportunities   Discuss and agree which adverts to watch on television.

Discuss the content of adverts which use pets and express your own views.

Discuss the results of interviews with a variety of people.

Element   1.2/2.2 Produce written material.

Opportunities   Record advert review information.

Write a letter to a television station or product advertiser for information about the use of pets.

Compile a list of questions to ask people about pets in advertising.

Element   1.4/2.4 Read and respond to written materials.

Opportunities   Read information received about pets in advertising and use to write questions for an interview.

Evaluation Exercise

Discuss your work on this project about pets and people. Will you think carefully before getting a pet? Will you be careful about dog litter and make sure a child in your care doesn't come to any harm? Will you think about how cute, cuddly animals used in adverts might persuade you to buy products you don't really need?

Do you feel more confident now about giving a talk? Do you feel your presentation skills have improved? What progress have you made towards gathering evidence for assessment? Do you feel more confident about making arrangements for a special event or being part of a group event?

Check your Skills Record Sheet is up to date in case you need to refer back to it. Record details of skills you have practised and resources you have used. Fill in your Skills Summary Record. Record the evidence you have of competence towards an accreditation you are studying for. Write down details of your achievements and progress so far. Which skills do you need to practise further? Write down details of skills you need to work on next.

A guide for pet owners

Think about your guide

Write a guide which helps people decide which pet is the right one for them. List advice under a series of headings, e.g. time, money, space. Provide choices with tick boxes to help people decide on a suitable pet. List a series of popular pets. Give information about each one such as the care the animal needs and whether it is an ideal pet for a child, single person or family.

Present your guide

Present a small brochure or leaflet. Design an attractive cover, have a contents page, use pictures, diagrams and photographs.

or

Present a fact pack. List all the important facts about each animal you feature, so they can be seen at a glance. Include photographs. Add addresses to write to for more information about each pet or useful books to read.

or

Present linked cards. Use pieces of coloured card linked together at the corner. Each piece features one pet or one area of concern such as cost, space, etc. Provide a contents card so someone using your card system can find the card they need.

Example layout
(Include a drawing or photograph of the pet)

Garter snake   Grows to about 1 metre and is completely harmless. Can live to about 12 years of age.

Housing   Large tank with lid and controlled heating for snake to bask. Large water dish for snake to lie in. Needs rocks and hiding places.

Food   Feed weekly on whole fish or earth worms or strips of meat. Include vitamin powder.

Handling   Don't handle after feeding. Pick up the snake near the centre of its body. Support the body as it moves through your hands.

Cleaning   Remove droppings, making sure you wear rubber gloves. Wash tank out well once a month.

Comments   Very interesting pet to watch. Need a friend also interested in snakes to leave pet with when you go on holiday.

Multi-use ■ *Use this worksheet for ideas on planning a talk.*

Plan a talk

Plan

Draw a diagram of what you could include in your talk. Write down ideas just as they come to you without thinking too much about them at this stage. For example:

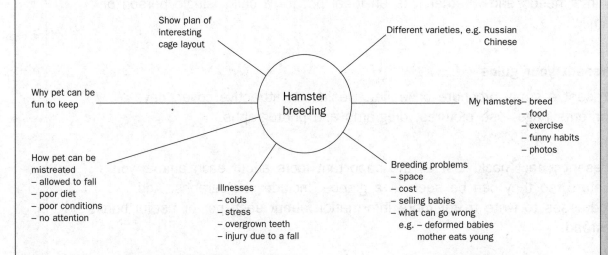

When your ideas are written down, look over them and cross out anything you don't need. Number the rest of your ideas in the best order to talk about them. Think about what you would like to say about each numbered point.

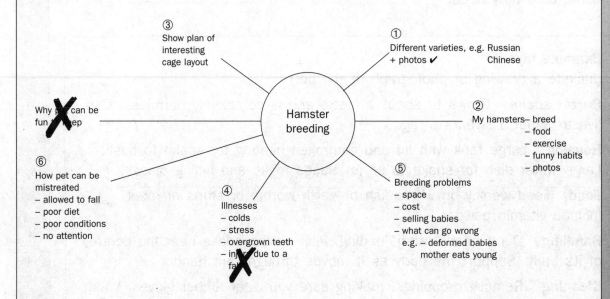

Write some notes to remind you of your plans and collect the visual aids you need.

Final tips

■ **Practise**   Practise your talk in front of a mirror or tape it. Get rid of any irritating habits you didn't realise you had! Imagine yourself giving a very successful talk. It will give you confidence!

■ **Smile**   If you look as if you are enjoying yourself, your audience will.

■ **Questions**   Keep questions until the end. This way interruptions won't put you off.

■ **Nerves**   Take a few deep breaths. Count four in and four out. It really does work! Don't worry about making mistakes. Just pause for a moment and then carry on.

■ **Visual aids**   Give people a chance to look at the things you show. It's hard to look and listen at the same time, so pause before you carry on talking.

Record of pet costs

Repeat the format of this worksheet for every pet you find out about.

Pet	Cost of buying pet

Minimum equipment needed

Description		Cost
1.		
2.		
3.		

Type of food

Description and quantity	How often purchased	Cost
1.		
2.		
3.		

Bedding

Description and quantity	How often replaced	Cost
1.		
2.		
3.		

Common problems

Treated by vet	How often problem likely to occur	Cost
1.		
2.		
3.		

Other expenses e.g. electricity, kennel fees, licence, etc.

Details	How often?	Cost
1.		
2.		
3.		

Multi-use ■ *Use this worksheet for ideas on organising a fund-raising event.*

Organise a fund-raising event

Write out a large version of the chart shown below. Use it to keep track of all the tasks which must be completed. Decide who is responsible for each one.

Two weeks to go	One week to go	On the day

Tick off each item as you complete your arrangements

1. Agree on the event and stick to your idea. ☐

2. Allocate tasks to each other. Arrange for a review on agreed dates to check on progress. ☐

3. Agree on the budget you have to spend. ☐

4. Book a space for the event, for example a room, hall, gym or field. Check there are enough power points and where they are located. ☐

5. Book equipment, e.g. a microphone or P.A. system. ☐

6. Organise publicity for the event, for example poster, flyers, word of mouth, local radio, etc. Check your publicity is accurate – date, time, place. ☐

7. Shop around for the best deal for any equipment or consumables you need to buy. Keep receipts so you can see how money is spent. Ask for discount or for free items. People can be very generous! ☐

8. Print sponsor sheets or tickets if you need them in good time. Sell them in advance or ask for sponsors. ☐

9. If you are having a sponsored event you may need an adjudicator. Ask someone who is reliable! ☐

10. Collect raffle prizes or tombola prizes from local businesses. ☐

11. Issue any special invitations in good time. Is someone going to open the event? This can be an attraction if it is someone well known. ☐

12. Arrange to clear up after the event. Check you allocate these tasks fairly as it can be hard work! ☐

Record of advert information

Use this layout to help you record information and comments on each advert which uses pets you review. Repeat the format for each advert.

Advert one

Description of product advertised

Does the product have anything to do with animals?   Yes/No

Channel   Frequency of advert over a day

Length of advert (seconds)

Times shown during day

Who is the target audience?

Animal(s) used in advert

Is the animal a popular pet?   Yes/No

Description of how the animal is used:

   seen behaving naturally   Yes/No

   seen working   Yes/No

   seen in natural setting   Yes/No

   seen in relationship with people   Yes/No

   given human thoughts or words   Yes/No

Why do you think the animal was chosen for this advert?

In your opinion does the use of the animal in the advert make you:

Remember the advert?   Yes/No

If yes, explain why

Go and buy the product?   Yes/No

If yes, explain why

Choose the product rather than another similar product?   Yes/No

If yes, explain why

Back to basics

Answers on pp. 315–16.

Careful reading

Read the following text carefully and then answer the questions which follow. Write your answers in complete sentences.

Anne was waiting to see her dentist and was feeling very nervous. She glanced through a pile of magazines stacked on a small table nearby and picked up one about gardening. She tried to read an article on how to make a compost heap, but her attention soon wandered. She looked over towards the window and noticed a fish tank in the corner.

It was an attractive tank. Its colours and the movement of the fish caught Anne's attention. She moved closer for a better look. Strands of weed swayed gently, stirred by the bubbles rising from the air tube. Orange and white fantails idled slowly around a miniature sunken ship. Anne was fascinated. Tiny, bulgy-eyed, black fish wiggled clumsily through the weed looking quite comical beside the sleek comets. A small basket floated on the surface of the water. The fish darted at it hungrily to grab mouthfuls of food.

Suddenly, Anne heard her name called and realised it was her turn.

1. Why was Anne feeling nervous?

2. What did Anne do to help pass the time as she waited?

3. Why did the fish tank attract Anne's attention?

4. Which different varieties of goldfish did Anne notice?

5. Why did Anne think the black fish were comical?

6. Would you find watching fish relaxing while you were waiting for an appointment and if so, why?

Muddled and missing words

Sort out the muddled-up words below, which are all names of common small pets.

stremah	bartib	brileg
gerigrabud	neagui gip	dolgshif

Use the pet names you have just sorted out to replace the missing words in the sentences below about pets and pet care.

a) Handle it with care and a _____ will become very tame.

b) A _____ enjoys the company of other familiar animals.

c) Never pick a _____ up by its ears, support it underneath its body.

d) A _____ enjoys eating cereals and plenty of fruit and green vegetables.

e) A large tank with a lid to keep out dust is ideal for _____.

f) If trained early a _____ should talk to its owner.

Quick reading

Look through this advert, which could have been taken from the Yellow Pages, and answer the questions below.

Angus Pet Foods

All major brands of foods and dried food stuffs.

** Trade enquiries welcome
** Competitive prices
** Delivery service
** For expert advice with
   friendly personal service

Telephone Angus Birtwell 01729 726591

1. Who is advertising?

2. What kind of service does this business promise?

3. What do you think the phrase 'competitive prices' means in this advert?

4. What would make you notice this advert among many others in the Yellow Pages?

Living with animals: people working with animals

INTRODUCTION

In this individual project on *people working with animals* you will be able to:

■ Research how working dogs benefit people.

■ Write a report or leaflet explaining the work of a charity which uses working dogs.

■ Carry out an interview to find out about a working animal.

■ Write an advert for a working or open farm.

■ Carry out an investigation into the Freedom Food Scheme.

■ Design a display for an exhibition about a working animal for a local Heritage Centre.

■ Write a guide for how to arrange a group outing.

■ Investigate a range of products to find out which have been tested on animals.

■ Write a shopper's guide for cruelty-free products in your local area.

■ Research and write a profile of a race horse.

■ Evaluate your work on the project.

Choose activities which interest you from the wide range of suggestions provided in the project. You can choose to do just part of an activity if you wish. The choice is yours. There are more suggestions in the Alternative Ideas section (p. 304), so you should find enough activities to suit your interests and needs. Finish with the Evaluation Exercise as this will help you think about your work on the project and remind you to record the skills you covered.

For each activity you choose to do use the information provided for you in the activity text and worksheets, as well as your own experiences and knowledge. If you need to look for more information consider resources such as books, newspapers and magazines as well as television, radio, video and CD-ROM. You can also use resources such as writing to an organisation or telephoning for information, talking to people you know and talking to other people who may be able to give you the information you need.

Optional task   If you have more time available and would like to try another task to develop the skills you have already used in an activity, you can look for the Optional Tasks which are linked to many of the project activities.

You will find the following worksheets useful:

Living with animals: people working with animals

Activity 1   **Write a report about working dogs**

Dogs are often used to help people who have special problems and needs. Through poor eyesight or blindness, a person may have difficulty moving around outside their home. They may need to travel as part of their job and a dog can help them become more mobile and independent. Hearing dogs are trained to alert their owners to sounds such as the telephone ringing, the door bell or a baby crying. Dogs can become hospital visitors. These animals will be people's pets. They will be well behaved, gentle dogs and friendly towards people. They are taken into hospitals, hospices and homes for the elderly for people to make a fuss of and enjoy contact with an animal again. The work these dogs do is thought to be very useful and adds to the therapy of giving patients laughter and enjoyment.

Carry out some research about one type of working dog. Find out how they are used to help people cope with special problems.

 Ask yourself some questions to answer by collecting information. For example:

- what problems are experienced by the person needing the dog?

- which breeds of dog are most commonly used to help and why?

- how are the animals selected?

- what are the different stages of their training?

- how are the dogs taught special skills?

- how do these skills meet the needs of the people who use the dogs?

- who pays for the training and how is the money raised?

- how are dogs matched to people?

- does the owner need to be trained as well?

- what happens to the dogs when they are too old to work?

Find out about the problems people have to cope with and the work of your chosen dog. Collect photographs, pictures and newspaper articles. Find out which charity, if any, is associated with the work of the animals. Write to them or telephone for information. They may be able to send you leaflets or put you in touch with someone in your area who can answer your questions. Use the worksheet provided to help you plan and record your research.

 When your research is complete, use the information you have collected to present a detailed outline of the work of your chosen animal.

Imagine you are a volunteer for a charity or local group who support the work of the dogs you have been finding out about. The group needs money for its work. You have been asked to write a detailed outline of the work of the group. It will be sent to local businesses in the hope of receiving a donation to help the group's work. Explain in your outline the work of the dogs and the needs of the people who use the dogs. Use photographs or diagrams to illustrate your outline.

Set out your outline as a short report or leaflet. Use the worksheet provided to help you plan your writing.

 Check your written outline. Do you think your description would persuade someone to make a donation? Show your outline to a friend or someone you work with and discuss whether it is clear and gives interesting information. Would it persuade them to make a donation?

Optional task   Arrange to interview someone who has a working dog. Ask them questions about the benefits the dog brings to their life. Prepare your questions carefully. Record the replies you receive either by making notes or by taping the interview.

Write a description of a typical day the dog and its owner experience and how they overcome common problems together.

(*See also* Worksheets: working dogs, part one and part two)

From this activity you may have evidence for:

Skills list	1, 3, 4, 6, 7, 8/9, 10, 11, 12, 13/14, 15, 16.
Core skills	Communication level 1 and 2.
Element	1.1/2.1 Take part in discussions.
Opportunities	Telephone for information about the work of a charity which uses dogs.
	Ask a variety of people for information about working dogs.
	Discuss your written outline with someone and ask for feedback.
	Interview someone about their working dog (optional).
Element	1.2/2.2 Produce written material.
Opportunities	Make notes about research material.
	Write an outline on the work of a dog.
	Write a description of a typical day for a working dog and its owner (optional).
Element	1.3/2.3 Use images.
Opportunities	Collect and use photographs and pictures to support a written outline.
Element	1.4/2.4 Read and respond to written materials.
Opportunities	Read books, magazines and leaflets for information about a chosen working dog for use in a written outline.
	Read information received from a charity.

Activity 2 Write an advert for a working farm

Many small working farms open up to the public as a way of making extra money. They also provide a chance for families with young children, clubs and school groups to find out how animals are reared and cared for. A visit to an open farm can give children a realistic idea of how food is produced, and how some working animals live.

Visitors to a small open farm may see cows being milked and learn about milk production. They may see the conditions in pig rearing sheds, for example. They may be able to see a variety of machinery and the process of transporting live animals. Children may be able to help feed or clean animals.

Design a flyer to advertise a working or open farm in your area. The flyer will be picked up by interested people visiting the Tourist Information Centre.

Find out about the facilities and attractions at your chosen open or working farm by writing or telephoning for information. Visit your local Tourist Information Centre and ask for information. Collect and look at the design of flyers on display for ideas on how to present your own advert. Ask friends or relatives who have visited your chosen farm for comments on the facilities. Visit the open farm yourself if possible and make notes and photograph what you see.

Present your advert on a coloured flyer to be picked up by groups or families looking for somewhere interesting to go. Give details of opening times, costs, how to find the farm, and the attractions. Include a map or plan of the farm's location so it can be easily found. Give information about facilities such as picnic sites, play areas and toilets. There may be seasonal attractions to advertise such as lambing times, piglets to view, harvests or demonstrations of butter making, for example.

Consider the colour of your flyer. What colour would be eye-catching? What other devices can you use to attract people's attention? Consider the following points when you are planning your flyer:

■ Give clear information about the farm which would help someone plan their visit, e.g. cost, opening times, location.

■ Check your advert sounds interesting. Does it suggest there is plenty to do to make a visit worthwhile?

■ Decide how you can make the farm sound attractive to groups, e.g. educational aspects.

■ Use a slogan which sums up the kind of experience a visitor would have at the farm.

■ Use pictures, photographs, drawings or cartoons.

Look at your finished flyer and decide if it's attractive and informative. Would people pick it up and read it? Show it to friends or people you work with and ask them for comments. Do they think the open farm you have advertised sounds worth visiting? Amend the flyer if you receive any helpful suggestions.

Optional task The RSPCA monitors the way in which animals such as chickens, turkeys, pigs and calves are reared and cared for on farms which are registered with their Freedom Food Scheme. Under the scheme, animals must live without pain and discomfort. They must receive enough food and water and be allowed to express their normal behaviour. The Freedom Food Scheme does not allow battery cages for chickens or sows feeding piglets in stalls without room to even turn around. Research has shown for example that hens find nest making very important. If they are allowed access to nests their egg yields improve.

The Freedom Food Trademark shows which products have been produced under this scheme. You may find eggs, bacon, pork and chicken in local supermarkets showing the Freedom Food label.

Write to Freedom Food Ltd., Manor House, Causeway, Horsham, West Sussex RH12 1HG and ask for an information leaflet. Ask about where to find foods produced under the scheme in your local area.

When you have found out more about the Freedom Food Scheme, talk to friends and people you work with about it. Ask them if they would choose these products if they knew where to find them.

Design a customer information card which could be put on shelves in local shops, explaining what the Freedom Food Scheme is all about. Use the information you received from the RSPCA to help you list the main points of the scheme. Design your customer information card so it is easy and quick to read.

(*See also* Worksheets: design a flyer)

	From this activity you may have evidence for:
Skills list	1, 3, 4, 6, 7, 8/9, 10, 11, 12, 13, 14, 15, 16.
Core Skills	Communication level 1 and 2.
Element	1.1/2.1 Take part in discussions.
Opportunities	Ask or telephone for information about an open farm.
	Ask friends for information about a farm.
	Ask people for comments on the farm advert.
	Talk to friends about Freedom Foods (optional).
Element	1.2/2.2 Produce written material.
Opportunities	Design a flyer advertising a local working farm.
	Write a letter to an open farm asking for information.
	Write to the RSPCA for information on the Freedom Food Scheme (optional).

Design a customer information card which gives details about Freedom Food products (optional).

Element 1.3/2.3 Use images.

Opportunities Use maps, diagrams, drawings or photographs in an advert for an open farm.

Element 1.4/2.4 Read and respond to written materials.

Opportunities Read leaflets, posters and replies to a letter for information about a local open farm.

Read flyers for ideas on how to design an advert for a local open farm.

Read information received from the RSPCA about the Freedom Food Scheme (optional).

Activity 3 Design a display for an exhibition

You see an advert in your local paper for the opening of a new gallery in the Heritage Centre in your town. The gallery was built with money from the Lottery Fund. There is one small display space left to fill in a new exhibition. The exhibition is about the working conditions of animals used in your local community in the past. The Heritage Centre is advertising for ideas from members of the public to fill the last display space.

Find out about the life, conditions and treatment of a working animal used in your local community in the past. Write a proposal for a display for the exhibition at the Heritage Centre.

For example, have any of the following working animals been used in your community in the past? Consider:

■ **Horses used to pull canal narrow boats** Did this happen in your area? Find out what kind of life the horses led. What kind of loads and weight did they pull? How far did they travel along the canal networks?

■ **Pit ponies** Do you live in an old coal mining area where ponies were once used down the mines? Find out what kind of work they did and who looked after them. Were they ever brought up to the surface to graze? What happened to them when they were too old to work?

■ **Doves and pigeons** Do you live near a large historic house which has a dovecote in the gardens? Find out about how doves and pigeons were once kept for food. Find out about dovecote designs. They were built with hundreds of nesting holes on the inside of the walls. The birds and their eggs were eaten for food and their droppings used for fertilizer.

■ **Cock fighting** Did cock fighting once go on in your area? Cock pits were specially built for the fights. People bred prize cockerels which fought to the death, making or losing money for their owners and the spectators who placed bets on them. An Act of Parliament put a stop to the sport in 1835, but it sometimes happens today. The RSPCA becomes involved if there are reports of cock fighting today.

■ **Brewery horses**   Do you live near a brewery which once delivered casks of beer or cider in carts or drays pulled by heavy horses? They may still be used today for parades in carnivals or galas. Find out how the horses were cared for, and what breeds were used for the heavy work.

 Collect information about your chosen working animal at your local library. Make use of your reference librarian who is usually very knowledgeable about where to look for unusual information and can suggest resource ideas to you. Use magazines or videos. Look out for any useful programmes on television and use a CD-ROM if you have access to one. Contact a local history group who may be able to offer some help. Use the worksheet provided to help you plan your research.

 Decide what kind of display you are going to propose about your chosen animal. A Heritage Centre in a town will attract quite a few visitors. Some of these will be tourists. Other people using the Heritage Centre will be school and college groups from the local area. Plan a display which involves people and gives them more to do than just looking.

Choose one of the following ideas:

■ an audio-visual display with slides fading into each other, music and commentary

■ a life-size model setting with press buttons for sounds and commentary

■ a short video, activated by people sitting to watch

■ a computer game, activated by people sitting to play it

■ a working model demonstrating loads and weights moved

■ a display of photographs, with push-button commentary

Present your proposal for a display at the Heritage Centre. Include information and illustrations you have selected from your research material.

Present the plan for your proposed display in the exhibition space in one of the following ways:

■ a short report

■ a storyboard

■ a flow chart

■ a labelled diagram

Use the worksheet provided to help you write out your proposal for a display at the Heritage Centre.

Look carefully at the proposal you have produced. Have you put in full instructions for how your planned display will look? Does the planned display sound interesting and attractive? In what ways would people enjoy looking at or using your display?

(*See also* Worksheets: research and presentation plan)

From this activity you may have evidence for:

Skills list	1, 3, 4, 6, 7, 8, 9, 10, 11, 13, 14, 15, 16.
Core skills	Communication level 1 and 2.
Element	1.1/2.1 Take part in discussions.
Opportunities	Ask a variety of people for help with research activities.
Element	1.2/2.2 Produce written material.
Opportunities	Write to a local organisation for information about a working animal.
	Write out a proposal for a display in an exhibition.
Element	1.3/2.3 Use images.
Opportunities	Use diagrams, pictures and photographs in a plan for a proposed display.
Element	1.4/2.4 Read and respond to written materials.
Opportunities	Read books, magazines and replies to letters for information about a working animal.

Activity 4 Write a guide on how to arrange a group visit

You have a friend who belongs to a club which is planning a group outing. Your friend has been asked to make the arrangements and isn't sure what to do. It's a club for people who are involved in animal welfare. They are going to visit a centre which rescues injured and ill-treated birds of prey. The centre rescues birds such as kestrels which people have tried to keep as pets. The birds have often been rescued from miserable conditions. The centre releases some birds back into the wild. It cares for those which cannot be released and uses them for breeding and education. Some birds are flown in demonstrations of skill for the public.

Write a 'Guide to arranging a group outing' for your friend to follow. Include tips on making arrangements, gathering information about the chosen venue, dealing with problems and how to keep a record of the tasks to be covered.

Note down some ideas for your guide. What kind of arrangements have to be made to enable a group to go on an outing together? For example, transport and places must be booked in advance and money collected from the group. What kind of information do you need to find out about before going on a visit? For example, you need to check opening times, costs and what attractions are on offer at your chosen destination.

Ask friends for ideas and use your own experience of trips you have taken. Find out from your nearest Tourist Information Centre about a bird of prey sanctuary in your area or something similar. Find out what kind of facilities are offered for groups visiting.

Ask well as making arrangements and finding information, include a problem buster section in your guide. Give advice on typical problems which can happen on a group outing and how to prepare for them. Write down a list of possible problems and think how you would solve them.

Use and add to the following ideas for the problem section in your guide:

■ **The weather**   If the venue is all outside, bad weather can ruin the day. Give advice in your guide about preparing for bad weather, for example by taking waterproof clothing. Suggest choosing a venue which has some attractions under cover.

■ **Food**   If people expect to buy food at the venue and then find they can't, they might get hungry and grumpy! Suggest in your guide that people prepare for meals by taking their own food or telephoning in advance and asking about refreshment facilities.

■ **Poor travellers**   If there is someone in the group who is usually travel sick, it can be unpleasant for everyone concerned. Suggest in your guide some sickness prevention methods such as pressure bands, nibbling dry biscuits or sucking mints. Suggest taking a travel pack which includes a large bag, damp cloth and towel and bottle of fresh drinking water.

■ **Money**   An outing can be ruined if everything costs more than people expect. Suggest in your guide how to find out about all the possible expenses before setting off.

■ **Access**   It would be a serious problem if the venue were reached only to find some members of the group could not get into all of the parts. Suggest in your guide how to check the venue offers full access to all the members of the group, including wheel chair users.

■ **People**   The most unreliable factor! For example, the outing can be upset if someone is very late, someone forgets to bring any money, or someone gets lost. Suggest in your guide how the group can prepare for arrangements going wrong at the last minute! Suggest everyone agrees on some simple and fair rules for the outing which everyone must keep.

 Use your notes and ideas from talking to other people to present a 'Guide to arranging a group outing'. Illustrate your guide with pictures or cartoons. Include a simple record sheet in your guide which helps the group keep track of all the arrangements. Allow space on the record sheet for:

■ booking details and contact address
■ number of people going on the outing

- times of departure and return
- details of pick-up points
- information about attractions and costs
- advice on what to bring on the day, e.g. food, camera
- details of tasks allocated to each group member

 Read through your guide carefully and check it all makes sense. Does it look attractive? Is it easy to use? Would your guide help a group successfully arrange an outing for themselves? Show your guide to a friend or someone you work with and ask them if they think it is practical and useful.

Optional task Imagine the group outing to a Bird of Prey Centre actually took place. Write the entry which appeared in your friend's diary later that day. Use the problems you have thought about for your guide to imagine what might have happened. Use information you received from the Tourist Information Centre to help you record what birds of prey the group may have seen. Make the diary entry descriptive, using personal comments, humour and details of sights, sounds, tastes and smells.

From this activity you may have evidence for:

Skills list   1, 3, 4, 6, 7, 8, 10, 11, 13, 14, 15, 16.

Core skills   Communication level 1 and 2.

Element   1.1/2.1 Take part in discussions.

Opportunities   Ask friends for ideas about arranging group outings.

Ask for information at the Tourist Information Centre.

Ask for feedback on your guide.

Element   1.2/2.2 Produce written material.

Opportunities   Make notes on what to include in your guide.

Write a list of problems to feature in the guide.

Write a 'Guide to arranging a group outing'.

Write a diary entry (optional).

Element   1.3/2.3 Use images.

Opportunities   Use pictures or cartoons to illustrate your guide.

Element   1.4/2.4 Read and respond to written materials.

Opportunities   Read leaflets about a bird of prey centre and use ideas in your guide and diary entry.

Activity 5   Carry out an investigation to find cruelty-free products

Consumers like to buy products which are 'natural' or cruelty-free. Some of the labels on these products can be misleading. The final design of a product may have been tested on human volunteers, and so the labels state 'not tested on animals'. However, many of the individual ingredients which make up a product may have been tested on animals. Projects for new products must be licensed and inspectors will make spot checks on the use of animals for testing to ensure it is necessary.

Many companies, for example Boots, The Body Shop, Tesco and Rimmel offer products which have not been tested on animals. Beauty Without Cruelty is a company which offers a guarantee that no ingredient has been tested on animals for at least the last five years.

 Select ten categories of body care products which you enjoy using such as bubble bath, bath oils, perfumes and colognes, combination shampoos, hair colours, skin toners, skin cleansers, anti-ageing creams, shaving products and a variety of cosmetics. Carry out an investigation to find a product for each of the body care categories on your list which you would be happy to use and which has not been tested on animals.

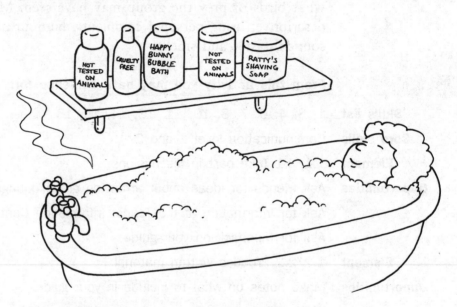

 Write a list of your ten body care categories. Visit local supermarkets, shops and chemists and find ten products which are not tested on animals. Check you are happy with each product you find.

■ do you like the smell?

■ does it do the same job as your usual product?

■ is the cost reasonable?

■ are you sure it has not been tested on animals?

Check by reading labels and packaging. Look for a leaflet about the products or ask an assistant to tell you about a product. Get information by writing to the maker of a range of products you are unsure about. You should find an address on the packaging. Write to The Vegan Society for information about why it is worth choosing cruelty-free products and advice on which products you could choose. Find the address in health magazines or from your local library or local health food store.

Use the worksheet provided for ideas on how to record your investigation.

Present the results of your investigation as a shopper's mini-guide to body care products which have not been tested on animals. Include where to find the products and reasons for buying cruelty-free products. Design your mini-guide so it is a small, handy size to be carried around in a bag, purse or wallet.

Talk to friends about your shopper's mini-guide. Ask them for suggestions of products they like to use which have not been tested on animals. Improve and add to your guide, using their ideas. Divide your guide into sections covering products for skin, hair, bath, shaving and perfumes, for example. Make copies for friends who are interested.

(*See also* Worksheets: cruelty-free product investigation)

From this activity you may have evidence for:

Skills list	1, 4, 6, 7, 8, 10, 11, 13, 15, 16.
Core skills	Communication level 1 and 2.
Element	1.1/2.1 Take part in discussions.
Opportunities	Ask a variety of people questions about product information.
	Ask people for cruelty-free product suggestions.
Element	1.2/2.2 Produce written material.
Opportunities	List body care categories for investigation.
	Record results of investigation on cruelty-free products.
	Write a letter to an organisation asking for information about cruelty-free products.
	Write a mini-guide to products which are cruelty-free.
Element	1.4/2.4 Read and respond to written materials.
Opportunities	Read product labels, packaging and leaflets for information on product testing.
	Read information received in reply to letters.

Activity 6 Write a profile of a race horse

Horse racing has been a popular sport for hundreds of years, providing work for people and animals. The work is hard, so the horses are carefully bred and chosen for the job. They are trained by experts until they are fit and strong enough for the work.

In the UK there are two types of racing, flat racing and National Hunt racing, which involves fences and hurdles. A horse may start flat racing at around two years old but a horse trained for jumping won't race until around four years of age. The National Hunt season is from August until May and the flat racing season runs from March to November. The season ends at this time as the ground is beginning to be too hard and may cause serious injury to a horse's legs. The horses are rested for a while and then begin training again for the start of the new race season.

Produce a profile of a race horse of your choice which is racing at the moment. Pick a name which appeals to you from a daily newspaper or pick a horse you have already heard of. Follow its progress for a day. Write a detailed profile which gives a full picture of your chosen horse and its racing performance that day.

Find the information for your written profile by watching racing on television or listening to the radio. Ask for information from any friends or people you work with who are keen on horse racing. Find information about your chosen horse from national newspapers or specialist papers such as *The Sporting Life*. Look at newspapers and ask for information in your local library.

You may find extra information about your chosen horse in tips or reviews of races. Find out what kind of ground your horse likes, how successful it's been in the last few races and who the trainer, jockey and owner are.

The diagram which follows explains how to work out the entries you may find in a newspaper about your horse on the day of the race. Look for the race meeting, place and time and list of the horses entered for the race. The diagram describes some of the most common pieces of information you will find about your chosen race horse.

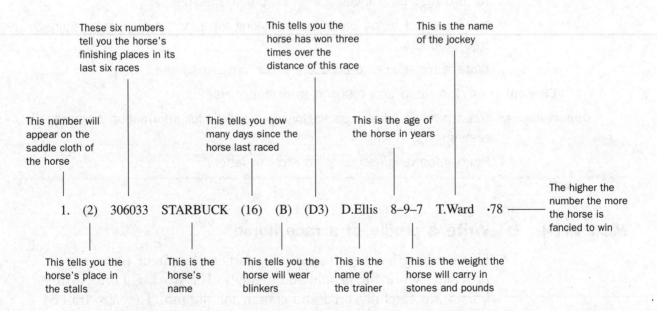

Write the profile of your chosen horse on a card with headings for each section of information. Include a photograph of your horse. Make a prediction, based on what you have found out, on whether your horse will win on the day you are following its progress.

Check the results of the race on television or in the newspaper the next day. Include your prediction and the result in your profile.

Talk about the profile you have written with a friend or someone you work with. Discuss why horse racing has been such a popular sport for so long. What do you think attracts people to watch and bet on horse races?

(*See also* **Worksheets: race horse profile**)

From this activity you may have evidence for:

Skills list	1, 2, 3, 4, 6, 7, 8/9, 10, 12, 13/14, 15, 16.
Core skills	Communication level 1 and 2.
Element	1.1/2.1 Take part in discussions.
Opportunities	Ask a variety of people for information about horse racing.
	Discuss the profile and horse racing with another person.
Element	1.2/2.2 Produce written material.
Opportunities	Write a profile of a selected race horse.
Element	1.3/2.3 Use images.
Opportunities	Use a photograph to illustrate a profile of a race horse.
Element	1.4/2.4 Read and respond to written materials.
Opportunities	Read books, newspapers and magazines for information about a race horse for use in a written profile.

Evaluation exercise

Think about the work you have done on this project. Will you try to buy foods with the Freedom Food label from now on? Will you look out for body care products which have not been tested on animals?

Do you feel more confident about carrying out a variety of research activities? Do you feel your written skills have improved? What evidence of competence have you collected to show a variety of presentation skills?

Fill in your Skills Record Sheet so it is up to date. You may need to look back at this when you come to plan more work or to remind yourself about skills you practised. Write down the variety of resources you have used during work on the project. Complete your Skills Summary Record so you have details of the evidence you have collected of assessment for an accreditation you may be working towards. Write down information about your achievements and progress. Think about which skills you need to practise further and write down details of your plans.

Working dogs

Follow the prompts suggested on this worksheet to carry out your research on working dogs. Part two of the worksheet helps you with presentation ideas.

Part one: research on working dogs

Details of chosen working dog

What do I already know about the work this dog does?

What special difficulties do people have who need the help this dog can offer?

Where can I look for information?

- ■ **Library**   Books, magazines, videos, leaflets, addresses.
- ■ **People**   Ask the Reference Librarian for help. Ask someone who has a working dog about their experiences.
- ■ **Organisations**   Write to a charity or support group which funds and trains the dogs. Get an address from the library or telephone book.
- ■ **Television**   Look out for any documentaries which might give some information.

What questions do I need to find answers to?

How are the dogs chosen for the work?

What kind of nature does the dog need?

Which breed of dog is usually chosen?

Does the dog need to be particularly fit/young/strong/agile?

How is the dog trained and who does the training?

What kind of skills does the dog have to learn?

How long does the training process take?

How does the dog benefit the person it is trained to help?

What kind of problems can the dog or its owner have?

Part two: **write an outline**

Present the information on your chosen dog as a written report or leaflet.

Title of report or leaflet

Think of a good title for your report or leaflet which describes the dog you have chosen and the work it does.

Ideas:

Introduction

Write a brief description of the work the dog carries out. Describe the type of problems or special needs the people who use the dogs may have.

Ideas:

Section one

Explain how the dog is chosen and trained and the kind of skills it learns. Include photographs and diagrams you have collected.

Ideas:

Section two

Describe how the dog's skills can benefit the life of the person who uses it. Refer to any newspaper reports you have collected.

Ideas:

Section three

Describe the follow-up support or life-long support the dog and handler receive. Describe how the charity or support group keeps in touch with the people who need their help.

Ideas:

Section four

Provide names and addresses for the charity. List resources you have used such as newspapers, television programmes, people interviewed.

Ideas:

Design a flyer to advertise a working or open farm

Checklist: what information should you include?

Use the headings below to help you decide what to include in your flyer to advertise a local working or open farm. Fill in details from your own research to use in your flyer design.

Location: use a diagram or photocopy part of a map to show where the farm is and how to get there.

Your ideas:

Transport: give details of bus routes or bus numbers if the farm is on a public transport route. Give road numbers.

Your ideas:

Costs: give details of adult and child entry costs and any special rates for groups and families.

Your ideas:

Opening times: give details of opening times and any seasonal changes. The farm may be closed to the public in the winter.

Your ideas:

Facilities: e.g. parking, toilets, picnic area, café or a place to buy food and drink, access for wheel chair users, etc.

Your ideas:

Attractions: e.g. play area, craft shop on site or nearby, baby animals at various times of the year, feeding or milking times, demonstrations at harvest time or of butter making, etc.

Your ideas:

Research and presentation plan

Part one

Use this worksheet to help you plan your research about a working animal once used in your local community.

Tick which suggestions you will try:

I will look for information and illustrations at the library:

Ask the Reference Librarian for help ☐

Use the subject catalogue to find reference numbers ☐

Look for local history information (old copies of a local paper) ☐

Borrow useful videos ☐

I will find useful addresses or contact numbers and write or telephone for information:

Local history society ☐

Animal welfare group ☐

Local museum ☐

Other sources of information worth trying:

Television / Radio programmes (use weekly guides) ☐

CD-ROM ☐

What I hope to find out about the working animal:

Work done and how important it was for local people ☐

Conditions of work for the animal ☐

What kind of people owned or worked with the animal ☐

How should I plan my time?

Collect information from a variety of sources ☐

Write for information, make telephone calls or visits ☐

Collect illustrations, e.g. photos, cuttings, etc. ☐

Read through collected material ☐

Select what is useful for my planned display ☐

Write a rough outline of a plan for a display ☐

Make a good copy of the plan ☐

Research and presentation plan

Part two

Use the ideas in this worksheet to help you write your proposal for a display your local Heritage Centre.

Report Have you planned an audio-visual display at the Heritage Centre? How can you present this plan? Use a report style. Describe each feature of the audio-visual display in separate sections of your report. The audio-visual display may be slides fading into each other with realistic sound effects, music and a commentary. For example:

1. Write about the music and sound effects.

2. Write about the commentary.

3. Write about the pictures and images which will be shown.

Flow diagram Have you planned an interactive game at the Heritage Centre? How can you present this plan? Use a flow diagram. Draw out a series of boxes with arrows pointing to the next one. Fill in each box with information about each part of your interactive game. For example:

1. Show pictures of your animal at work with information to read about the scene.

2. Questions appear on the screen which must be answered to go on to the next set of pictures.

3. Give instructions for how to play the game.

Storyboard Have you planned a display of photographs with a push-button commentary? How can you present this plan? Use a storyboard. Divide a large piece of card into squares and sketch each photograph in your display. Make notes to explain the commentary. For example:

1. Show the sequence of photographs in order. Your sketching does not have to be wonderful!

2. Explain in simple notes on the storyboard how the push-button commentary will work.

3. Give some details about what the commentary will include.

Labelled diagram   Have you planned a model of your chosen animal as a display? How can you present this plan? Use a labelled diagram. Draw out a diagram of your model and label all the features. For example:

1. Sketch out a picture of how the model will look.

2. List materials and features of the model.

3. Describe what kind of information the labels will give.

Cruelty-free product investigation

List of categories e.g. shampoo, bath oil	**Products found which are not tested on animals**
List A	List B
1.	1.
2.	2.
3.	3.
4.	4.
5.	5.
6.	6.
7.	7.
8.	8.
9.	9.
10.	10.

What information have you found which proves the products in List B are not tested on animals?

Information on labels?	Yes/No
Information on packaging?	Yes/No
Leaflets given with product?	Yes/No
Responses from shop staff?	Yes/No
Replies to letters asking for product guides?	Yes/No
Is it easy to obtain suitable information on cruelty-free products?	Yes/No
Do shops offer product information when asked?	Yes/No

Are products which have not been tested on animals:

  more expensive / less expensive / about the same?

Are the 10 products you have chosen for List B readily available
and easy to find in shops?   Yes/No

Race horse profile

Name of horse:

Details of breeding:

Description of appearance:

Any unusual habits:

Photograph

The owner is:

The racing colours are:

The trainer is:

Stable companions are:

The favourite jockey is:

Horse's preferred ground:

Placing in last six races:

1.

2.

3.

4.

5.

6.

Details of race prediction (day, race, place):

Race result:

Back to basics

Answers on p. 317.

Proof-reading

Read through the following text carefully and put in the punctuation. Capital letters, commas and full stops are all missing.

the freedom food labelling scheme is carefully checked by the rspca it is a step forward in improving the care and rearing of farm animals in the uk the freedom food label can be found on meat eggs and dairy produce the foods produced under this scheme may cost a bit more but when you buy them you know the animals concerned have not suffered pain or discomfort they have also been allowed to move around in a natural way

Missing words

Rewrite the sentences below, putting back the missing words. The words you need are listed for you in the box below. Make the task harder for yourself if you wish by covering up the list of words.

track	police	tested	Freedom
sensitive	RSPCA	Open	welcomed
pet	reared	Cruelty	enjoyment

a) _____ farms give families a chance to find out how animals are _____ and cared for.

b) The _____ Food Scheme is monitored by the _____.

c) Friendly _____ animals are _____ into homes for the elderly to create interest and _____ for the residents.

d) The _____ use dogs to _____ people and objects as the dogs have a very _____ sense of smell.

e) Beauty Without _____ products are a range of items which have not been _____ on animals.

Careful reading

Read the short text carefully and then answer the questions which follow. Write your answers in complete sentences.

Many people like and respect guide dogs. However, people sometimes forget that the safety of a blind or partially sighted person depends on how well his or her dog is concentrating on its job. Never distract a guide dog who is working. Don't pat it, talk to it or give it treats to eat. Any of these things can distract the dog and may cause an accident. When a guide dog is at rest, relaxing without its work harness, then with the owner's permission, you may be able to make a welcome fuss of a hard-working dog.

1. What do some people forget about guide dogs?

2. In what ways can people distract a working guide dog?

3. What may happen to the owner if a guide dog is distracted from its work?

4. When may you make a fuss of a guide dog?

Alternatives Other ideas for activities on living with animals

Any activity from the group or individual projects can be replaced with an idea from the list below. Use the list to give you more choice of activities to do which suit your needs, interests and the amount of time you have available.

- Find out about allergies caused by pets. What kind of symptoms do people suffer from? Write a description of what you find out. Discuss what it must be like to give up a much loved pet because someone in the family is allergic to it.

- Find out how to get your pet into show business. Find a pet agency or talk to people who have had a pet working in a film or stage play or in advertising. Write a checklist on how your pet can work for a living safely and with enjoyment.

- Find out about pet psychologists and how they can help a pet and its owners to sort out problem behaviour. Write a guide to common problems and what advice would be offered to owners to cope with the problem.

- Find out about the different diseases which can be spread by birds, reptiles, cats and dogs to their human owners. Write a guide to how to handle each pet to avoid contracting any illness.

- Discuss why people will give money readily to charities which help animals.

- Find out what happens to pets when their owners go on holiday. Find out about costs, conditions and what can be done to make a pet feel as happy as possible in a cattery or kennels. Write a checklist for owners to follow.

- Visit a working animal event, such as an agricultural show or sheep dog trials. Take photographs and write a report as if it is for the local newspaper.

- Find out about the history of the Spanish bull ring and how animals are used today. Write your opinion about the sport.

- Find out about bee-keeping. Draw a diagram of the equipment and how the hives are built. Comment on any dangers involved in keeping bees. Describe the work of the bees and why they sometimes swarm. Describe some of the folk lore which surrounds bees.

- Find out about puppy farms. Dogs may be kept in poor conditions, and are bred only for the purpose of producing as many puppies as possible for profit. Write a checklist for anyone thinking about getting a puppy. Suggest what questions they should ask and what information they should be given about the puppy. Write to the RSPCA for information and advice.

■ Find out about the use of animals in the circus today. Visit a circus if possible and ask questions, write to the RSPCA for information or find information in your local library. Find out about codes of practice for circus animals.

Back to basics: answers

Safety at work

Missing words

Here are the statements about safety in the workplace with the missing words replaced.

a) Inspectors have powers to **prosecute** a firm for breaking the **Health** and **Safety** Regulations.

b) Leave your **work** area **clear** and **tidy** ready for the next shift or person.

c) Make sure you know how to use and **store** your **protective** clothing properly.

d) Make sure you know who is your **First Aider** or **Appointed** person in case of an accident.

e) Your work area should have enough **space** for you to **move** about safely.

f) Do not store **dangerous** substances in spare bottles which are not properly **labelled**.

g) Make sure you know the **correct lifting** procedures if you are going to move loads about the workplace.

Muddled words

Here are the answers to the muddled words about protective equipment and the body part the equipment protects.

Muddled word	Correct word	Body part	Why protect?
sloggge	**goggles**	**eyes**	from dust or chemical splashes
feasty toobs	**safety boots**	**feet**	from chemicals and falling objects
tenraih	**hairnet**	**hair/scalp**	prevents hair from tangling in machinery
reaglups	**earplugs**	**ears**	prevent hearing damage and loss

Careful reading

Here are the answers to the questions about the short text on safety in the workplace. You may not have written exactly the same but you should have something very similar.

1. Around 50 people every year are killed at work from an electric shock.

2. If someone you work with receives an electric shock you should be able to help by knowing some First Aid.

3. Plenty of socket outlets should be provided in the workplace so there is no temptation to dangerously overload one of them.

4. You should check plugs are fitted properly to make sure wires are clamped and cannot be pulled away from the terminals.

5. A properly trained electrician should carry out electrical repairs in the workplace to make sure the work is done to a safe standard.

Safety in and around the home

Write a note

You may not have written exactly the same as the example note below but you should have something very similar. It is a good idea to put in the day, date or time of your note. The person reading your note will then know it is not an old one, left lying about from a previous day. Write the name of the person the note is for at the start of your message. Make it clear why the iron should not be used. Sign the note so it is clear who has written it.

> Friday
>
> Ian,
> Please don't use the iron today. I noticed this morning the plug is very loose and it may be dangerous. I'll check it when I get home at 5 pm.
>
> Love Tina

Proof reading

Here is the passage about cold compresses written out correctly.

Cooling an injury such as a nasty bruise or sprain can help reduce swelling. Place the injured part under cold running water, or in a bowl of cold water. When injuries need longer cooling use a cold compress. If you have no ice cubes handy you can make a cold compress from a bag of frozen peas. Never put the ice bag directly onto skin, always wrap it in a cloth first. Apply the compress to the injured part and hold it in place for 20 minutes.

Advertisement

Your card won't be exactly the same as the example below but you should have written something similar.

Friendly, reliable baby-sitter, with own transport, seeks work in local area. Experienced in caring for children, with a special interest in the pre-school child.

References provided on request.

Telephone 667488 and ask for Sallie Robinson.

Time for recreation

Muddled words

Here are the muddled-up words written out correctly. How did you get on?

recreation	activity	leisure
enjoyment	fun	benefit
problem	relax	time

Careful reading

Here are the answers to the questions about the short text. You may not have written exactly the same, but your answers should be very similar.

1. Kerry was feeling nervous when she walked into the classroom.

2. Peter was writing on the board when Kerry walked in.

3. The group were talking about recreation and trying to decide on their favourite activities.

4. Kerry sat next to Chris because Peter asked her to.

5. Kerry may have been feeling nervous because she was joining the class later than everyone else and knew she had missed some of the work. She may have been anxious as she thought she didn't know anyone there. It may have been some time since Kerry had joined a study class and so she wasn't sure what to expect.

Read and order

Here are the instructions about how to meditate written in the correct order. Don't worry if you have one or two differences as long as your instruction list is also in a sensible order.

1. Choose a warm, quiet place.

2. Set an alarm clock or timer so you don't have to worry about the time.

3. Close your eyes and relax.
4. Breathe deeply.
5. Count up to four on each breath as you breathe out.
6. Don't try to change your breathing.
7. If your mind wanders just bring your attention back to your breathing.
8. Finish your meditation with a stretch.

Recreation and exercise

Careful reading

Here are the answers to the questions about the text on exercise. You may not have written exactly the same, but your answers should be very similar.

1. Twenty to thirty minutes of exercise, three times a week is the suggested amount of exercise to keep you fit.
2. Some benefits gained from exercise can be enjoyment, reducing high blood pressure, relaxation and feeling more energetic.
3. Feeling fit means being supple, strong and having plenty of stamina.
4. Anyone can try a new activity, whatever their age may be.

Missing words

Here are the sentences about recreation and exercise with the missing words correctly replaced. How did you get on?

a) Choose **activities** which you enjoy.
b) Try to follow the **instructions** carefully in an exercise class to avoid **injury**.
c) Yoga and gymnastics keep you **supple** and **flexible**.
d) Walking is a good all round exercise for all **age** groups.
e) For jogging you need a pair of shoes which give **support** and **cushioning**.
f) Swimming is a **refreshing** form of exercise.

Fast reading

Here are the answers to the questions about the ski course advert.

1. You can try the sport of skiing for a day.
2. The course begins at 10 am.
3. You can find out more about the course by telephoning for further information.
4. The course costs £9.50.
5. All of the equipment is provided for you.
6. If you take a size 4 boot you would not be able to join the course as the minimum boot size is a 5.

Personal care: feet and hair

Careful reading

Here is the correct order for the hair care routine.

- Comb dry hair with wide-toothed comb to prevent tangling when wet.
- Wet hair with warm water and gently comb fingers through hair to make sure it's completely wet.
- Rub shampoo between the palms of your hands then smooth into hair. Massage gently over your whole scalp.
- Rinse hair well using clear, warm water. A common cause of dull hair is poor rinsing.
- Smooth conditioner over hair with the palms of your hands, concentrating on the ends of the hair. Rinse well again.
- Blot your hair dry gently with a towel. Comb your hair with a wide-toothed comb to get rid of any tangles.

Here are the answers to the questions about the hair care routine. You may not have written exactly the same, but you should have a similar answer each time.

1. You should comb your hair before washing it to remove any tangles.
2. You should rub the shampoo between the palms of your hands and massage it gently onto your hair and scalp.
3. A common cause of dull hair is not rinsing shampoo out of the hair properly.
4. You should put conditioner on all of your hair right down to the ends, using the palms of your hands.

Muddled words

Here are the muddled-up words about foot care written out correctly.

nails	athlete's foot	verrucae
bunions	footwear	cotton socks
bare foot	flexible	blister

Leaving a note

Sandra would need to know which appointment Mrs Waters had cancelled (the date and time). She would also need to know which Wednesday Mrs Waters wanted another appointment for (again the date and time). Jackie should have said exactly what Mrs Waters wanted as 'the usual' is too vague. Finally, Jackie should have reminded Sandra that Mrs Waters needed her appointment confirming.

You may not have written a note which is exactly the same as the example shown but you should have something similar.

Tuesday 7th Nov.

Sandra,

One of your ladies, Mrs Waters, telephoned just as I was leaving. She's had to cancel her appointment for Thursday, 9th November, at 10 am. There's some emergency at home she said. She wants to make another appointment for next Wednesday, 15th November at 9.30 am, just for a wash and blow dry. Write it in the book please and telephone Mrs Waters to confirm her appointment. Her number is in our file.

Thanks, Jackie.

Personal care: teeth, skin and body

Missing words

Here are the completed sentences about caring for your teeth and body, with all the missing words replaced. How did you get on?

a) A bad attack of spots is called **acne**.

b) The skin acts as a **barrier** to stop **germs** getting in.

c) The top layer of your skin is called the **epidermis**.

d) **Clean** your teeth thoroughly as part of a **regular** routine.

e) Use **fluoride** toothpaste and **dental** floss to keep your teeth and gums **healthy**.

f) **Sugar** left in your mouth after eating turns to **acid** which can attack the hard **enamel** on your teeth.

Muddled words

Here are the words about teeth, skin and body care written out correctly.

enamel	plaque	toothpaste	decay
sebum	dermis	skin cancer	nails

Reading for information

Here are the answers to the questions on the short text about sweat. You may not have written exactly the same, but you should have something very similar.

1. You have about two million sweat glands.

2. Your sweat is made up of water, salt and a small amount of body waste.

3. If you are frightened you may sweat from the palms of your hands and soles of your feet, where you have a lot of sweat pores in the skin.

4. Sweat starts to smell unpleasant when it has been on your skin for a long time. Bacteria start to breed and cause an unpleasant smell.

Colour choices

Mixed sentences

Here are the sentences written out in the correct order. How did you get on?

1. Blue is a cool colour.

2. A colour linked to danger is red.

3. The primary colours are red, yellow and blue.

4. Complementary colours are opposite each other on the colour wheel.

5. Feelings are often linked to colours, for example, green with envy.

Careful reading

Here are the answers to the questions about the text on the colour blue. You may not have written exactly the same, but you should have something very similar.

1. The European Community flag has a blue background.

2. Exposure to the colour blue can have a calming effect and may reduce your pulse rate.

3. Blue is used in safety codes to remind people to wear protective equipment.

4. The answer to this question will depend on your own opinion. Blue may be popular because it is such a peaceful and relaxing colour.

Missing punctuation

Here is the short text about the colour yellow with the missing punctuation correctly replaced.

Yellow brightens a room. Often used in kitchens, it produces a feeling of welcome and friendliness. Yellow is just as useful in a small room which looks out over a dull city view. It helps make a room seem light, sunny and cheerful. The painter Monet's house in France has a famous yellow dining room.

Seeing colour

Match up

Here are the two lists with the colour names in list one matched up to the correct descriptive words in list two.

List one	List two
Blue	sapphire turquoise
Green	leaf lime
Yellow	mustard golden
Red	ruby scarlet
Purple	foxglove plum
Brown	tan chocolate
Orange	amber apricot

Proof-reading

Here is the short text about colour in advertising with the punctuation replaced.

The customer judges the quality of a product by its colour. Pink is used in hand creams as it is a colour which suggests a soft, tender mildness. Green is used successfully on toilet cleaner containers as it suggests a clean, natural freshness. If the customer wants a mild coffee they look for a blue labelled jar. Coffee jars with red labels suggest a stronger flavour.

Careful reading

Here are the answers to the questions on the text about the eye. You may not have written exactly the same but you should have something very similar.

1. The lens in your eye focuses the light.

2. The iris controls the amount of light getting into your eye by altering the size of the pupil.

3. When you see something you like your pupils open wider and more light is allowed to enter your eye.

4. When you see something you don't like your pupils narrow and less light is allowed to enter your eye.

Pollution and noise

Missing words

Here is the short text about noise pollution with the missing words correctly replaced.

Noise is a part of our daily lives. If **noise** is at a reasonable **level** it can do you no **harm**, but if noise is very loud it may cause **damage** to your hearing which can be **permanent**. The **risk** of damage depends on how **long** you are **exposed** to the noise and how **loud** the noise level is. After a time listening to very loud music can damage the **delicate** workings of your ear. Working with noisy machinery without any ear **protection** can also cause you harm. Sometimes people who have damaged hearing may suffer from **tinnitus**, which is a constant ringing or buzzing in their ears.

Careful reading

Here are the answers to the questions about the newspaper article. You may not have written exactly the same but you should have something very similar.

1. The residents of Quarry Street are upset about the amount of noise one of their neighbours, Mrs Robinson, is making.

2. Mrs Robinson has a collection of 59 drums which she keeps in her front room.

3. Alice plays her drums every morning and evening.

4. The residents of Quarry Street have asked the Noise Team from their local council for help.

5. Mrs Robinson's neighbours seem to have a reasonable complaint. The drum playing must make a lot of noise if people can't hear themselves speak in the street. It must be very irritating to hear the drums every morning and evening.

Matching up

Here are the two word lists rewritten so each word in the first list is opposite a word which has a similar meaning in the second list. It's useful to know words with similar meanings as it can help you make your own writing more varied and interesting.

List one	List two
damage	impair
delicate	fragile
loudness	high volume
noise	sound
danger	hazard
permanent	lifelong
protect	guard

Pollution and waste

Missing punctuation

Here is the text about packaging with the punctuation replaced.

Packaging is important to protect, preserve and keep products fresh. When the customer buys goods they expect them to be in good condition. Safe packaging of medicines can help keep dangerous drugs away from children. Most packaging is thrown away as soon as the goods are brought home from the shops. We can help to protect our environment by choosing products which use the least amount of packaging wherever possible. Packaging removed from products should be recycled by taking it to a local recycling centre.

Jumbled sentences

Here are the jumbled sentences written out correctly.

1. Recycling reduces the waste of raw materials.
2. Choose items which can be recycled.
3. Don't drop litter.
4. You can be fined for dropping litter.
5. Dangerous litter can harm people and wildlife.
6. Try to recycle household items such as glass, paper and drinks cans.

Scan and read

Here are the answers to the questions about the Mother and Toddler Group meeting. You may not have written exactly the same, but you should have very similar answers.

1. Woolton Mother and Toddler Group has organised the meeting.
2. The name of the speaker is Dr Andrew White.
3. The speaker is going to talk about the dangers to children of dog waste.
4. The meeting is going to take place in Woolton Community Centre.
5. There is a free crèche where young children can be looked after while mothers listen to the talk. Refreshments are also offered.
6. The logo means dispose of your dog's waste, don't leave it lying about in public places. If it is cleared up children can play safely with no danger of contracting infection.

Living with animals: pets and people

Careful reading

Here are the answers to the questions on the short text about Anne. You may not have written exactly the same but you should have something very similar.

1. Anne was feeling nervous because she was waiting to see the dentist.

2. Anne tried to read a magazine and then spent time watching fish in a tank.

3. The fish tank caught Anne's attention because it was attractive, colourful and full of movement.

4. Anne noticed the fantails, comets and bulgy-eyed black fish.

5. Anne felt the black fish were comical because they looked different and seemed to behave in a rather clumsy way compared to the other sleek fish.

6. The answer to this question is of course your own opinion. Many people do find fish very relaxing and soothing to watch as the fish move about in such a smooth, easy manner.

Muddled and missing words

Here are the names of common small pets written out correctly.

hamster   rabbit   gerbil
budgerigar   guinea pig   goldfish

Here are the sentences about pets and pet care with the missing pet names replaced.

a) Handle it with care and a **hamster** will become very tame.

b) A **gerbil** enjoys the company of other familiar animals.

c) Never pick a **rabbit** up by its ears, support it underneath its body.

d) A **guinea pig** enjoys eating cereals and plenty of fruit and green vegetables.

e) A large tank with a lid to keep out dust is ideal for **goldfish**.

f) If trained early a **budgerigar** should talk to its owner.

Quick reading

Here are the answers to the questions about the advert. You may not have written exactly the same but you should have very similar answers.

1. Angus Birtwell of Angus Pet Foods.

2. The business promises a friendly, personal service.

3. The phrase 'competitive prices' means Angus Pet Foods claim to charge the same or even less for their pet foods than any similar business in the area.

4. You may notice this particular advert in the Yellow Pages because the bold print would make it stand out on the page. The list of attractive services which is easy to read may also attract your attention.

People working with animals

Proof-reading

Here is the text about the Freedom Food Scheme with the punctuation back in place.

The Freedom Food labelling scheme is carefully checked by the RSPCA. It is a step forward in improving the care and rearing of farm animals in the UK. The Freedom Food label can be found on meat, eggs and dairy produce. The foods produced under this scheme may cost a bit more but when you buy them you know the animals concerned have not suffered pain or discomfort. They have also been allowed to move around in a natural way.

Missing words

Here are the sentences with the missing words replaced in the correct places.

a) **Open** farms give families a chance to find out how animals are **reared** and cared for.

b) The **Freedom** Food Scheme is monitored by the **RSPCA**.

c) Friendly **pet** animals are **welcomed** into homes for the elderly to create interest and **enjoyment** for the residents.

d) The **police** use dogs to **track** people and objects as the dogs have a very **sensitive** sense of smell.

e) Beauty Without **Cruelty** products are a range of items which have not been **tested** on animals.

Careful reading

Here are the answers to the short text about guide dogs. You may not have written exactly the same but you should have very similar answers.

1. People forget that the safety of the blind or partially sighted person depends on their guide dog doing its job properly.

2. People can distract a guide dog by patting it, talking to it or offering it food treats.

3. The guide dog's owner could have an accident if their dog is distracted.

4. You may make a fuss of a guide dog when it is obviously not working and you have the permission of the owner.

Group project: Safety at work

Activity	Skills list																Core skills: communication							
	1	2	3	4	5	6	7	8	9	10	11	12	13	14	15	16	1.1	1.2	1.3	1.4	2.1	2.2	2.3	2.4
1. Write a safety checklist for using a computer or word processor		✓	✓	✓	✓	✓	✓	✓		✓			✓	✓	✓	✓	✓	✓	✓	✓	✓	✓	✓	✓
2. Write a summary of action for a case study	✓	✓	✓		✓	✓	✓	✓					✓			✓	✓	✓	✓	✓	✓			✓
3. Find out about safe manual handling methods	✓	✓	✓		✓	✓	✓	✓	✓				✓	✓	✓	✓	✓	✓	✓	✓	✓			✓
4. Write a checklist on fire prevention at work	✓	✓	✓		✓	✓	✓	✓	✓				✓	✓	✓	✓	✓	✓	✓	✓	✓			✓
5. Design a chart to warn about dangerous substances	✓	✓				✓	✓	✓	✓				✓	✓	✓	✓	✓	✓	✓	✓	✓			✓
6. Find out how to move about the workplace safely	✓	✓	✓		✓					✓	✓		✓	✓	✓	✓	✓	✓	✓	✓	✓			✓

Individual project: Safety in and around the home

Activity	Skills list																Core skills: communication							
	1	2	3	4	5	6	7	8	9	10	11	12	13	14	15	16	1.1	1.2	1.3	1.4	2.1	2.2	2.3	2.4
1. Carry out a survey on safety in a children's play area	✓	✓	✓	✓	✓	✓	✓	✓	✓	✓	✓	✓	✓	✓	✓	✓	✓	✓	✓	✓	✓	✓	✓	✓
2. Investigate toy safety	✓	✓	✓	✓	✓	✓	✓	✓	✓	✓	✓	✓	✓	✓	✓	✓	✓	✓	✓	✓	✓	✓	✓	✓
3. Carry out a safety review of your home	✓	✓	✓	✓	✓	✓	✓	✓	✓	✓	✓	✓	✓	✓	✓	✓	✓	✓	✓	✓	✓	✓	✓	✓
4. Write a top ten for DIY safety tips	✓	✓	✓	✓	✓	✓	✓	✓	✓	✓	✓	✓	✓	✓	✓	✓	✓	✓	✓	✓	✓	✓	✓	✓
5. Design a handbook for baby-sitters and parents	✓	✓	✓	✓	✓	✓	✓			✓			✓	✓	✓	✓	✓	✓	✓	✓	✓	✓	✓	✓
6. Design a mini-guide to home security	✓	✓	✓	✓	✓	✓		✓					✓	✓	✓	✓	✓	✓	✓	✓	✓	✓	✓	✓

Group project: **Time for recreation**

Activity	Skills list																Core skills: communication							
	1	2	3	4	5	6	7	8	9	10	11	12	13	14	15	16	1.1	1.2	1.3	1.4	2.1	2.2	2.3	2.4
1. Discuss the benefits of recreation and list activities	✓	✓	✓	✓	✓								✓	✓	✓	✓	✓	✓	✓	✓	✓	✓	✓	✓
2. Write a guide on how to cope with recreation problems	✓	✓	✓	✓	✓	✓	✓	✓	✓		✓	✓	✓	✓	✓	✓	✓	✓	✓	✓	✓	✓	✓	✓
3. Write a directory for recreation	✓	✓	✓	✓	✓	✓	✓	✓	✓	✓	✓	✓	✓	✓	✓	✓	✓	✓	✓	✓	✓	✓	✓	✓
4. Write a schedule for a radio breakfast show	✓	✓	✓		✓	✓	✓		✓	✓	✓	✓	✓	✓	✓	✓	✓	✓	✓	✓		✓	✓	✓
5. Research and present information about a new leisure activity	✓	✓	✓	✓	✓	✓	✓	✓	✓		✓	✓	✓	✓	✓	✓	✓	✓	✓	✓	✓	✓	✓	✓
6. Watch and review a television programme	✓	✓	✓	✓	✓	✓	✓	✓	✓	✓	✓	✓	✓	✓	✓	✓	✓		✓	✓	✓	✓	✓	✓
7. Eating out	✓	✓	✓	✓	✓	✓	✓	✓	✓	✓	✓	✓	✓	✓	✓	✓	✓	✓	✓	✓	✓	✓	✓	✓

Individual project: Recreation and exercise

Activity	Skills list																Core skills: communication							
	1	2	3	4	5	6	7	8	9	10	11	12	13	14	15	16	1.1	1.2	1.3	1.4	2.1	2.2	2.3	2.4
1. Carry out a survey of exercise videos	✓			✓	✓	✓	✓	✓	✓	✓	✓	✓	✓	✓	✓	✓	✓	✓	✓	✓	✓	✓		✓
2. Compile a personal exercise record	✓		✓	✓	✓	✓	✓	✓	✓	✓	✓	✓	✓	✓	✓	✓	✓	✓	✓	✓	✓	✓		✓
3. Investigate sports energy foods and drinks	✓		✓	✓	✓	✓	✓	✓	✓	✓	✓	✓	✓	✓	✓	✓	✓	✓	✓	✓	✓	✓		✓
4. Write a guide to fitness and recreation	✓		✓	✓	✓	✓	✓	✓	✓	✓	✓	✓	✓	✓	✓	✓	✓	✓	✓	✓	✓	✓	✓	✓
5. Find out about safe footwear for exercise	✓		✓	✓	✓	✓	✓	✓	✓	✓	✓	✓	✓	✓	✓	✓	✓	✓	✓	✓	✓	✓	✓	✓
6. Write a safety checklist for exercise	✓		✓	✓	✓	✓	✓	✓	✓	✓	✓	✓	✓	✓	✓	✓	✓	✓	✓	✓	✓	✓	✓	✓

Group project: Personal care: feet and hair

Activity	Skills list																Core skills: communication							
	1	2	3	4	5	6	7	8	9	10	11	12	13	14	15	16	1.1	1.2	1.3	1.4	2.1	2.2	2.3	2.4
1. Research and present information on footwear fashion				✓	✓	✓	✓	✓	✓	✓	✓	✓	✓	✓	✓	✓	✓	✓	✓	✓	✓	✓	✓	✓
2. Design a questionnaire on footcare	✓	✓	✓	✓	✓	✓	✓	✓	✓	✓	✓	✓	✓	✓	✓	✓	✓	✓	✓	✓	✓	✓	✓	✓
3. Design a chart about common foot problems	✓	✓	✓	✓	✓	✓	✓	✓	✓	✓	✓	✓	✓	✓	✓	✓	✓	✓	✓	✓	✓	✓	✓	✓
4. Design a shoe	✓	✓	✓	✓	✓	✓	✓	✓	✓	✓	✓	✓	✓	✓	✓	✓	✓	✓	✓	✓	✓	✓	✓	✓
5. Investigate hair style and colour choices	✓	✓	✓	✓	✓	✓	✓	✓	✓	✓	✓	✓	✓	✓	✓	✓	✓	✓	✓	✓	✓	✓	✓	✓
6. Investigate hair care routines and hair products	✓	✓	✓	✓	✓	✓	✓	✓	✓	✓	✓	✓	✓	✓	✓	✓	✓	✓	✓	✓	✓	✓	✓	✓
7. Carry out research into common hair problems	✓	✓	✓	✓	✓	✓	✓	✓	✓	✓	✓	✓	✓	✓	✓	✓	✓	✓	✓	✓	✓	✓	✓	✓
8. Design an advert for a hair care product	✓	✓	✓	✓	✓	✓	✓	✓	✓	✓	✓	✓	✓	✓	✓	✓	✓	✓	✓	✓	✓	✓	✓	✓

Individual project: Personal care: teeth, skin and body

Activity	Skills list																Core skills: communication							
	1	2	3	4	5	6	7	8	9	10	11	12	13	14	15	16	1.1	1.2	1.3	1.4	2.1	2.2	2.3	2.4
1. Write a checklist for caring for teeth and gums		✓	✓	✓	✓	✓	✓	✓	✓	✓	✓	✓	✓	✓	✓	✓	✓	✓	✓	✓	✓	✓	✓	✓
2. Carry out an investigation to find the best toothpaste		✓	✓	✓	✓	✓	✓	✓	✓	✓	✓	✓	✓	✓	✓	✓	✓	✓	✓	✓	✓	✓	✓	✓
3. Write a low sugar snack plan		✓	✓	✓	✓	✓	✓	✓	✓	✓	✓	✓	✓	✓	✓	✓	✓	✓	✓	✓	✓	✓	✓	✓
4. Design a guide to good skin and nail care		✓	✓	✓	✓	✓	✓	✓	✓	✓	✓	✓	✓	✓	✓	✓	✓	✓	✓	✓	✓	✓	✓	✓
5. Investigate sun protection methods and products		✓	✓	✓	✓	✓	✓	✓	✓	✓	✓	✓	✓	✓	✓	✓	✓	✓	✓	✓	✓	✓	✓	✓
6. Write your opinion about body image		✓	✓		✓	✓		✓	✓		✓	✓		✓	✓		✓	✓	✓	✓	✓	✓	✓	✓

Group project: Colour choices

Activity	Skills list																Core skills: communication							
	1	2	3	4	5	6	7	8	9	10	11	12	13	14	15	16	1.1	1.2	1.3	1.4	2.1	2.2	2.3	2.4
1. Find out about the meaning of colours you like to wear		✓	✓	✓		✓	✓	✓	✓		✓	✓	✓	✓	✓	✓	✓	✓	✓	✓	✓	✓	✓	✓
2. Carry out research into colour healing		✓	✓		✓	✓	✓	✓	✓		✓	✓	✓	✓	✓	✓	✓	✓	✓	✓	✓	✓	✓	✓
3. Discover colour preferences		✓	✓		✓	✓	✓	✓	✓		✓	✓	✓	✓	✓	✓	✓	✓	✓	✓	✓	✓	✓	✓
4. Design new colours for a household item		✓	✓		✓	✓	✓		✓		✓	✓	✓	✓	✓	✓	✓	✓	✓	✓	✓	✓	✓	✓
5. Colour in festivals, ceremonies and celebrations		✓	✓	✓	✓	✓	✓	✓	✓		✓	✓	✓	✓	✓	✓	✓	✓	✓	✓	✓	✓	✓	✓
6. Collect information about warning and safety colours		✓	✓		✓	✓	✓		✓		✓	✓	✓	✓	✓	✓	✓	✓	✓	✓	✓	✓	✓	✓

Individual project: Seeing colour

Activity	Skills list																Core skills: communication							
	1	2	3	4	5	6	7	8	9	10	11	12	13	14	15	16	1.1	1.2	1.3	1.4	2.1	2.2	2.3	2.4
1. Using colour inside your home	✓	✓	✓	✓		✓	✓	✓	✓	✓	✓	✓	✓	✓	✓	✓	✓	✓	✓	✓	✓	✓	✓	✓
2. Street colours	✓	✓	✓	✓		✓	✓	✓	✓	✓	✓	✓	✓	✓	✓	✓	✓	✓	✓	✓	✓	✓	✓	✓
3. Write a description for a holiday guide	✓		✓			✓	✓	✓	✓	✓		✓	✓	✓	✓	✓	✓	✓	✓	✓	✓	✓	✓	✓
4. Find out how colour is used in High Street signs	✓		✓			✓	✓	✓	✓	✓	✓	✓	✓	✓	✓	✓	✓	✓	✓	✓	✓	✓	✓	✓
5. Find out how colour is used in product packaging	✓		✓			✓	✓	✓	✓	✓	✓	✓	✓	✓	✓	✓	✓	✓	✓	✓	✓	✓	✓	✓
6. Write a questionnaire to find out about the importance of colour in food	✓	✓	✓	✓		✓	✓	✓	✓	✓	✓	✓	✓	✓	✓	✓	✓	✓	✓	✓	✓	✓	✓	✓

Group project: **Pollution and noise**

Activity	Skills list																Core skills: communication							
	1	2	3	4	5	6	7	8	9	10	11	12	13	14	15	16	1.1	1.2	1.3	1.4	2.1	2.2	2.3	2.4
1. Find out about noise pollution	✓	✓	✓								✓	✓	✓	✓	✓	✓	✓	✓	✓	✓	✓	✓		
2. Carry out a survey on local noise pollution	✓	✓	✓	✓	✓	✓	✓	✓		✓	✓	✓	✓	✓	✓	✓	✓	✓	✓	✓	✓	✓	✓	✓
3. Write a checklist on how to be a noise-free neighbour	✓	✓	✓	✓	✓	✓	✓	✓	✓				✓	✓	✓	✓	✓	✓	✓	✓	✓	✓	✓	✓
4. Find out how to complain about noise pollution	✓	✓	✓	✓	✓	✓	✓	✓		✓		✓	✓	✓	✓	✓	✓	✓	✓	✓	✓	✓		✓
5. Find out about noise at work and ear protection	✓	✓	✓	✓	✓	✓	✓	✓	✓	✓	✓	✓	✓	✓	✓	✓	✓	✓	✓	✓	✓	✓	✓	✓
6. Investigate car alarms	✓	✓	✓	✓	✓	✓	✓	✓			✓	✓		✓		✓	✓	✓	✓	✓	✓	✓		✓

Individual project: Pollution and waste

Activity	Skills list																Core skills: communication							
	1	2	3	4	5	6	7	8	9	10	11	12	13	14	15	16	1.1	1.2	1.3	1.4	2.1	2.2	2.3	2.4
1. A survey on litter in your local area	✓		✓	✓		✓	✓	✓	✓	✓	✓	✓	✓	✓	✓	✓	✓	✓	✓	✓	✓	✓	✓	✓
2. Design a questionnaire to find out about litter habits	✓		✓	✓		✓	✓	✓	✓	✓	✓	✓	✓	✓	✓	✓	✓	✓	✓	✓	✓	✓	✓	✓
3. Consider a case study about a litter problem	✓		✓	✓		✓	✓	✓	✓	✓	✓	✓		✓	✓	✓	✓	✓	✓	✓	✓	✓	✓	✓
4. Find out about easy recycling	✓		✓	✓		✓	✓	✓	✓	✓	✓	✓	✓	✓	✓	✓	✓	✓	✓	✓	✓	✓	✓	✓
5. Write a plan for making money from recycling	✓		✓	✓		✓	✓	✓	✓	✓	✓	✓	✓	✓	✓	✓	✓	✓	✓	✓	✓	✓	✓	✓
6. Carry out a survey on the use of packaging	✓		✓	✓		✓	✓	✓	✓	✓	✓	✓	✓	✓	✓	✓	✓	✓	✓	✓	✓	✓	✓	✓

Group project: Living with animals: pets and people

Activity	Skills list																Core skills: communication							
	1	2	3	4	5	6	7	8	9	10	11	12	13	14	15	16	1.1	1.2	1.3	1.4	2.1	2.2	2.3	2.4
1. Write a guide to being a pet owner	✓	✓	✓	✓	✓	✓	✓	✓	✓	✓	✓	✓	✓	✓	✓	✓	✓	✓	✓	✓	✓	✓	✓	✓
2. Give a planned talk about a pet	✓	✓	✓	✓	✓	✓	✓	✓	✓	✓	✓	✓	✓	✓	✓	✓	✓	✓	✓	✓	✓	✓	✓	
3. Carry out an investigation into pet costs	✓	✓	✓	✓	✓	✓	✓	✓	✓	✓	✓	✓	✓	✓	✓	✓	✓	✓	✓	✓	✓	✓	✓	
4. Find out about the work of an animal charity	✓	✓	✓	✓	✓	✓	✓	✓	✓	✓	✓	✓	✓	✓	✓	✓	✓	✓	✓	✓	✓	✓	✓	
5. Find out about the dangers of dog litter	✓	✓	✓	✓	✓	✓	✓	✓	✓	✓	✓	✓	✓	✓	✓	✓	✓	✓	✓	✓	✓	✓	✓	
6. Review the use of pets in advertising	✓	✓	✓	✓	✓	✓	✓	✓	✓	✓	✓	✓	✓	✓	✓	✓	✓	✓	✓	✓	✓	✓	✓	

Individual project: People working with animals

Activity	Skills list																Core skills: communication							
	1	2	3	4	5	6	7	8	9	10	11	12	13	14	15	16	1.1	1.2	1.3	1.4	2.1	2.2	2.3	2.4
1. Write a report about working dogs	✓	✓	✓	✓	✓	✓	✓	✓	✓	✓	✓	✓	✓	✓	✓	✓	✓	✓	✓	✓	✓	✓	✓	✓
2. Write an advert for a working farm	✓	✓	✓	✓	✓	✓	✓	✓	✓	✓	✓	✓	✓	✓	✓	✓	✓	✓	✓	✓	✓	✓	✓	✓
3. Design a display for an exhibition	✓	✓	✓	✓	✓	✓	✓	✓	✓	✓	✓	✓	✓	✓	✓	✓	✓	✓	✓	✓	✓	✓	✓	✓
4. Write a guide on how to arrange a group visit	✓	✓	✓	✓	✓	✓	✓	✓	✓	✓	✓	✓	✓	✓	✓	✓	✓	✓	✓	✓	✓	✓	✓	✓
5. Carry out an investigation to find cruelty-free products	✓	✓	✓	✓	✓	✓	✓	✓	✓	✓	✓	✓	✓	✓	✓	✓	✓	✓	✓	✓	✓	✓	✓	✓
6. Write a profile of a race horse	✓	✓	✓	✓	✓	✓	✓	✓	✓	✓	✓	✓	✓	✓	✓	✓	✓	✓	✓	✓	✓	✓	✓	✓